Football – Bloody Hell!

Also by Patrick Barclay

Mourinho: Anatomy of a Winner

Football – Bloody Hell!

The Biography of Alex Ferguson

CANCELLED

Patrick Barclay

Yellow Jersey Press
LONDON

Published by Yellow Jersey Press 2010

2 4 6 8 10 9 7 5 3 1

Extracts from *The Blair Years* by Alastair Campbell (Hutchinson, 2007)

First published in Great Britain in 2010 by
Yellow Jersey Press
Random House, 20 Vauxhall Bridge Road,
London SW1V 2SA

www.rbooks.co.uk

Addresses for companies within The Random House Group Limited can be found at:
www.randomhouse.co.uk/offices.htm

The Random House Group Limited Reg. No. 954009

A CIP catalogue record for this book
is available from the British Library

ISBN 9780224083058

The Random House Group Limited supports The Forest Stewardship Council (FSC),
the leading international forest certification organisation. All our titles that are
printed on Greenpeace approved FSC certified paper carry the FSC logo.
Our paper procurement policy can be found at www.rbooks.co.uk/environment

Mixed Sources
Product group from well-managed
forests and other controlled sources
www.fsc.org Cert no. TT-COC-2139
© 1996 Forest Stewardship Council
FSC

Typeset in Minion by Palimpsest Book Production Limited,
Falkirk, Stirlingshire
Printed and bound in Great Britain by Clays Ltd, St Ives plc

To The Moon

Contents

List of Illustrations

NO DOUBT ABOUT IT

Among the Idiots

The winds from the North Sea still howled at the back wall of the Beach End, which didn't even blink. The Beach End had seen all this before, night after black night. The Beach End: although the most exposed part of Aberdeen Football Club's Pittodrie Stadium is accurately named, it is fair to add that neither Malibu nor Manly need fear for its place in the hierarchy of balmy suburban strands.

The winds still howled, but the noise of the crowd had long since ceased. All 24,000 paying spectators had drifted back up Merkland Road towards the city centre, the autograph hunters and their parents being the last as usual, and it was left to the journalists, the game's diligent janitors, to sweep up what was left of an Under-21 international match between Scotland and England, a quarter-final of the European Under-21 Championship which had ended goalless, eliminating the Scots because they had lost the first leg at Coventry.

The earnest Alex McLeish on his home ground, the mournful Steve Archibald, a fresh-faced Alan Brazil – all had had their expressions of regret dutifully sought. The triumphant English, whose ranks featured such giants in the making as

Terry Butcher and Glenn Hoddle, had tried not to look too superior as they assessed their chances of going all the way and taking the European title that spring. But naturally they exuded optimism (it proved excessive, because they were beaten home and away by East Germany in the next round). For football journalists it is a familiar routine — our rite of passage to bed or bar — and on this March night in 1980 the little group of travellers from England, having assessed the so-called 'quotes', adapted them for publication and telephoned the consensus of import to their offices in London (transmission by laptop computer had yet to be introduced), duly spilled out on to the dark thoroughfare in search of comfort.

At that moment the headlights of a sleek saloon, easing itself out of Pittodrie's official car park, obligingly swivelled to point them up Merkland Road. The driver-side window rolled down, revealing the face of Alex Ferguson.

Although he had yet to work in English football, Ferguson was recognisable to some of us as the potent young manager of Aberdeen, who were about to claim the first of three Scottish championships under his leadership. 'Where are you heading for, lads?' he asked. The nearest taxi that could sweep us to our hotel, he was told. If Ferguson experienced a temptation to grin at Sassenachs appearing to mistake Merkland Road for Park Lane in the West End of London, he resisted it. 'You'll never get a taxi here this time of night,' he said. 'Jump in.'

Due to this and other encounters, Ferguson became known on the fringes of English football as a good bloke. It was a reputation that survived his arrival at Manchester United, whose manager he became in 1986 when Ron Atkinson was dismissed with the team placed nineteenth in England's old twenty-two-club First Division. Results improved, but not steadily. By the end of the 1986/7 season, though safe from relegation, United had lost to Wimbledon (twice), Oxford United, Norwich City and Luton Town, among others, and a luminary of a former Old Trafford era mentioned that fans, including his grown-up sons, were unconvinced about Ferguson. My friend said he kept telling his sons to be patient and bear in mind that everyone at the club thought the Scot a 'good lad'. This never mollified them. 'Good lad!' they would splutter. 'We don't want a good lad. What we want is a bastard who'll win us the League.'

They got both in the sense that Ferguson, in guiding United to eleven League titles, became recognised as one of the hardest men in football, significantly less popular with some former players than their public pronouncements might suggest. And certainly less anxious to throw open his car door to an English journalist. Some twenty-two years after his generosity in Aberdeen – in May 2002, the day before Arsenal came to Old Trafford to confirm that they would be borrowing the title for a year – he sat down with the daily-paper representatives and was immediately asked by the man from the *Sun* to assess the first season at United of Juan Sebastián Verón. He threw the question back at the reporter, who replied that he did not think Verón had been worth the fee paid. Ferguson erupted and ended the briefing almost before it had started.

'Out of my sight,' he yelled. 'I'm not fucking talking to you any more. Verón's a great fucking player. You're all fucking idiots.'

It was true to the extent that Verón had inhabited the verge of greatness. I had first seen him playing for Argentina in a friendly match against Brazil at the Maracanã in Rio de

Janeiro in 1997. He was not quite twenty-two and already with Sampdoria in Italy, and such was his indefatigable midfield craft that Argentina's 1-0 win flattered their hosts. He looked a potential star of the forthcoming World Cup in France but, despite a gently impressive performance against England in the match in which David Beckham was sent off, did not quite stamp the expected authority. Afterwards he moved to Parma and then Lazio, whom Ferguson had paid more than £28 million for him.

After the outburst, Ferguson kept Verón for one more season and then sold him for £15 million to Chelsea, where he did not last long either. He had a spell with Internazionale back in Italy before returning to Argentina to join Estudiantes de La Plata, with such success that Diego Maradona restored him to the national team and took him to the 2010 World Cup.

Why had Verón flopped in England? The best guess would be that the physical determination required for a player to flourish in England was incompatible with his mid-career comfort zone. It was, however, beyond conjecture that the idiots had got this one right — and Ferguson cannot have enjoyed being exposed by a breed he appeared to regard as inferior.

It was not always so. He had grown up as a footballer in Scotland in an age when it was possible to engage with the common man, who often turned out to be a journalist. Once, Ferguson claimed, when suspended for a Rangers match abroad, he and a clubmate, Sandy Jardine, had sat in the press seats and penned the report that appeared under the name of the man from the *Scottish Daily Express*. But over the years, while retaining friendships with old-timers, above all the great Hugh McIlvanney of the *Observer* and later the *Sunday Times*, he seemed to develop a contempt for what the press had become.

It was not unreasonable, given the tendency to speculation and point-stretching that contaminated even some of the formerly broadsheet sections of the industry, not to mention such perceived coups as the bugging of conversations involving, among others, Sven-Göran Eriksson and the ill-fated FA chairman Lord Triesman (who stood down in May 2010 after he had been caught making ill-advised comments concerning the 2018 World Cup bid). 'It's not so much the reporters,' Ferguson once told me, 'as what their newspapers make them do now.' And it was easy to agree.

He was less persuasive in disparaging some of the younger reporters for wearing 'torn jeans' at his briefings, as if he himself did not often turn up in a tracksuit or even shorts. Self-awareness seldom appeared to be a strong suit of Ferguson's and mounting success made it less and less evident. He might bemoan injustice at large while being unfair to, say, referees. He demanded respect while, increasingly, lapsing into rudeness. Asked a fair question by the television reporter Rebecca Lowe at Birmingham, he brusquely replied: 'Were you watching the match?'

This was early in the 2009/10 season, when he was sixty-seven. Sir Bobby Robson, whom Ferguson admired, was around the same age when I interviewed him in connection with a biography of José Mourinho. 'Let me tell you what happens to successful managers,' said Robson. 'It's happened to me. It happens to all of us. We acquire a bit of power, don't we? That success . . . you know what you stand for . . . you know what people think of you. And this power, this control you have over people, becomes ingrained into you. You use your position to be more powerful. More powerful than you basically are.'

Late in the summer of 2009 a memorial service was held for Sir Bobby in Durham Cathedral and Ferguson gave a wonderfully sensitive address, as he invariably does when called upon to pay tribute (it is said that no one has attended more funerals, in itself a remarkable reflection on a man with so much else to do). On the train back to London, I sat with McIlvanney and took the opportunity to ask how he would describe his friend. 'Alec,' he said (Ferguson's shortened name began to be pronounced 'Alex' only after he left Scotland), 'is a good man.' Quite deliberately McIlvanney left it there, knowing that I wanted a distillation. But no one, of course, is that simple.

A Hero and an Inspiration

McIlvanney was to remain a close friend of Ferguson even after going into print with elegant advice to him to quit after United's early exit from the Champions League in 2005. He had written of Ferguson that 'his achievements are already so monumental that recent events could not conceivably cast a shadow . . . a personally choreographed exit would be bathed in the dignity and honour that are his due . . . he must never run the risk of being dispatched by remote control from Florida . . . there must come a time when the best and bravest of fighters shouldn't answer the bell'. Although I have never been emboldened to consider myself a friend of Ferguson's, let alone an intimate such as McIlvanney, I have known Ferguson for longer than most observers of the game.

And to me, despite the odd professional kindness Ferguson has done, he has always been more of a hero and an inspiration than a chum. This is not to imply that the choice has been offered. One of my favourite stories about Ferguson is of the journalist sent to Manchester to take over the United beat for a tabloid. At the first Ferguson briefing he attended, he boldly advanced through the group of colleagues, shook hands and introduced himself. Afterwards, he quietly returned to Ferguson. 'Alex,' he said, 'now that we're going to be working together, I wonder if I could have your home phone number.' Ferguson's reply was more of a derisive snort and, as the chastened scribe withdrew, he added: 'And don't read too much into the bloody handshake either!'

Ferguson is a hero and inspiration for a variety of reasons. Above all is his gift for time management. I confess that, when the day contains too much to contemplate, I find myself asking: 'What would Ferguson do?'

An especially memorable conversation with him took place towards the end of 2008, when a mutual friend was dying. Hymie Wernick was a car dealer in Manchester whom I had met many years earlier through a fellow journalist, Roy Collins. Hymie was not hard to like and yet, whenever I drove from London to Manchester on journalistic duty, I cursed myself for the common affliction of never quite having time to see him. Once I asked Ferguson how Hymie was. 'Not good,' he said, pausing before entering a press conference to impart every detail of Hymie's medical condition, including, at length, the certainty that it was terminal. When he added that Hymie was in reasonably good spirits but occasionally forgetful, I realised that Ferguson had been a frequent visitor to his bedside. Ferguson, with infinitely more calls on his time, had proved an infinitely better friend than me.

One of Ferguson's friends in high places – at least when Tony Blair ran the country – was Alastair Campbell and often Ferguson would define 'the real friend' for him as 'the one who walks through the door when the others are putting on their coats to leave'.

Anecdotal evidence of his willingness to stretch the day

for a good reason was frequent. Walking to Piccadilly railway station after United's late victory in the derby at the City of Manchester Stadium in April 2010, I was assailed by a voice from a van halted in traffic: 'Hey, lay off our Fergie!' I guessed it was to do with an article linking the unpopular ownership of United by the Glazer family with Ferguson's erstwhile friendship with the Irishmen – the racing people Magnier and McManus – who had sold out to the Americans in 2005. The piece had irked a lot of Ferguson's admirers. So I walked over to have a chat with the man and only then noticed that the van had been converted; he and his companions were physically disabled. 'Fergie's brilliant', I was told. 'He's always got time for us.'

There are some, on the other hand, with reason to attest that time, tide and adulation have soured him. In 2008, though obviously comfortable in an extended television interview with Sir David Frost, he reacted with sudden aggression to a reminder that Gary Lineker had criticised him for maintaining a refusal to speak to the BBC. Lineker, he said, after what appeared to be a hasty search for a verbal weapon, 'has had stuff stopped going in the papers'. Ferguson went on to claim that he never bore a grudge, adding: 'What I'm doing to the BBC is a *stance*.' Funny though it sounded, it was a genuine distinction to draw.

A good man or not, Ferguson is very much his own man. This sets him apart. In more than time management, he makes his own rules. In the early years of the present century, the entire British nation seemed in a permanent state of astonishment; everything was 'awesome' or 'amazing'. Ferguson, seldom bowing to fashion in words or anything else – his hairstyle remained as it was in his playing days and his dress sense owed much to the neat Crombie coat once proudly purchased with a Rangers wage — actually did amaze people. Even McIlvanney must have been surprised by the response to his well-intentioned piece in 2005. Ferguson had been beaten by José Mourinho to one championship and was to lose out again in 2006 — before winning three in a row, plus a second European title.

Ferguson time somehow permitted hobbies. There was the horse-racing, to which he gradually returned, mixing business with pleasure, after recovery from a chastening defeat in his court case with Magnier and McManus over the stud rights to Rock of Gibraltar. There was wine, in particular French red, in which he took a keen interest after being introduced to the nuances of its character by an hotelier while in France to watch Montpellier before a European tie in 2001; coincidentally or not, his favourite wines often turned out to be very expensive ones. And there was politics.

Michael Crick, the distinguished broadcaster, journalist, United fan and chronicler of Ferguson's life, once described his politics thus: 'Like Alastair Campbell's, Ferguson's socialism is pragmatic: like a committed football fan, his prime concern is to see the team win.' To that I should add that he is tribal. His responses are less those of an intellectual than a partisan. In an interview with Campbell for the *New Statesman* in 2009, he declared: 'I grew up believing Labour was the party of the working man, and I still believe that.' The first reader to respond emailed from Glasgow: 'Ferguson is remembering a dream.'

Nor, despite his disparagement of Margaret Thatcher – 'Don't compare me with that woman,' he once snapped, after being told that each of them got by on a few hours' sleep a night – has his stewardship of Manchester United involved much restraint on the extremes of capitalism, as the Glazers and, before them, Magnier and McManus, would delightedly testify.

But then Ferguson might be quite happy to accept a definition of a football club as a profit-making dictatorship. In a *Times* article about Mourinho's pre-eminence after success with Inter Milan in the 2010 Champions League final, Matthew Syed wrote: 'Ferguson's tendency is more towards megalomania than narcissism, but the consequences are the same. The central tenet of life at Manchester United is the primacy of Ferguson.' This was hardly unique; 'Arsenal' could have been substituted for 'Manchester United' and 'Arséne Wenger' for 'Ferguson'. But the subtle difference between Ferguson and Mourinho was identified: Ferguson's is a dictatorship of conviction rather than ego.

You get a sense of it in his fondness, perhaps unwitting, for the phrase that leaves no room for argument; he often suffixes an assertion with something like 'there's no doubt about that'. The more substantial a man, however, the more he must be challenged and it is precisely because of the tirelessly sharp-eyed predatory tendencies that have helped him to thrive – to Ferguson, referees and all other incarnations of footballing authority are so many mice and voles – that we must watch him like a hawk.

The Rich Loam of Home

There may never be another Ferguson. There will certainly never be another football environment like that which nurtured him.

By the time of his arrival at Aberdeen, where he was to complete his journey to a wider recognition, he had spent two decades in the Scottish game. He had played for six clubs and managed a further two. Yet today you could take a car after breakfast and with a bit of the planning required to avoid traffic delays, complete a tour of his career to that point before returning for supper. For the Scottish football in which he grew up had a wonderful intensity. You got an awful lot of passion and commitment to the acre.

It was embodied by Hampden Park, the great Glasgow arena where world attendance records had been set. Ferguson had contributed to one. As a teenager he had joined the crowd of 135,000 who watched Real Madrid beat Eintracht Frankfurt 7-3 in the European Cup final of 1960, a match of unforgettable spectacle and significance: everyone who saw it (Ferguson and his fellows on the slack-jawed slopes, we who could only gape at our monochrome screens) fell deeper in love with football, just as we were to do when colour television brought us the majesty of Brazil in the 1970 World Cup.

Yet the 135,000 had rolled up that May evening in 1960 not knowing what they were to witness. Scots in the overwhelming majority (relatively few, in those days of more carefully limited tourism, would travel from Germany or Spain for even such an occasion), they had come out of a pure and simple desire to appreciate the game's finest. There was no national or sectional interest, no cause to support except the game itself. It was just that Real had become champions of Europe in each of the previous four years since the competition began and Eintracht had looked such promising challengers in disposing of Scotland's champions in the semi-finals, beating Rangers 6-1 at home and, as if that were not swashbuckling enough, 6-3 at Ibrox.

Ferguson had been to the second Rangers match and, as a young aspirant with Queen's Park, who played at Hampden, was admitted free to the final. He recalled that the Queen's Park boys had trained at adjacent Lesser Hampden the night before and taken the opportunity to gaze at the stars during their final pre-match session: 'It was fairytale stuff. I'd been to the semi-final and, as Rangers fans and young boys, we thought, "The Frankfurt players are gods, they must win". They got slaughtered 7-3! This game epitomised all the dreams of European football.'

So fitba' for its own sake drew Ferguson and his horde of compatriots and never in the world, surely, had so many turned up to watch clubs play a match on a neutral ground. Nor, given the small and diminishing number of stadiums with a capacity of 135,000 (Hampden now holds 52,000), can it have happened since. Scotland is entitled to be proud of that and to cite it as evidence when people ask why the nation has spawned so many football managers of distinction: not just Ferguson but Jock Stein and Matt Busby, who preceded him in guiding teams to the summit of the European game, but Bill Shankly, who laid the foundations at Liverpool. Even after the flow of players to England began to slow in the 1980s (the widespread presumption was that the youngsters who used to practise for fun had found other things to do, including nothing), Scottish managers continued to affect the great issues of the English game: Kenny Dalglish at Liverpool and then Blackburn Rovers, George Graham at Arsenal.

Scots care about football. Ferguson was raised in an environment of nurture. It was like putting a seed in rich loam. To that extent, he was lucky.

It used to be said of the French that, if they could play football as well as think about it – Frenchmen were fundamental in conceiving just about every form of international competition – they would be unstoppable. Between 1984 and 2000, they won the European Championship twice and the World Cup, hushing the gentle jibe.

Only briefly could the Scots swat away accusations that, for all the achievement of their managers, their players seldom obtained a close view of the glittering prizes. Stein's Celtic put paid to that for a while. In 1967, seven years after young Ferguson had marvelled at Alfredo Di Stefano and Ferenc Puskás in the all-white of Real, the green and white hoops of Celtic thrilled in Europe in sweeping aside Internazionale in a Lisbon final that seemed to establish verve and adventure as the height of footballing fashion.

And, for all Celtic's Irish tradition, they did it with a team drawn from within a thirty-mile radius of Glasgow. West Central

Scotland also produced the great managers. Not just Stein but Busby and Shankly, all of whom flourished as Ferguson grew up. Only one other bit of Britain could offer a challenge to its status as a breeding ground: the relatively short stretch of England's north-eastern coastline that, having given us Bill Nicholson, came up with Don Revie and then Brian Clough.

You could have a sense of the intensity of Scottish football even in the rural east of the country, where a bike ride into Dundee's hinterland might take you to a crossroads with a signpost bearing mileages that might be mistaken for a slightly implausible set of lower-division results: Arbroath 7, Brechin 4, Montrose 6, Forfar 8. But the heavily industrial West of Scotland, Ferguson's country, was always different, harder, special, and somehow those Lisbon Lions of Stein's came to represent it, to embody its potency.

For all the beauty and greatness of Real, which was to survive all the changes of a half-century that encompassed globalisation, Celtic on their greatest day had no need of an Argentine-born Colombian who was later to represent Spain (Di Stefano) or a galloping major from Hungary (Puskás). Celtic were the glorious harvest of the loam in which Ferguson grew and Ferguson saw it all burgeon at close quarters, even becoming a close friend of Stein's. In 1983 he was himself to lead a team of Scots into conflict with Real in a European final in Gothenburg and prevail, before reaching the outer limits of what could be done at Aberdeen and graduating to the wider world in which borders were there only to be crossed and cultural differences so taken for granted that Ferguson's players came to Manchester United from almost every ethnic source.

Almost. I write with fingers trembling in uncertainty, for this is 2010 – but thus far United have yet to sign an Inuit.

IN THE BEGINNING

A Govan Childhood

There can be no doubting Sir Alex Ferguson's affection for the Govan of his youth. His autobiography paints such a touchingly romanticised picture – streets bustle with organ-grinders, singers, fruit-sellers and bookies' runners – that the reader is sorely tempted to accept his comparison with a movie Manhattan. But to state that he was a product of his upbringing would be simplistic.

The Govan of Ferguson's happy childhood, after all, produced countless men who were to make no discernible mark on the world beyond the shipyard cranes, men for whom ambition, as he writes with admirable sensitivity, was practically synonymous with survival. A proportion are deemed by Ferguson to have wasted their lives through excessive drinking (and again he makes the point without a trace of loftiness or scorn) or even to have gone to prison. Others have advanced with equanimity and been casually insulted, throughout Ferguson's career, by the ascribing of fiery lapses to his background; to them it is no excuse for a belligerent or bullying manner.

Ferguson was born on New Year's Eve 1941, shortly after the

Japanese attack on Pearl Harbor, more than two years into the Second World War (lest there be any assumption that, with an early outburst against perceived injustice, he started it). He and his brother, Martin, a year his junior, grew up in a modest but respectable tenement household, sharing one of two bedrooms. There was an inside lavatory but the bath, a zinc tub, had to be used in the sitting room. The boys were scrubbed once a week and given simple principles, which, far beyond childhood, they remained touchingly eager to follow. Ferguson was sixty-seven when he told Robert Phillip in an interview for the Scottish newspaper the *Sunday Herald*: 'The greatest fortune in life is to be born into a loving family.' His parents had instilled 'all their traditional working-class values – discipline, good manners, honesty, decency'. When his father said something, he meant it, but he was 'a very, very fair man'. He was 'a stickler for punctuality' and one of his favourite sayings had been that 'if a thing's worth doing, it's worth doing well'.

Ten years earlier, in *Managing My Life: My Autobiography*, Ferguson had written: 'Basically, you are what your parents are.' His father, Alexander Ferguson, though an introvert, was given to eruptions of the temper that referees, journalists and even fellow managers were to experience later from his elder son. Lizzie Ferguson, who loved to dance, was strong. Ferguson described her as 'our rock throughout our lives'. On her death from lung cancer he was mining his own quarry of resilience. It was during the early years at Manchester United.

Between them his parents, with help from their own parents and other members of a family as close as was the custom in those post-war days, did their best to guide the boys away from the trouble always available in a Glasgow notorious for its gangs. 'My parents suggested things to keep me out of trouble,' he said, 'like joining the Life Boys and later the Boys' Brigade.' Alex and Martin still got into fights. Yet when they came home it was to an unlocked door; often his mother would return from work to find a note from a neighbour who had borrowed tea or sugar.

Both of his parents had to work (and both served as shop stewards, a tradition Ferguson was to maintain), so he and Martin spent a lot of time with their grandparents. 'You never had a lot,' he recalled, 'but I wouldn't call it poverty. You always had your meals, you never missed school, you were always clean and tidy.'

Somehow, too, it symbolised the values the boys received that Alex Ferguson, nominally a Protestant like his father, was to marry Cathy Holding, a Roman Catholic like his devout mother (such aspects of a marriage were remarked upon in the West of Scotland then, and occasionally they still are). In doing so Ferguson benefited from the local habit of mating early and for life: Cathy was to provide a classic example of the creative power of female selflessness.

Not that anyone she married would necessarily have gone on to become a gloriously successful manager of Aberdeen and Manchester United. Not that Martin Ferguson, for all the parental exhortation to do his best, could have been expected to achieve parallel fame and fortune.

Martin did forge a playing career as a creative midfielder with Partick Thistle and Greenock Morton in Scotland and Barnsley and Doncaster Rovers in England's lower divisions. He became player/manager of Waterford Town in Ireland and then manager, briefly, of East Stirlingshire – following in his brother's footsteps – and Albion Rovers. He was a part-time assistant to Alex Miller for three years at another of his brother's former clubs, St Mirren, and a further ten years at Hibernian.

When Miller was sacked by Hibs in 1997, so was Martin. But his brother made sure he fell on his feet by inviting him to join the Manchester United payroll; from then, while remaining based on the outskirts of Glasgow, he acted as a globetrotting scout for the club. Mischievous United supporters noted his perceived recommendations of the likes of Kléberson, Liam Miller and Eric Djemba Djemba. The more charitable gave him credit for Ruud van Nistelrooy and Jaap Stam. But mostly, like the vast majority of Britain's football community, he lived in the shadow of a particular greatness.

Who can say exactly why Martin's brother was to walk so tall for so long? Let us just ascribe the extraordinary career of Sir Alex Ferguson to a genetic and environmental cocktail whose secret will never be fully revealed, even by the close study his association with football so richly merits.

Street and School

On those Govan streets you could still hear the noise from the shipyards day and night. It was slowly to be stilled. Yards such as Fairfield's where his father worked were shut down, despite campaigns that made celebrities out of trade union leaders, notably Jimmy Reid, whom Ferguson was to get to know. But as a boy he knew only the streets and school, where, though neither angelic nor delinquent, he made a friendship with his favourite teacher, Liz Thomson, which proved so durable that she would come to stay with him and Cathy in Cheshire half a century later.

On a Saturday, he would join the vast crowds who watched Rangers at Ibrox (he and Martin favoured the blue prevalent in Govan even though their father discreetly wore Celtic's green) and then come home and, during street games, imagine scoring for them. Scoring goals was always close to the heart and soul of Ferguson's game.

He played football with the Life Boys (a vaguely nautical equivalent of the Wolf Cubs, designed to fill young heads with wholesome and constructive and above all disciplined thoughts) and the Boys' Brigade, to which Life Boys graduated at around the age Cubs became Boy Scouts. He played for boys' clubs and, at his secondary school, Govan High, began to represent Glasgow Schools. A further sign that his football was acquiring wings came when he was invited to join the Drumchapel Amateurs club, a footballing academy remarkable for the number of graduates it has produced for the professional ranks.

Ferguson was fourteen when the remarkable man who ran Drumchapel, Douglas Smith, knocked on his parents' door. Smith was to die in 2004 at the age of seventy-six having helped to groom nearly thirty full internationals for Scotland, including Kenny Dalglish, Andy Gray, Archie Gemmill, Asa Hartford, John Robertson, John Wark and Paddy Crerand, plus an estimated three-hundred other footballers, among them Ferguson and David Moyes, who was to become a friend and rival as manager of Everton. Moyes's father had been one of many parents enlisted by Smith to run his series of teams starting with the Under-14s. Ferguson was to describe Smith as 'a fantastic man' and 'a massive influence'.

Smith came from a wealthy middle-class family and, after Cambridge, served in the army. An accident caused him to be invalided out in 1949 and he returned to Dunbartonshire to run the family shipbreakers' business. He had a passion for football that initially he expressed through a Boys' Brigade team in Drumchapel, a village that grew into a vast council estate for Glaswegians. And he had a strong moral sense, as Ferguson was to recall in the *Sunday Herald* interview: 'Douglas didn't just teach you about football. He also instilled in you a code of life.'

It fitted comfortably with his parents' code: 'Discipline, cleanliness, good time-keeping, no swearing, good sportsmanship but also how to be competitive as well.' Ferguson was to find time-keeping and competitiveness easier to observe than some of the others, but his gratitude for Smith's unselfish guidance – 'it helped that he was very rich . . . but he devoted an incredible amount of time to us' – is matched only by admiration for his vision in taking the boys to Europe for tournaments in which they played equivalents from the likes of Barcelona, Milan and Juventus. He even compared Smith with Matt Busby, Manchester United's European pioneer, and implied that his 'meticulous' organisation and preparation lodged in the mind; those boys who had to play for their schools on a Saturday morning before representing Drumchapel in the afternoon, for instance, would be collected by car from the first match and taken for lunch. 'The bother Douglas went to on our behalf was simply unbelievable.'

Now and again, he would entertain them on Sundays. 'Eight or nine of us would pile into his big Rover,' said Ferguson, 'to be taken for lunch at Douglas's huge mansion where we trooped through his orchard to play football on his private bowling green. He didn't care about your background . . . or his beautiful grass – only if you could play football.' Nor had he any time for the sectarian divide and so Ferguson, who followed the blue, happily wore the green and white hoops of Drumchapel.

Shortly before his fifteen birthday, Ferguson was chosen for Glasgow Schools' annual match against Edinburgh and encountered John Greig. They were to become great friends after Ferguson realised his ambition to join Rangers. By then Greig was an established international, a more distinguished figure in Scottish football than Ferguson the player was ever to become. But as Greig first faced Ferguson he felt intimidated: 'Not by him. I don't even remember him. I just remember the sight of the team we faced — I thought we were playing a man's team, not Glasgow boys! As we were being beaten 4-0, it just felt as if we were being overpowered by a much bigger and stronger side. They bullied us, almost — maybe that's where he got that streak in him!'

A midfield player that day, Ferguson remembers being in direct opposition to Greig and thinking how small he was. He also remembers scoring from a penalty, and playing well.

Tools of the Trade

Ferguson left school, became apprenticed to the toolmaking trade at Wickman's on the Hillington industrial estate – and took his first serious step towards a football career by leaving Drumchapel to join Queen's Park shortly after his sixteenth birthday.

Queen's Park, too, was an amateur club, but by far Scotland's most distinguished, one which could proudly claim not only to have won the Scottish Cup ten times but twice to have reached the final of the FA Cup, albeit towards the end of the nineteenth century, when those conquered on the way to successive defeats by Blackburn Rovers at Kennington Oval included Aston Villa, Notts County, Blackburn Olympic and Old Wykehamists.

In 1903, Queen's Park built the biggest stadium in the world, which Hampden Park was to remain until Rio de Janeiro's Maracanã was prepared for the 1950 World Cup. In 1958, as memories faded of a midsummer in which Brazil had at last taken their first world title, the teenage Pelé startling and delighting the sporting planet by scoring a hat-trick in the final against the Swedish hosts (Scotland had begun to set their own form of precedent by returning home after the group stage), Hampden echoed to the sound of Alex Ferguson demanding the ball.

He had swiftly advanced through the club's youth ranks and was a month short of his seventeenth birthday when he made his first senior appearance, at Stranraer.

Ferguson had joined the rest of the players at Glasgow's Central Station for the journey of several hours to a town that still felt that the absence of an invitation to join the Scottish League until 1955 might not have been entirely unconnected to its remote location at Scotland's south-western tip, where the ferries left for Ireland.

Another reason, of course, might have been the presence in Stranraer's team of a left-back, identified by Ferguson only as 'McKnight', who bit him during a tussle in the match. Bemoaning it in the dressing room at half-time, the youngster was told by Queen's Park's equivalent of a manager to 'bite him back'. Whether or not the advice was taken, the senior players had heard it and, in a combative second half, a member of each side was sent off. It was all experience. As was defeat: 2-1.

A newspaper cutting records, however, that Ferguson scored Queen's Park's goal, 'ending a great solo run with a flashing drive'. Oddly, this is omitted from his book. An instance of self-effacement? Or a lapse of memory? Either would be a collector's item, for Ferguson's memory has often been described as 'photographic' and this picture he would certainly consider worth a thousand words.

In the late 1950s and early in the supposedly swinging 1960s, as Scots went about their business unaware of the impending arrival of Labour government, the Beatles and the Rolling

Stones and, less happily on the cultural front, the World Cup triumph in store for their big brothers to the south, Scottish football presented a relatively interesting face.

It was Hearts, rather than Celtic, who vied with Rangers for supremacy, taking the championship to Edinburgh in 1958 and 1960. Dundee acceded to the title in 1962 and Kilmarnock were to do so in 1965, before Celtic under Jock Stein emerged from semi-hibernation to begin a sequence of nine consecutive championships during which the club also brought the European Cup to Scotland.

By now Queen's Park were struggling to keep in touch with it all. They had genuflected to their past with two seasons in the top division and, despite relegation a few months before Ferguson's debut, the side contained players who were to surpass Ferguson's own career in the sense that they played for Scotland.

One was Willie Bell, who figured in Leeds United's rise under Don Revie. The other, Davie Holt, went to Hearts after representing Great Britain in the Olympic Games of 1960 in Rome. At Queen's Park, he and Ferguson used to travel to training together by bus from work at the Hillington estate. They were happy and, Holt later insisted, purely amateur days. 'People sometimes ask me if I had money slipped in my boot,' he said, 'but, believe me, you never got a brown penny out of Queen's Park. You were playing for the history of the club, and it was a fabulous history.'

At Stranraer, chastened, the Queen's Park players slipped out of the little Stair Park ground and across a railway track to await the train back to Glasgow.

They beat Alloa Athletic 4-2, Ferguson scoring at Hampden, and he went on to make sporadic first-team appearances. Bill

Pinkerton, the Queen's Park goalkeeper, recalled Ferguson as being 'difficult to knock off the ball because he was all elbows and hands'.

In training, Pinkerton surprisingly added: 'A few of us felt he could have worked a lot harder. I remember thinking some-times that his heart wasn't in it. He had a few run-ins with the trainers, Willie Gibson and Frank Lyon. It was always about the type of training we did. We would start with two laps of the cinder track at Hampden. Next it was up and down the terracing, every stairway, right to the top and back again. Then ten sprints. That was your training. Alex kept complaining, saying this was not the sort of stuff we should be doing. But we had no option because, being amateurs with jobs, we trained in the evenings and Hampden in those days had no flood-lights. There were only the lights along the front of the main stand – it was like training in the dark. We couldn't do any work with a ball until the light evenings came along.'

The gloom did bring Ferguson one benefit. 'Two or three of us were good quarter-milers,' Pinkerton recalled, 'and some of the other players didn't like it. After we'd set off on our laps, we'd look round for the next group and there'd be no one there. They'd be hiding in the tunnel or somewhere, waiting to join us on the track when we came round. Alex was always one of them. So he wasn't the most enthusiastic. Nor did he stand out as a player. But he was a good lad.'

A Saint at Perth

Impatience nagged at Ferguson and, although his first-team opportunities became more frequent in his second season at Queen's Park, he was vulnerable to the wooing of Willie Neil, the Glasgow scout of St Johnstone. This was ardent and not wholly scrupulous; although Neil was entitled to point out that the Perth club had been promoted to the First Division, he also promised Ferguson a regular place in the team. Naively, Ferguson believed it and signed for a year.

He remained an amateur – by now his toolmaking apprenticeship had been transferred to the Remington Rand factory, also on the Hillington estate – and the journey to and from Perth for training twice a week was costly. A combination of buses, trains and taxis enabled the eighteen-year-old Ferguson to leave Hillington at 4 p.m., reach St Johnstone's ground with the other Glasgow-based players in time to train with their clubmates and arrive home after midnight for a few hours' sleep before rising at 6.45 and setting off for work again.

On the rail journey, he enjoyed the players' banter. So the travel might have seemed a lighter sacrifice if his expenses claims had been promptly met. But, again, promise and the reality of St Johnstone proved distant strangers.

The first-team place? Ferguson began to appreciate it had never been reserved for him when, clearly in order to fill it, the club signed Jimmy Gauld, an ageing pro picked up from Everton, one with a respectable career, all of which turned out to be behind him because he was beckoned back to England to help police and ended up in prison after being named the ringleader behind British football's most infamous match-fixing scandal. Two England internationals, Peter Swan and Tony Kay, were also put behind bars along with their former Sheffield Wednesday colleague David 'Bronco' Layne.

There was, Ferguson wrote in his book four decades later, a suspicion among players in Scotland that corruption stalked dressing rooms closer to home. More than a suspicion, according to Ian Ure, the Dundee and Scotland centre-half who went on to play for Arsenal and Manchester United before succeeding Ferguson in his first managerial post at East Stirlingshire.

'Without ever being certain,' wrote Ferguson, 'I had the uneasy feeling that there were games played in Scotland at the beginning of the Sixties which were at least in the doubtful category.' Ure had no doubt that one would have taken place at St Johnstone's Muirton Park on the final day of the 1961/2 season, when a draw would have guaranteed Dundee the championship and St Johnstone survival in the top division, but for the visiting players' rejection of an offer of £30 (a little under a week's wages) to share the two points at stake. The disdain of the Dundee dressing room was not unanimous, according to Ure. 'One or two of ours,' he said, 'wanted to take the money.'

Ferguson played that day. He had spent his first Perth season in the reserves but then, after his father had undergone an operation for what later proved to be bowel cancer, one of the effects being that he was no longer fit for hard work in the shipyard, Ferguson decided to turn professional, signing a part-time contract that enabled him to keep his job in Glasgow. He played more often and began to score goals for a struggling side.

Not enough, though, to put fate in their own hands on that deciding day when Dundee made the twenty-two-mile journey along the River Tay followed by some 25,000 supporters, who, aided by 5,000 of the Muirton faithful, broke the ground's attendance record.

'Dundee at that time,' wrote Ferguson, 'were a team without a conspicuous weakness, an amalgam of all the attributes needed to win a championship.' Forty years on, he rattled off the line-up: 'Slater, Hamilton, Cox, Seith, Ure, Wishart, Smith, Penman, Gilzean, Cousins and Robertson.'

While conceding that it wasn't a bad effort, I have to correct Ferguson here and there. The goalkeeper was not Bert Slater, who arrived from Liverpool in time for the following season's European Cup campaign, but Pat Liney. Alan Gilzean wore the No. 10 shirt and Alan Cousin (singular, though many people made Ferguson's mistake of using the plural) the No. 9.

I know because I was among the dark-blue throng that day in the blazing sun, fourteen years old and sweatily stumbling towards the packed terraces to await a celebration that was to remain unique nearly half a century later. It was my first time in the presence of Ferguson, though if I knew who he was, I soon forgot; our eyes, on this historic day, were for Dundee alone. At least until St Johnstone's defenders started to kick our wonderfully elegant veteran of a winger, Gordon Smith. Then the notion of St Johnstone's relegation seemed quite appealing.

They had begun the day with optimism. Even if defeated, they could hope that one of the teams just below them – Falkirk, St Mirren, Airdrieonians – would fail to win and thus keep them up. If the defeat were narrow, too, they might conceivably survive. But a point would ensure the drop beyond question, and this point someone from their camp resolved to buy.

Ian Ure would not say who he was, except that he was a reserve player. 'He offered a couple of our players money to draw and, when we discussed it and it became apparent that one or two of ours wanted to take it, I threatened to go to our manager [Bob Shankly, brother of the Liverpool legend Bill] and report it. That was the end of the argument. It went no further.'

Such approaches were not unusual at the time. It was believed that players, even internationals, organised results to take advantage of fixed-odds betting – a double of successful away-win forecasts, paying 10/1, was said to be especially popular. When Gauld and the Sheffield Wednesday trio were brought to justice, there, but for the grace of God, went plenty of contemporaries.

The attempted fix at Muirton Park was known about in the St Johnstone dressing room – though not necessarily by every member of the team – and one player told me many years later that his reservations about it might have been shelved had he been aware that the clubs fighting St Johnstone for survival had themselves been up to no good that afternoon.

The defender Jim Lachlan finds the subject embarrassing. Asked about Ure's story, he replied: 'I can't say yes or no.' He was aware that 'rogues, real rogues' abounded in the game and had known it from early in his career when, throughout a 5-0 defeat at Airdrie, an opponent kept whispering phrases like 'chuck it' and 'take it easy'. Lachlan remembered being incredulous. 'I was never one,' he said, 'for taking it easy.'

Ferguson was of the same attitude, 'a decent lad', said Lachlan. 'There was a group of them who came up from Glasgow and some were kind of wide boys. Alex was different. He didn't even smoke or drink'.

Not that his good habits helped on the day of St Johnstone's relegation. Dundee played for themselves alone, and very well, and were winning 3-0 when Ferguson headed into the net only for the referee to spot an infringement. Had the goal stood, he implied, St Johnstone would have stayed up – but under the system of goal average used before goal difference, which entailed dividing the total number scored by the number conceded, St Mirren would still have finished above them after winning 4-1 at home to Dunfermline.

Under his agonising misapprehension, Ferguson went back to work at Hillington.

When the new season started, he did not suffer financially as much as the full-timers from the descent to the Second Division, but his supervisor at Remington Rand had insisted he stop travelling to train in Perth and the manager, Bobby Brown, responded by putting him in the reserves.

St Johnstone were promoted again and his career seemed becalmed, not least to Ferguson, who, on the eve of a reserve match at home to Rangers, arranged for his brother's girlfriend to ring Brown from Glasgow, pretending to be his mother, and say he had flu. Brown, seeing through the ruse, sent a telegram to Ferguson's house demanding that he himself ring immediately. His parents, furious, insisted on it, but when Brown answered, the message he had to impart was mixed: while he was irked by the lie, several senior players had contracted actual flu and Ferguson was to report to St Johnstone's hotel in Glasgow a few hours before the first-team match at Ibrox the next day.

Not only did he play, Ferguson scored a hat-trick at the theatre of his boyhood dreams. St Johnstone won 3-2 and the wind was in his sails. He walked home beaming to be congratulated by his mother, who said his feat had even been mentioned on television. Meanwhile, his father, to whom he had given a complimentary ticket, sat reading a book. Ferguson asked what he had thought of the match. 'Okay,' he replied, before almost praising his son for the successful observance of one of his principles: if you don't shoot, you won't score.

Less than twenty-four hours after being threatened with ejection from the house, Ferguson was a respectable member of the family again. He had also begun to learn how to keep a youngster's feet on the ground.

Another lesson he was to carry into management lurked around the corner. The local boy was enjoying the bachelor's life. He had a car and an expensive Crombie coat and plenty of friends (some of whom he was to keep for life). But it was clearly going to take more than an Ibrox hat-trick to land him anywhere near the top of Scottish football. He needed a stimulus. It came in the form of love. Or the seeds of it. One night, in a dance hall in Sauchiehall Street, he spotted Cathy Holding, a girl he had seriously fancied at Remington Rand. He approached her and almost immediately they began a steadily deepening relationship. Ferguson resolved to get a transfer from St Johnstone and make the most of his career.

Into Europe with Dunfermline

Opportunity knocked in the form of Dunfermline Athletic. There had been rumours which excited Ferguson because, under Jock Stein, the Fife club had performed notable deeds in the old European Fairs Cup (later Uefa Cup), knocking out Everton. Stein then left for Hibernian but his successor and erstwhile assistant, Willie Cunningham, a former Northern Ireland full-back, also wanted Ferguson. The deal was quickly done and, although initially Ferguson decided to keep his job, he realised within months that it was a false economy and threw everything into his footballing career.

He did, after all, now have it in mind to get married and start a family (as a manager, he was always to encourage young men to settle down). Toolmaking had given him memories to treasure – everything from the strike he prompted in support of a sacked colleague (it ended unsuccessfully after six weeks), to that first sight of Cathy – but now he knew clearly what he wanted and it didn't involve taking a smoke-filled bus to a factory every morning.

Dunfermline provided not only a proper footballer's life but a vision of life beyond. 'As soon as I became a full-time footballer,' he was to recall, 'I was committed to staying in the game. As an apprentice toolmaker, I'd get up and sit on a crowded bus to Hillington with everyone puffing away at their fags. Then to get my first car and be able to drive over to Dunfermline in the fresh air every morning — what a difference! I made up my mind I was going to stay in the game and started to get my coaching qualifications the following summer.'

Ferguson was lucky to arrive at East End Park, where Stein's invigorating influence was manifest in a brightly refurbished stadium. It housed a happy club, like a family, in which most of the players had been brought through the ranks together by Stein.

Cunningham had gone outside to recruit Ferguson, swapping him for the attacker Dan McLindon, but the new boy was instantly accepted. 'A right down-to-earth boy' is how one of the leading players, Willie Callaghan, remembers him. 'Fergie had no airs and graces. But Dunfermline was an easy club to come to. There were no big names. We were all on the same wages and would even show our wage slips to each other, when the packets were handed round on a Wednesday, just to compare the tax. I don't think you'd get that now. And, if you got picked for Scotland [as Callaghan did on a couple of occasions], the whole team were delighted. It was a happy dressing room.'

After training the players would lunch together at a cinema café and discuss tactics in the time-honoured manner, with salt and pepper pots. 'As time went by,' Cunningham recalled, 'Fergie got more and more into it and started bringing all sorts of information and statistics. He got into it a lot deeper than some of us.' But the main thing was to score goals.

They came steadily in his first season, 1964/5, and he made his first European appearance away to Örgryte of Gothenburg (in the same Ullevi Stadium nearly nineteen years later, he was to guide Aberdeen to the triumph over Real Madrid in the Cup-Winners' Cup final). A scoreless draw was enough for Dunfermline, who had won 4-2 at home. Next they beat Stuttgart 1-0 on aggregate before losing to Athletic Bilbao in a third match in the San Mamés Stadium (it was before the institution of penalty deciders and the Spanish club won the toss for choice of venue).

Back home, Dunfermline were in a three-horse race for the title which Kilmarnock eventually won on goal average from Hearts after Ferguson's team had been inconsistent in the run-in, beating Rangers (Ferguson had been dropped that day) but only drawing with St Johnstone (Ferguson played, but missed chances). Dunfermline had, however, one more chance to take a trophy, for they reached the Scottish Cup final, in which the opponents were Celtic, now managed by Stein but having gone eight years without silverware.

Cunningham had to choose two strikers from three: Ferguson, his leading scorer; Harry Melrose, who had scored in the semi-final against Hibs; and John McLaughlin, restored after injury, a regular starter whose place Melrose had taken in the previous round.

To the manager's mind, the argument for Ferguson was the least resonant, but he kept his line-up from the players until fifty minutes before the kick-off, when, some suffering more tension than others, they gathered in the Hampden Park dressing room to hear Cunningham – flanked by the club chairman and secretary – read out the names. Towards the end came those of Melrose and McLaughlin. Ferguson exploded. 'You bastard!' he yelled at Cunningham, who remained silent as he continued to vent his fury, ignoring instructions from the chairman, David Thomson, to behave.

The other players just watched. 'We were shocked,' said Willie Callaghan, one of those most friendly with Ferguson, 'but we had to get on with the game. I found it very surprising that Fergie was not playing. But you never know the inside story.'

The relationship with Cunningham, which was to last many years and be to Ferguson's considerable advantage, could almost be described as love/hate. 'Willie Cunningham was a very stubborn man,' said Callaghan. 'And Alex Ferguson was a *very* stubborn man.' He chuckled. 'So it was quite a clash of personalities.' That Cunningham was later to offer Ferguson a route into management was proof that the damage could be permanently mended. 'Oh, they soon sorted it out,' said Callaghan. 'Man-to-man, the way it should be.'

But not right away. There being no substitutes in 1965, Ferguson stayed in his suit and told his parents the news as they waited outside Hampden. He then watched Dunfermline lose 3-2 – their goals came from Melrose and McLaughlin – and, having sought and been refused a transfer (phlegmatism was never a Ferguson characteristic), turned his lingering resentment into a positive force.

A happy private life can only have helped. Towards the end of the following season, in March 1966, he married Cathy and they moved into a semi-detached house in the Simshill district of Glasgow which they had been sanding and painting for months. There was no honeymoon; they wed on a Saturday morning and not only did Ferguson play against Hamilton Academical at East End Park the same afternoon but the next day he went with the team to a hotel to prepare for a Fairs

Cup quarter-final at Zaragoza. Dunfermline, despite two goals from Ferguson, went out 4-3 on aggregate.

In the Scottish League they finished fourth, Ferguson's contribution giving him a tally of forty-five goals in fifty-two matches at home and abroad. He rejected Dunfermline's pay offer for the next season amid reports that Rangers, the club of his heart, and Newcastle United, who had a traditional fondness for signing Scots, were interested and headed for the Scottish FA's coaching centre near Largs on the Ayrshire coast to complete his qualifications for a career beyond playing.

Learning to Coach

At Largs, Ferguson shared a room with Jim McLean, who, in years to come, as Dundee United manager when Ferguson was at Aberdeen, was to help him to break the Rangers/Celtic duopoly.

They were taught by Bobby Seith, a member of the Dundee team whose finest hour and a half had brought about Ferguson's relegation with St Johnstone four years earlier; Seith was to be on the staff at Rangers when Ferguson secured a move there in the summer of 1967, and to be fondly remembered by Ferguson. 'Both Alex and Jim were good pupils,' said Seith. 'Even then, you had the impression that they would go far. They were always so keen to think about things, to learn and to ask.

'They first came the previous year to do the prelim, which involved very basic things like how to set up a session. But when they came back to do the full badge it was much more complicated and related to the game itself. We'd do something then put it into a game and see the effect.

'We'd work on systems of play like 4-3-3, which was coming in at that time [that very summer in England, Sir Alf Ramsey was using a version of it to such effect that his so-called Wingless Wonders won the World Cup]. And other systems including *catenaccio*, with which the Italians had had a lot of success.

'Not that you should ever fall into the trap of fitting players into a preconceived system. A good example of it occurred at Dundee. After we won the championship, we started the next season badly and it was worrying because in the European Cup we were due to play Cologne, who'd been built up as favourites to win the competition. So two days before the match Bob Shankly devised a system to stop the Germans scoring.

'He withdrew me to play almost alongside Ian Ure and brought back Andy Penman, who played in front of me, into midfield. Now Andy, who was a natural and hated anything tactical, was like a fish out of water. After twenty minutes the reserves were beating us 3-0 and Shankly called a halt. "Och," he said, "I'm washing my hands of you – just get on with it." And we beat Cologne 8-1. Those were the sort of practical examples we gave the students and I like to think they gleaned something.

'I've certainly never thought Alex was fitting players into a system rather than the other way round, even at Manchester United, for all the money he's had at his disposal.'

Ferguson left Largs a coach at twenty-five. He spent one more season with Dunfermline after being given a pay rise and a promise of a move the following summer. A high-octane European tie with Dynamo Zagreb, who won on away goals, proved the highlight. Domestically, Dunfermline slumped to eighth place. Ferguson had an unusually long spell without goals, then an injury.

Events elsewhere were, however, working in his favour. Because Rangers were getting angry and frustrated. Stein had launched Celtic's great era and, a few months before they could clinch the second of their nine consecutive championships (to which that year they were to add the European title), Rangers' woes were compounded by a first-round Scottish Cup defeat by tiny Berwick Rangers: arguably the greatest shock in the competition's history. Rangers ruthlessly sold their strikers and, as part of the task of replacing them, began the process that was to lead to a record transfer between Scottish clubs at the time: £65,000 was to change hands when Ferguson's dream of joining Rangers came true.

Playing for Scotland?

He had developed considerably at Dunfermline, said Willie Callaghan. 'Of course I'd known him before as an opponent, an old-fashioned centre-forward with no respect for anybody. With us he retained his *that's-ma'-ba'* attitude but also began coming back to get the ball and start moves – as well as getting into the box to finish them. There was more football in his game. Being with better players helped. For instance, we had a right-winger, Alex Edwards, who was that good a crosser he just bounced the ball in off Fergie's head. Mind you, you could always rely on Fergie to be there. Coming to Dunfermline did a lot for his career, as it did for plenty of others, and along with me he got picked to go on a world tour.'

Picked by whom? We are entering sensitive territory here, for in his book Ferguson states: 'I was selected to go on a world tour with Scotland in the summer of 1967.' In fact it was far from a full Scotland party which set out under the captaincy of Ferguson's old adversary Ian Ure, now with Arsenal: a point the Scottish FA recognised in declining to award caps.

The players of some clubs were excused because of European commitments, most notably Celtic's momentous date with Internazionale of Milan on the outskirts of Lisbon. 'And before any wiseacre,' Ferguson continued, 'observes that Rangers, Celtic and Leeds United withdrew their players, reducing the travelling party to the status of a B squad, let me point out that I was chosen in the original pool.' No doubt. But it is also true that Ferguson was one of seven of the nineteen travellers destined never to play a full international for their country.

He did get closer than ever to it that spring. His former St Johnstone boss Bobby Brown, now manager of Scotland, did select him for the Scottish League side who lost 3-0 to the English League at Hampden and Ferguson points out that he was on standby for the full international with the world champions at Wembley, in case his hero Denis Law failed to recover from injury. But hardly anyone remembers that apart from Ferguson. Every Scot around at the time does, however, vividly recall Law and Jim Baxter taunting the English as they won 3-2.

Ferguson's father and brother, who had flown hopefully to London, were among the exultant tartan throng and everyone was happy, even Dunfermline's leading scorer having no complaints as he joined the celebrations. After all, he could hardly call Brown a bastard for preferring the great Law.

The tour featured only one Scot who played at Wembley that day: Jim McCalliog, who made the most of Bobby Murdoch's absence with Celtic by scoring the third goal.

According to Ferguson, Brown ought also to have included Kate Adie in the tour party, given that the first destination, Israel, was experiencing the skirmishes that led to the Six Day War and the second, Hong Kong, coping with riots that were an overspill from the Cultural Revolution in China, where the activities of the Red Guards were to induce second thoughts about a proposed match by the Scots. In Israel Ferguson heard rockets and in Hong Kong he reported demonstrators menacing a training session before, buoyed by the news of Celtic's historic victory in Europe, the party moved on to the tranquillity of Australia.

Callaghan's recollections were jollier than Ferguson's. 'In Israel,' he said, 'we met Mandy Rice-Davies.' Miss Rice-Davies was best known for her part in the John Profumo scandal that had discredited the Conservative Government of Harold Macmillan in 1963 and, in particular, for her courtroom riposte to a suggestion that Lord Astor would deny ever having met her, let alone slept with her: 'Well, he would, wouldn't he?' She had converted to Judaism and married an Israeli businessman. 'Mandy had a club there – I think her husband ran it and Ian Ure knew them.

'We had left and reached New Zealand by way of Hong Kong and Australia by the time the war broke out. The television was on somewhere and we just gaped at the scenes. Later we heard that Mandy had turned her club into a hospital during the war.'

Callaghan and Ferguson, being clubmates and such pals that Ferguson would stay overnight at Callaghan's parents' house after midweek matches at Dunfermline instead of driving the fifty miles back to Glasgow, naturally roomed together. 'It annoyed him,' said Callaghan, 'because everywhere we went the effect of my name was unbelievable.' It does seem to have been a case of people asking: who's that guy with Willie Callaghan?

'Imagine me sitting in Hong Kong and getting a phone call. It's a member of the Hong Kong Government who's from

Dunfermline and he asks me — as captain of Dunfermline Athletic Football Club, representing the town with the Scotland party — if I'd like to come to his house for a meal. He said I could bring a friend, so I invited Alex and, as we were waiting for the Government car to pick us up, he said, "How come you got the phone call?" and I said "It's the name, son. Callaghan — known all over the world".

'So we had a beautiful night at this guy's house. Next day there was the game and, after playing a one-two with Fergie, I scored, but in doing so I fell and broke my wrist. So from then Fergie had to write my postcards to my wife. Every city we went, I'd dictate to him "Dear Mary, I'm writing this on behalf of Willie . . .".

'The next stop was Australia and in Sydney this lassie comes over saying "Willie! Willie! Willie!" Her mum and dad had the Silver Birch pub in Cowdenbeath. And again Fergie can't believe it.

'When we get to Melbourne, there's a dinner-dance and I says to Fergie, "That lassie over there's from Lochgelly [another mining village near Dunfermline]." She's a hairdresser. I used to work in the cooperative, you see, and the hairdresser's was across the road. So I go over. "Oh, Willie!" she says, "I thought you were never going to talk to me!" Fergie's mouth is wide open.

'Then we go to New Zealand and I get a call from the son of the guy we'd had dinner with in Hong Kong, wondering if it's all right to come and pick me up and show me round Auckland. Again Fergie comes along.

'And then we land in Canada and he says, "Who are we going to meet here, then?" and I say, "No idea". But I knew. My mum and dad got married in Canada and my eldest brother is Canadian. So we go through with the luggage and suddenly I go, 'Bridget! How are you?' It's my sister-in-law. That was it for Fergie.

'Of course, if we did that trip now, everyone would be asking "Who's that man with Sir Alex Ferguson?" But he was a great guy to have as your room-mate. A smashing guy.'

When Dunfermline played at home in Europe, the club's habit was to entertain the visitors to a meal. One day the Dunfermline players welcomed the Hungarians of Újpest Dózsa to the dining room of an Edinburgh hotel. 'We're sitting there at the table,' said Callaghan. 'There's me, then a Hungarian, and then Fergie, then another Hungarian. And we're describing the menu to them, going through the various steaks. And I'm telling the guy next to me to have fillet. And Fergie, who's got a wee bit of a speech quirk, is trying to say the same. He's trying to recommend fillet. And he's saying, "Have fowet – *fowet!*" And we're all just looking at Fergie and trying to imagine this Hungarian going home and telling his friends how much he'd enjoyed the Scottish speciality – *fowet.*'

There were a lot of laughs. And lasting affection. 'After a night game,' Callaghan said, 'Fergie would always ask if he could stay and I'd tell him my mum and dad were waiting for him. My mum used to call him "my laddie". When he moved to Rangers, she said, "I've lost my laddie." And then at Christmas this card came through the door. And she wouldn't take it down. A Christmas card with the Rangers crest on the front and inside "To Mum and Dad, from Fergie". And it stood on top of the sideboard after all the other cards had been thrown out. She used to dust round it.

'He's never changed. When one of our Dunfermline pals, Jim Leishman, lost his wife, he was first on the phone. When

George Miller, our captain, died, the first guy there was Alex Ferguson [it was early in 2009, as Manchester United's thoughts turned to the knockout stages of the Champions League]. That's the type of boy he is. Never forgets his roots.'

He grasped those roots at the end of that summer of 1967 by joining Rangers. Life was good. On the Hong Kong leg of the world tour he had scored his first pair of goals for 'Scotland' and by the end of his travels with Callaghan he had notched nine in seven matches. The statistic is put in a certain context by the tally of Morton's nineteen-year-old Joe Harper, who got eight in three matches against the likes of New Zealand Under-23s and a Vancouver XI.

Later Ferguson became Harper's manager at Aberdeen, without a great deal of comfort on either side; Harper, though a fans' favourite and a prolific scorer for most of his career, liked a drink and was ageing. But before Ferguson could further his education in the arts of management, he had to learn his limits as a player, and this he was to do, quite painfully, at Ibrox.

Rangers: Welcome to Hell

The deal taking him to Rangers was completed despite Cunningham's dismissal as Dunfermline manager. Ferguson, having anxiously phoned Cunningham from Vancouver, was promised that the verbal contract to release him would be honoured. On returning to Glasgow he was beset by reporters, most notably Jim Rodger (known, with some irony, as 'The Jolly'), a tabloid man with a bit too much weight for his modest height, a twinkling eye and an almost complete lack of writing ability that was massively outweighed by an extraordinary gift for producing exclusive stories for his newspapers.

Rodger would do it by taking part in these stories, personally oiling the wheels of transfers and managerial movements. He did it in a manner that suggested he had seen too many spy films, but people trusted him and, when Rodger assured Ferguson he was Rangers-bound, Ferguson knew he need only wait for the call. In a typically cloak-and-dagger operation organised by Rodger, he was driven from his home to that of Scot Symon, the manager of Rangers, from whom he agreed to take a signing fee of £4,000 and a double-your-money £80 a week.

He also negotiated a slice of the transfer fee out of Dunfermline; it was a familiar Ferguson ploy. But from Rangers he was to get more than he bargained for. 'No other experience in 40 years as a professional player and manager,' he was to write, 'has created a scar comparable to that left by the treatment I received at Ibrox.'

It began on the day he signed when a club director asked if his wife was a Roman Catholic and then if they had been married in a Catholic church. Upon hearing that the ceremony had taken place in a registry office, the director almost audibly sighed with relief, yet Ferguson buried his distaste under the joy of having at last joined Rangers.

The Protestant bigotry still evident at the club – it was barely disturbed until, in 1989, under the chairmanship of David Murray and with Graeme Souness manager, they signed Maurice Johnson, the first of many Catholics (though piety was not the most noticeable feature of our Mo's lifestyle) to score and prevent goals for Rangers – was to haunt him.

Rangers were under abnormal pressure because of their enemies' rise under Jock Stein. Even their achievement in not only reaching the European Cup-Winners' Cup final but taking the Bayern Munich of Franz Beckenbauer, Gerd Müller and Sepp Maier to extra time had been recorded in the shadow of Celtic's historic triumph over Internazionale. Yet Symon, in his thirteenth year as manager, had been equipped with new players in the long and wince-inducing aftermath of the Scottish Cup defeat at Berwick: not just Ferguson but Andy Penman from Dundee and the almost equally stylish Örjan Persson, a Swedish winger, from Dundee United, plus the goalkeeper Erik Sørensen from Morton.

On the coaching front, Bobby Seith had been engaged and

it is a measure of how Rangers lagged behind Celtic off the field that Seith's introduction of afternoon sessions for individuals, Ferguson included, was considered revolutionary. 'Rangers had broken with tradition to appoint me,' Seith recalled. 'I was their first coach – as opposed to trainer – and the first member of the backroom staff not to have been a Rangers player.'

Although Symon's new team were to prove no match for the Stein Machine in the long term, they did beat Celtic despite losing their left-back, Davie Provan, after a tackle by the notoriously abrasive Bertie Auld that broke his left leg and his Ibrox career, and were League leaders in November.

Then Symon was sacked. He went, moreover, in a manner that showed bigotry was not the only bad smell in a boardroom, giving the lie to the old American saying that nice guys finish second. More than a whiff of cowardice could be detected as the directors responded to terrace discontent during a home draw with Dunfermline. It was resolved that Symon, a man of dignity and presence as well as achievement, whose distinctions included having played for Scotland at both football and cricket (he had taken five wickets in an innings against the 1938 Australians), would have to go. But thirteen years, during which Rangers had collected fifteen trophies, did not entitle him to a decent farewell. 'They sent an accountant to his house to offer him terms of resignation,' said Seith, 'and, when he refused them, wouldn't even allow him back to Ibrox to clear his desk. I had to go and get his belongings for him.'

When Ferguson heard, he was furious. 'He didn't want to be associated with a club that could do such a thing,' said Seith, 'and came to me so angry he was about to demand a transfer. So I took him into a sort of gymnasium place and gave him a bit of a talking-to.' Ferguson remembers being stunned by the normally 'sedate' coach's passion. 'It wasn't a bolllocking as such,' said Seith, 'I was just trying to make Alex see that it made no sense, at least from his own point of view. "Look," I said, "if you want to do something for Scot Symon, go out there and show the people – the directors who have sacked him, the fans who have lost faith in him – that he did the right thing in signing you, that he knew a player when he saw one." Alex went out and scored twice in the next match.' It was a 3-0 victory over Cologne in the Fairs Cup and Ferguson went on to be the club's leading scorer in his first season.

Seith, however, had long since left the club. Within days of dissuading Ferguson from taking his protest against Symon's dismissal to the ultimate, he had himself resigned. 'I'd talked to my wife about it and decided to follow my conscience. I know I'd talked Alex out of that, but there was a difference in that Alex was at the peak of his playing career. I'd been Scot's coach and wanted no part in a club that could treat such a loyal servant in this way.' Symon was a benign disciplinarian, immaculately dressed. 'Okay, he might never have got into a tracksuit, and in the end it might have been held against him, but he dedicated his life to the football club, helping them to win a lot of trophies [including six Scottish championships]. He was a man to be admired, straight as a die.' It is understandable that Ferguson should have felt the same way about Seith, of whom he was to write so warmly more than thirty years later.

Although a return of twenty-three goals from that first season may have appeared bright enough, the clouds were gathering. Towards the end of the season, with Rangers still leading Celtic on points, Stein all but conceded the championship, saying it was in Rangers' hands and they could only throw it away (Ferguson was never to forget the ploy and would take it into management), which they eventually did by losing their final match at home to Aberdeen. Angry supporters broke dressing-room windows and it was hours before the players felt emboldened to go home; one kicked Ferguson on the leg. It had been an equally painful experience of Stein's mind games for the new Rangers manager, Davie White.

Ferguson never felt he had the confidence of White, who had been Symon's assistant, and was further troubled by bigotry most clearly discernible in the bowler-hatted form of Willie Allison, a former football journalist somewhat bizarrely employed by Rangers as public relations officer. In Ferguson's book, Allison is described as a 'muck-spreader' and 'diseased zealot' who even started rumours that the Fergusons' first-born son, Mark, was christened in a Catholic church (it happened to be untrue).

In truth, the whole atmosphere around Rangers was diseased. Seith remembered that once his wife, a Lancashire lass whom he had met while playing for Burnley, invited an English friend to a match at Ibrox. Neither could understand why they were being stared at with ill-concealed disapproval until Mrs Seith noticed that her friend, a member of the Church of England, had a crucifix on her necklace.

Antipathy towards anything vaguely Catholic was manifest in aggression once shown towards the club physiotherapist, Davie Kinnear, because he happened to be wearing a tartan tie that was predominantly green. Decent men like Seith became accustomed to swallowing their revulsion, just as Ferguson let pass the director's intrusiveness on the day he joined Rangers.

Was Willie Allison as bad as Ferguson paints him? 'I didn't know the guy well,' said John Greig. 'But you wouldn't have thought he'd been a press man. He wasn't the type. He was more close to the directors.' So Ferguson took a risk when, having phoned his wife while on tour in Denmark and been told about a newspaper story predicting (correctly) that his days at Rangers were numbered, he got drunk with Greig and others in a bar in Copenhagen's Tivoli Gardens and returned to the hotel to give Allison an earful of blame. 'Part of the trouble,' said Greig, 'was that Alex hardly drank alcohol, if at all.'

Just before the start of the next season, White told him he had been offered to Hibernian as makeweight in a deal for the centre-forward Colin Stein. Ferguson refused and was banished to train with the reserves, but Rangers still signed Stein, again breaking the all-Scottish record with a fee of £100,000. That he was an improvement on Ferguson is hard to deny. He scored a lot of goals, and at memorable times: in the European Cup-Winners' Cup final victory over Moscow Dynamo in 1972, for instance. Stein also played on twenty-one occasions for Scotland, scoring nine goals.

Ferguson continued to make the odd first-team appearance and near the end of the season, with Stein injured, was chosen for the Scottish Cup final against Celtic. Not for the first time, however, he disappointed White, who had directed him to mark Billy McNeill at corners. Although Ferguson had a spring, the disparity in size was too great. After two minutes, from a corner, McNeill headed the first of four unanswered goals and afterwards White's choice of scapegoat was simple. The atmosphere of suspicion had become mutual – during the manager's inquest into the Cup final, he had accused Ferguson of undermining him in the press (a not dissimilar charge to that levelled against Allison by Ferguson) – and that was the end. Ferguson was dropped for the last four matches of the season and never played for Rangers' first team again.

At the start of the next season, 1969/70, he was separated from the rest of the senior squad. At times he trained with the apprentices – until White found him coaching them at the suggestion of another staff member and banished him to train alone – and played for the third team against the likes of Glasgow University. 'It was embarrassing for the other players,' Greig recalled, 'but more so for him, because we could see him. We used to run round the track at Ibrox and he'd be kicking a ball against a boundary wall. [In his book, Ferguson defiantly states that his appetite for practice was undiminished.] And once they sent him down to England with the third team and he didn't even get a game – they left him on the bench.

'There were a few things which, being so friendly with him, I found hard to take. I don't know why he and the manager fell out and why it couldn't be repaired. It was sad because he was a Rangers supporter, born and bred half a mile from the ground. It must have broken his heart.'

But not his will. Or his ability to make the best of a bad job. When a £20,000 fee was agreed for his transfer to Nottingham Forest – he assumed the English club had been alerted by Jim Baxter, the great Scotland midfield player and party animal who had returned to Rangers from Forest – Ferguson negotiated a tenth of the sum for himself. Then he heard that his old Dunfermline boss Willie Cunningham, now with Falkirk in the Second Division, wanted him too. Cathy brightened perceptibly at the thought of remaining in Scotland

and all that was left for Ferguson to do was apologise to Forest for changing his mind.

A few days later, as a Rangers supporter, he went back to Ibrox to watch them take on the Polish club Górnik Zabrze. They lost and now Davie White, under whom he had been hauled from the dressing room and returned to the terraces, was sacked. It was too late for third thoughts, even though Ferguson had reason to believe the new man in charge, Willie Waddell, would have wanted him. But he did still get his £2,000.

What had caused Ferguson to fall short at Rangers? Was he unable to live up to a £65,000 price tag? Did he make his disdain for Davie White too obvious? Or was it a combination of those factors with his marriage to a Catholic? Many — including Ferguson himself — believed his battle for acceptance was harder than it needed to be.

We should dispose of the coincidental rise in tension between Catholics and the Protestant majority across the Irish Sea. Although it is true that the first civil rights marches by Catholics in Northern Ireland took place in March 1968, little over six months after Ferguson's arrival at Ibrox, Glasgow was more of a spectator to than a participant in the renewed troubles. It remained so as rioting spread from Londonderry to Belfast over the next eighteen months and British troops were sent in by the Prime Minister, Harold Wilson, to be generally welcomed by Catholics, even though they were to be dragged into a bloody conflict with the IRA that lasted for decades.

The songs of hate were incessant on the stadium slopes. Soon after the death of the Republican hunger striker Bobby Sands in May 1981, Rangers met Dundee United in the Scottish Cup final at Hampden Park, which echoed to gleefully repeated chants of 'Sands is dead' (to the tune of 'Hooray for the Red, White and Blue') and, had the martyr been a Loyalist, no doubt the same would have been heard at Celtic's Parkhead. But it was a soft sectarianism that football harboured.

The difference between Rangers and Celtic in that era was that, while Celtic would employ Protestants – Jock Stein and several members of his great side included – Rangers avoided giving Catholics work, reflecting the discrimination that had led to the civil rights movement in Northern Ireland. It would still be wrong to deny that Rangers had signed Ferguson knowing he had followed in the family tradition of marrying whom he pleased.

So was Ferguson just not up to the international standard Rangers expected? The words most frequently used in descriptions of his playing style were 'enthusiastic' and 'elbows' (though not necessarily in that order). He was even to allude to the latter in renaming a Glasgow pub he had acquired the Elbow Room. John Greig recalled: 'Obviously I played against him as well as with him [they were even sent off together after Ferguson had joined Falkirk towards the end of his career] and he was always a handful, a pest. He bustled about with his elbows parallel to the ground – and he was all skin and bone so that, when he got you, it was like being stabbed.'

Davie Provan said: 'I'd give him about seventy out of a hundred as a player. As far as effort was concerned, he was a hundred. And he did score quite a few goals for us.' Bobby Seith added: 'He was typical of good goalscorers. If you saw any picture of a match in which Alex was playing and the goalkeeper was on the ground with the ball, you could bet your bottom dollar that Alex would be standing over him, waiting for him to let it go. He was always looking for goalkeepers or defenders to make mistakes. So, if you were playing against him, you had to be very careful not to make a wee slip – because he'd be there and the ball would be in the back of the net.'

So why did Scotland prefer the likes of Colin Stein, let alone Law? 'He lacked a bit of pace,' said Seith, whose other criticism was more subtle. 'Perhaps his work rate was not all it could have been – certainly not what you'd expect in the modern game.' The modern striker, by harrying defenders in possession or obstructing their lines of communication with those further forward, acts as a first line of his own side's defence. 'People would cover for Alex,' said Seith. 'As they should when a striker's putting the ball in the net. But it is fair to say that he liked to save his energy for the business of scoring goals.' In which case he fooled a few. Newspaper accounts often spoke of his crowd-pleasing energy and combativeness. And Greig expressed surprise that Ferguson's industry had been questioned. 'I don't think Alex ever scored from outside the eighteen-yard box,' he said, 'but I've never before heard him accused of not working hard enough. He gave defences a lot to do. But you have to bear in mind that there was a lot of competition for Scotland places in those days.' Too much for Ferguson.

Fighting at Falkirk

Willie Cunningham still wanted Ferguson, so it was off to Falkirk and another dip into the Second Division, albeit a brief one. He joined in December and five months later the club were promoted with Ferguson contributing plenty of goals in partnership with Andy Roxburgh, later to succeed him as Scotland manager.

They were to have a long association, for they had met towards the end of Ferguson's spell at Queen's Park, when Roxburgh joined the youth team, and continued to meet for half a century because Roxburgh, after parting company with the Scottish FA, became a coordinator of elite coaches for Uefa, organising informal conferences at which the cream of the profession – the likes of Ferguson, Marcello Lippi, Louis van Gaal and José Mourinho – could exchange views.

At Falkirk, though, their relationship became strained – certainly on Ferguson's side – through a bizarre episode seen by millions on national television. It was in 1970, shortly after the club had been promoted, that they were invited to take part in a BBC programme called *Quiz Ball*.

For those too young to remember it – those old enough

certainly will — it was a competition between teams of four from various English and Scottish football clubs in which they scored 'goals' through making 'passes'. A pass was completed by the successful answering of a question. The more difficult the question, the longer the 'ball' travelled and when it reached the opponents' 'line' a 'goal' was scored. Each match made a half-hour programme. The excitement inherent in the format (and no sarcasm is intended here) was enhanced by interest in what these footballers, whom we had hitherto only seen rushing around on the field, were like in real life and, in particular, how clever they were.

Falkirk's team comprised Roxburgh, who was combining studies to be a PE teacher with his playing career; his classmate and team-mate Bobby Ford, a midfield player; Ferguson; and Chic Murray, a revered Scottish comedian who owed his place to the obligation to include a celebrity supporter. Murray was later to play Bill Shankly in the musical *You'll Never Walk Alone* and a headmaster in the football-themed film *Gregory's Girl*, the latter shortly before his death in 1985 at the age of sixty-five.

Ferguson, though, was the star performer of Falkirk's *Quiz Ball* team. By virtue of beating Huddersfield Town through a Ferguson 'goal', they qualified for the semi-finals, in which they met Everton, whose celebrity fan was the disc jockey Ed 'Stewpot' Stewart, and whose manager, Harry Catterick, took part along with the former grammar-school boys Joe Royle and Brian Labone. Ferguson also 'scored' against them but Labone got two and so Everton were leading when the final question of the evening was put to Roxburgh.

'Which jockey,' asked David Coleman, 'rode the winning horse in last year's Grand National?'

Ferguson knew but, as he tried to whisper what would have been an equalising answer to Roxburgh, the younger man panicked and guessed: 'Lester Piggott.' Ferguson was irate – incredulous that anyone could imagine the best known flat-race jockey winning the most famous steeplechase. And not for the first time, nor for the last, he left Roxburgh in little doubt about it. The fans caught on and, trotting out for the next home match, Roxburgh was greeted with chants of 'Lester Piggott'.

It was cruel luck, according to Bobby Ford, that he got the question. 'Neither Andy nor I took any interest in racing,' he said, 'while a group in our dressing room, with Fergie very much one of them, followed the horses every day. They used to set aside money for it. Every week we'd get our wages in little brown envelopes with the amounts written on the outside – basic, bonuses, total – and they would get blank envelopes from the secretary, put a proportion of the money in, reseal them and write the new amounts on. Then they'd give them to their wives. You'd hear their girls at the annual dance "Oh, he's so good, gives me his wage packet every week, unopened, bonuses and the lot . . ." If only they'd known.'

Ferguson apart, the Falkirk party did not let Roxburgh's gaffe ruin the adventure and were further cheered by an invitation from Murray to join him at a nightclub he happened to own in Birmingham, where *Quiz Ball* was recorded. 'Naturally we expected the VIP treatment,' Ford recalled, 'but he charged us to get in! Six pounds each – Chic was a true Scotsman! I was only on eight pounds a week as a part-timer. But Fergie and the others had a whipround to get me in.'

Ford had encountered Ferguson towards the end of his time at Rangers. They met in a reserve match when Ford, barely nineteen, was detailed to mark Ferguson at a corner. He went with Ferguson to the edge of the penalty area. 'Before I could even move, the famous right elbow went into my solar plexus. That was me being introduced to Alex Ferguson. He had his free run into the box and I was left winded, but wiser.'

Ford neglected to remind Ferguson of that when he arrived at Falkirk. It soon became obvious that Ferguson's aggression was not reserved for opponents. With his new team he went back to Ibrox for a Scottish Cup match and a minute from half-time, with the scores still level, the full-back John 'Tiger' McLaughlan made a mistake that led to Rangers taking the lead. In the dressing room, Ferguson went straight for him. 'I can't remember exactly what he called him,' said Ford, 'but "fucking useless bastard" would have come into it. Tiger wasn't the quiet and retiring type either and all of a sudden the two of them were at each other. They were like a pair of animals, rolling about on the floor. The manager, Willie Cunningham, just watched it all, leaning with his elbow against the wall. Eventually two of us younger ones separated them and we went out for the second half [Rangers won 3-0]. But it was a shock to my system to see such violence.'

Not that Ford himself would shrink from the challenge when he fell foul of Ferguson. In, of all things, a testimonial match for the East Stirlingshire player Arthur Hamill. Towards the end of it, Ford misplaced a pass. 'Fergie sprinted the length of the field to give me an earful while the game was going on. He was jabbing a finger in my face. I wasn't taking in what he was saying and I wasn't taking that finger either, so I gave him a bit back of what he'd given me.

'At the end, quite a few of the crowd spilled on to the pitch to congratulate Arthur, who'd been a popular player for East

Stirling. I'm walking off, through the throng of supporters, when suddenly Fergie comes for me and the arms are like windmill blades. Both of us. No blows actually land before we're pulled apart, but there are plenty of wild swings to entertain the astonished supporters.'

Despite the demise of his Rangers career and the general perception that his best days as a player were behind him, Ferguson believed his arrival at Falkirk had boosted morale and results remained good in the First Division the following season.

He was always drawn back to Ibrox and when, on 2 January 1971, Falkirk's match at Airdrie was postponed due to saturation of the pitch, Ferguson, Roxburgh and another team-mate, Tom Young, decided to watch the Old Firm match there. It proved a traumatic day.

Three minutes from the end, Jimmy Johnstone put Celtic ahead and Rangers fans began to stream, dejected, from the stadium. But Ferguson and his companions stayed just long enough to see Colin Stein, Ferguson's replacement, cause wild rejoicing among the blue majority with an equaliser. The trio did not, however, wait for the final whistle; they made for the exits.

Ferguson arrived at his parents' home to find them aghast. Television was reporting a death toll in the forties (it was to rise to sixty-six) from a crush on a stairway that had begun as the first wave of Rangers fans left early. The Fergusons feared most acutely for Alex's brother, Martin, who had been in that section, and began an anguished search of bars where he might have gone. Eventually they found him driving home from one, oblivious to the disaster. Martin had left after Johnstone struck for Celtic but avoided the fatal congestion.

There was a widespread theory – to which Ferguson subscribed – that the crush had been indirectly caused by Stein's goal in that Rangers fans near the bottom of the stairs had turned back upon hearing a great roar, or at least stopped to confirm their team's salvation. The official inquiry found otherwise, its report stating that all spectators were moving in the same direction when the barriers collapsed. The casualties included many children and, as in the case of the Hillsborough disaster that cost the lives of ninety-six Liverpool supporters in 1989, former players joined in trying to help the bereaved families. Ferguson was among them.

His friendship with John Greig, his old team-mate from the Rangers days, survived a confrontation on the field. Although Ferguson was around thirty, the physical side of his game was never far from the surface. Nor, when Falkirk met Rangers, was there any question of divided loyalty. 'We tangled on the centre circle,' Greig recalled. 'I was just recovering from an ankle injury and somebody had given me a whack. As I was rubbing the ankle, the ball came back to me, swiftly followed by Alex with, of course, the elbows up. He brushed past and, although he didn't catch me, I had a swipe at him with my boot. I missed too – completely. But the referee stopped the game and called me across.

'"Fair enough," I said to him. "I deserve to be booked." He said I deserved more than that – I was going off. I'd never been sent off in my career and so I had this conversation with him. Basically I told him that, if he sent me off, he'd be demoted from Grade One refereeing – the lot. That was in the days when Rangers had a good relationship with the Scottish FA.

'Anyway, it didn't work and I trooped off the park. In one

way I was pleased because I was going to a very good friend's daughter's wedding in Edinburgh that evening and now I could get back in time for the meal. So I got in the bath and was lying there when suddenly I felt a hand on my head and was pushed under the water. I came up gulping for breath and there was Alex telling me he'd got sent off as well. "But you didn't do anything," I said. And he said, "I know that." At the hearing, I think I got two weeks and a £100 fine and he got one week and £50. I spoke up for him – but he had a disciplinary record as long as your arm.'

Nor was that Ferguson's only equivalent of the red card when at Falkirk. He had always been aggressive, but his temper was not abating with age or even parenthood; in February 1972, Cathy, already the mother of Mark, gave birth to twin boys, Darren and Jason. A month after the happy event, Ferguson was wanted by Hibs and keen to go, his exchanges with Willie Cunningham, a manager plainly reluctant to let him leave, becoming so passionate that they squared up, Ferguson once again shelving the behavioural principles intended to turn Life Boys into fine men.

So, whatever possessed Cunningham to couple a pay rise with a promise to help him stay in the game as a coach, it was not evidence of maturity on the player's side.

Cunningham, being Cunningham, proved as good as his word. He began by sending Ferguson, when injured (Ferguson was no stranger to knee trouble), to assess and report on future opponents. The manager's reward was to discover that Ferguson, as representative of the players' union, saw his first duty as being to his fellow players, especially when Cunningham reacted to an especially supine defeat by ordering extra training and cutting expenses. The squad went on strike until, shortly before the next match, Cunningham, under pressure from club directors, relented.

Later Ferguson came to see his side of the argument, to understand the sense of isolation that caused him to punish the players so severely. But at that stage Ferguson was lucky that Cunningham — for all that he shared with Ferguson, most obviously a stubborn streak — had one significant difference from the younger man.

Such was his lack of vindictiveness that the following season he appointed Ferguson first-team coach, with responsibility for every aspect of match preparation except team selection — on which he would, however, be able to advise Cunningham.

According to Ferguson, performances improved, but he was just a month into his new role when, in the first half of a Cup match with Aberdeen, he swapped petulant kicks with Willie Young and was sent off. It was irresponsible enough behaviour for a player; for a player/coach it verged on a resignation letter. Nothing was said at half-time but late on the night of his sixth dismissal — a terrible figure to reach in an era when the walk of shame was comparatively rare — Cunningham took him aside and suggested he get wise if that future in football was to be rescued. Neither man knew that the incident had already cost Ferguson an interesting job offer: Jimmy Bonthrone, the Aberdeen manager, was having second and final thoughts about asking him to be his assistant.

The next day, Ferguson's apology to his fellow players was accepted, but the Scottish FA, tiring of Ferguson's rough edges, imposed a suspension of nearly two months.

Falkirk, for the second season in succession, avoided relegation, but Cunningham was dismissed. The new manager, John Prentice, let the firebrand Ferguson go and the next move was to the West Coast. To Ayr, wham ne'er a town surpasses (as Robert Burns wrote) for honest men and bonnie lasses. The national poet would have been proud of the local football club, too, in 1973/4 because, under the effervescent management of Ally MacLeod, later to supervise Scotland's calamitous appearance in the World Cup in Argentina, an Ayr United team of part-timers finished sixth in the First Division, the club's best performance ever.

Ferguson, partnering another former Rangers striker, the cheerful playboy George McLean, began with seven goals in eight matches, but his form and fitness deteriorated and by early spring he was usually a substitute. His last competitive match was for Ayr's reserves against their East Fife equivalents and, although there was potential for one last sending-off in that his craggy young opponent, Colin Methven, handled him with scant care, the devil in Ferguson had gone with his legs.

The devil in the player, that is; there was a hell of a manager to be made. 'By now I knew I was going to have to work hard at it,' he was to recall. 'When you're with Rangers and scoring in front of big crowds, you think it will never end. Then you're released and try for the Falkirk job and don't get it and you start thinking. I was at Ayr when the offer came along to manage East Stirling. I asked Ally about it. "You can't wait for the perfect job," he said.'

First the loose ends of his playing career had to be tied. The second half of his two-year contract was mutually waived in the early summer of 1974 and MacLeod did it with kindness, happily writing off the entirety of Ferguson's signing-on fee and erring on the side of generosity with his severance pay.

The University of Life

By now the Fergusons had completed their family. Mark, their first-born, was nearly six and the twins in nappies. Social life tended to revolve around the Beechwood pub and restaurant near Hampden Park, where the Fergusons got on especially well with Jock Stein and his wife. Ferguson was given a basic training in the catering business; helped by friendly staff, he learned to cook and met a publican called Sam Falconer who, at his own establishment, passed on the techniques of keeping beer in good condition and customers calm.

The latter was not always easy, as Ferguson discovered when he followed his instinct into the licensed trade.

First he took a pub called Burns Cottage in the Kinning Park area of Glasgow, bordering Govan. Despite the theme, few poets were among the customers and, in any case, Ferguson immediately renamed the place Fergie's in an ill-disguised attempt to capitalise on his lingering fame; the downstairs bit was the Elbow Room.

All human life was there: bloody brawls, but also family days out in the summer which Ferguson would organise. Stolen goods were routinely and blithely traded, as Ferguson was to confess, with only slight sheepishness. Shortly after he went into football management with East Stirlingshire, he acquired a second premises – Shaw's, on the opposite side of the city – in a partnership with Falconer that proved ill-fated.

Even in those days, his knack for cramming an unfeasible variety into twenty-four hours was remarkable. True, the part-time footballer's life had left plenty of hours spare, but management at East Stirlingshire was part-time only in terms of the wording on the contract and the salary it stipulated (£40 a week). Yet still he juggled the job with responsibility for Fergie's and a share of Shaw's.

He was, however, to devise an ingenious method of relieving the pressure when he left East Stirling for St Mirren; he called his old friend Davie Provan, the Rangers team-mate whose leg had been broken in an Old Firm match, back from England and handed him the triple role of player, coach and pub manager. How was that for delegation?

Ferguson had learned much in a playing career of 16 years, 432 matches and 222 goals.

At Queen's Park, though an amateur, he had begun to learn the ways of the professional game and how they could be improved.

At St Johnstone, he had learned first to be wary of promises and then how to cope with relegation.

At Dunfermline, where Jock Stein had laid down a frame-work for growth through youth development, he had learned how a football club should be run and how enjoyable the professional game could be.

At Rangers he had learned how a football club should *not* be run and experienced the ultimate in disillusion.

At Falkirk, reunited with Willie Cunningham, he had learned

coaching on a practical level and began to realise that the certificate he had obtained on the Ayrshire coast could prove the start of something big.

At Ayr, Ally MacLeod had believed in him. He had taken such encouragement in his stride – it is not an unusual trait in footballers – while resentfully absorbing the lessons of adversity. Such as being silently omitted from a Cup final by Cunningham at the last possible moment. When Ferguson himself became a manager, he resolved to give advance notice of disappointment to any player likely to be mistakenly expecting a shirt on a big occasion. 'It is basic to my philosophy of management,' he wrote in his autobiography in 1999.

A quarter of a century earlier, he had had thrown away his boots and collected the theories amassed over the span of his playing career, from the *catenaccio* classes with Seith at Largs to the salt and pepper sessions at Dunfermline to the spying missions on which Cunningham sent him at Falkirk. Now it was time for the university of managerial life.

EAST STIRLINGSHIRE

Small Wonders

There are only about 32,000 people in Falkirk and yet, despite its proximity to the footballing temptations of Glasgow and Edinburgh, the town supports two clubs in the Scottish League. One is Falkirk and the other East Stirlingshire. It is fair to say that East Stirlingshire is the smaller.

While Falkirk have won the Scottish Cup twice and not only produced several internationals – most memorably John White, who distinguished himself in Tottenham Hotspur's great Double team of 1960/61 – the twin peaks of East Stirlingshire's existence since 1880 have been promotions to the top division in 1932 and 1963.

Each lasted a single season. On the latter occasion, they rose in second place, behind the St Johnstone whose squad included Ferguson. St Johnstone stayed up and nine years later, under the astute management of Willie Ormond, sallied forth into European competition, achieving victories over Hamburg and Vasas of Budapest in the Uefa Cup. In contrast, East Stirlingshire were relegated in 1964 having lost twenty-seven of their thirty-four matches.

When Ferguson arrived at their modest Firs Park ground

(the word 'stadium' is not always appropriate) to take over as manager in the summer of 1974, they were at the very bottom of Scottish football's pile. Or so Ferguson would have us believe. In fact, East Stirling, as they are usually known, had finished fourth from bottom the previous season.

There is also some disputing his contention that the club had eight players when he was engaged three weeks before the start of the new season. In *The Boss*, Michael Crick's justly acclaimed and rigorously researched book about Ferguson, it is described as 'part of the Ferguson mythology' that he teased the chairman, Willie Muirhead, about it, observing that eleven men were needed to start a game of football. According to Crick, no fewer than twelve members of the previous season's squad played for Ferguson in his four months at the club.

The question of 'the Ferguson mythology' is one to which we shall naturally return.

What cannot be doubted is that Ferguson faced an uphill task. He had no goalkeeper, for a start, and signing Tom Gourlay from Partick Thistle took £750 out of an allocation of just £2,000 for reinforcements. He then paid a budget-busting £2,000 to keep the forward Billy Hulston, a former East Stirling favourite, out of Stenhousemuir's clutches.

Ferguson was thirty-two and already manifesting a relish for management reminiscent of Brian Clough, who had made his way from Hartlepool to Derby County a few years earlier. A defining Clough anecdote was that he drove to Archie Gemmill's home in 1970 to sign the Preston North End midfield player and, upon being told that Gemmill planned instead to join Harry Catterick's Everton, the champions, declared that he would sleep in his car in the hope of a change of mind by morning; Gemmill's wife offered Clough the spare room and the signing for Derby was agreed over a breakfast of fried eggs.

That Ferguson, too, had a flair for the persuasive gesture had been evident in the Hulston signing. Removing £50 from his wallet, he spread the notes in front of the player as an extra inducement to sign for East Stirling without first having the courtesy to inform Stenhousemuir. Nor did Ferguson waste any time in showing that applied psychology would be characteristic of his style of management.

From where did that come? Stein, Bill Shankly. And maybe Ally MacLeod, too. Ferguson's year at Ayr had been a happy and useful one, for all the injury problems that had persuaded him to quit as a player, and MacLeod had no hesitation in recommending him as a manager, first to Queen's Park, where Ferguson made a mess of his interview through nerves induced by having to face people under whom he had served as a young player, and then East Stirling. An East Stirling director, Bob Shaw, had encountered MacLeod at the World Cup in Germany and sought his opinion of the headstrong aspirant. It was positive and Ferguson now sailed through his interview, he and Muirhead taking to each other despite the limited resources the chairman was able to offer.

Ferguson accepted the notionally part-time job on £40 a week and, of course, did it full-time, despite his interests in the licensed trade and a young family. There were rows over money, not least when he was rebuked for paying a Glasgow junior club £40 in travelling expenses to come to test his young trialists, but plenty of encouraging moments. The players responded to him. One, Bobby McCulley, was famously quoted by Crick as saying: 'I'd never been afraid of anyone before but he [Ferguson] was a frightening bastard.'

He knew when to impose fear and when to remove it. In an early match at Forfar, his team came in for half-time trailing 3-0. Ferguson told them they had played well and could still win. They drew 3-3. On other occasions, he would exhibit a tendency to disturb half-time teacups. But the highlight of his 117 days at Firs Park came towards the end: a local derby. Falkirk had been relegated from the top division the season before and this enabled Ferguson to take a liberal portion of a dish best served cold.

The opportunity for revenge on the club and manager, John Prentice, who had rejected him came in October. A crowd of nearly 5,000 — about 12 times the number to which East Stirling had been accustomed — gathered to witness the fruits of the new manager's effort. But much was done before the match kicked off.

Ferguson, having informed the local paper that he was aware of all the strengths and weaknesses of the Falkirk players — he had been playing with and coaching them eighteen months earlier — arranged with Muirhead to have his team eat at a hotel where he knew Falkirk, too, would be having their pre-match meal. As his men arrived and walked past the window of the room where their counterparts were eating, he ordered them to laugh and joke as if carefree and confident.

Ferguson then got up to some more of what we now recognise as old tricks, telling his team the local press were biased in favour of the bigger club but then going through Falkirk's individual weaknesses — lack of pace, one-footedness and so on — to the extent that his men went out thoroughly believing they could win.

It was not all propaganda — the strikers, for instance, were advised to shoot early for a corner of the net rather than try to take the ball round Falkirk's goalkeeper – and East Stirling, fuelled by this heady cocktail of morale and useful information, won 2-0.

Soon they were in fourth place in their division, drawing crowds of more than 1,200 rather than a few hundred, but such clubs are seldom buoyant for long and the usual happened. It was later to happen to St Mirren, and Aberdeen. A club with more potential identified the secret of their success – and bought it.

To be fair to Ferguson, he accepted St Mirren's shilling with reluctance, or at least left East Stirling with a heavy heart, for he had grown genuinely fond of his first managerial charges, not to mention Muirhead. But quit he did.

The call had come even before the derby and, since the caller, the familiar Willie Cunningham, was at that time the manager of St Mirren, Ferguson could hardly have guessed at the motive behind an invitation to the club's Love Street ground in Paisley, a few miles from Govan. Cunningham said he was about to retire and asked if Ferguson would like to succeed him. Ferguson agreed to see the chairman, Harold Currie, but remained unsure. St Mirren were, without question, a bigger club, having spent much of their existence in the top division and with a sizeable ground that had once held more than 47,000 for a match against Celtic. However, they were below East Stirling in the Second Division table and pulling crowds no higher.

Ferguson rang Jock Stein, by now a friend as well as an inspiration, and the Celtic manager advised him first to go to the highest point of Love Street's main grandstand and look around, and then to do the same at Firs Park. We shall never know what Stein would have counselled had Ferguson got the job for which he was interviewed before East Stirling, for

Queen's Park's Hampden home then dwarfed not just Love Street but every other stadium in Scotland. Anyway, Ferguson got the message.

Later, when he became as big as Stein and even more widely sought after for assistance on managerial posts, he tended to give similar advice, telling people to go for potential. It was a principle Ferguson himself followed, for example in rejecting Wolverhampton Wanderers when that club was overreaching itself and about to take a tumble down England's divisions – and in going enthusiastically to Manchester United.

By 2009, when Ferguson was renewing his campaign to have the United board increase Old Trafford's capacity towards 90,000, the official figure for East Stirlingshire's ground was 1,800. This included two hundred seats, which made the Firs Park stand about the same size as Old Trafford's press box on a Champions League night. East Stirlingshire were still the smaller club of even their own small town – but they will forever be able to boast of having been the first of Alex Ferguson's managerial career.

SAINTS ALIVE:
THE LOVE STREET YEARS

Building on Baldy

So the first club to hire Alex Ferguson as a manager was East Stirlingshire. The first to fire him was St Mirren. But the stigma was hurled at a clean pair of heels because, by then, Ferguson was bound for Aberdeen; it was an untidy ending to an often troubled relationship.

The early signs had been promising. Ferguson knew the area and talked a good game, portraying St Mirren as potent enough to challenge Rangers and Celtic (although they tended to finish in the lower half of the First Division, they had won the Scottish Cup in 1959). He also found the seeds of a youth-development system that was to help make his reputation. But first he had to build a team of assistants.

One took about a year of cajoling. Ricky McFarlane had been a young physiotherapist at Falkirk, under John Prentice, and then East Stirling, but clearly had more than the treatment of injuries to offer, as he was to emphasise by training the players while still in his early twenties and eventually becoming manager of St Mirren.

While McFarlane took some time to be convinced that the Ferguson project was for him, Davie Provan leapt at the chance to join. When Ferguson rang his old Rangers team-mate, Provan was still playing, albeit not to the standard he had reached before his leg-break. Upon becoming surplus to requirements at Ibrox, he had gone to Crystal Palace on a free transfer but made only one League appearance and subsequently moved down a couple of divisions to Plymouth Argyle, where he played for five years.

Ferguson knew of his interest in coaching and called him back to Scotland. 'It sounded like a good move,' said Provan. 'I would play – but not a lot [he made thirteen appearances]. The main idea was to look after the St Mirren second team for Alex. I'd been to Largs and also to the English coaching centre at Lilleshall. I had my qualifications and was delighted to get the chance to use them.'

Especially as it involved a little extra money on the side. Because Ferguson needed help with his pub. Fergie's was proving such an avid time-consumer that, in his autobiography, Ferguson concedes that helping Cathy with their three young sons came third in his list of priorities, at least in terms of time; it almost beggars belief that in 1975 he became involved in the second pub, Shaw's.

So Provan took on a dual role, pulling pints and changing kegs at Fergie's by day and training young footballers at St Mirren in the evenings. 'It suited us both,' he said. 'The wages were handy for me – the money in football then wasn't like today's – and Alex would have had to get someone else into the pub otherwise. He knew he could rely on me and not have to worry all the time. So I'd work there before taking the reserves for training in the evening.'

Although Ferguson's job at St Mirren was again notionally part-time, he was in early and often stayed late (a habit that remained with him through the Manchester United years). He naturally shouldered such a burden that once he was in the middle of a pre-match address to his players when the dressing-room door burst open and a steward interjected: 'Boss, the toilets in the stand are blocked.'

So he could have done without the distraction of Fergie's, however rich the material it was to provide for his literary efforts in later life. There was a feeling that Ferguson, though he fell in with custom by taking home goods pilfered from the docks and sold in the pub at knockdown prices (Cathy's eyes would roll as these unwanted bargains appeared in the house), was as much sinned against as sinning in the licensed trade and he often seemed more short of money than you would expect of a football manager, even one in the habit of betting on horses.

He needed help and Provan was 'as conscientious and trust-worthy a man as you could ever have by your side'. Ferguson said Provan joined him as assistant manager but Provan, with characteristic modesty, toned this down. 'I helped Alex out with the first team from time to time,' he said, 'but didn't have a lot of input.' Ferguson valued him as a bridge between the youth and senior ranks. 'But really everything with the first team was down to Alex,' insisted Provan. 'There were three of us in the backroom team – Ricky McFarlane, Eddie McDonald and me – and we were all 100 per cent behind him.' And yet neither McFarlane nor McDonald is mentioned in Ferguson's book.

McFarlane is an especially glaring omission, given that he had followed Ferguson from East Stirling to St Mirren at Ferguson's instigation, become a key aide to the manager and later done well himself.

He had played football, once being on the schoolboy books of Celtic, but conceded that 'no one ever paid me to do it'. As a coach he became more valuable and McFarlane is in good company there, with Arrigo Sacchi, José Mourinho and the rest. Nor should anyone imagine that the transition from physiotherapist to manager was unique, there being the shining examples of Bertie Mee, under whom Arsenal won the Double in 1971, and Bob Paisley, who helped Liverpool to win just about everything between 1974 and 1983 (though Paisley had been a respectable player too).

McFarlane, having produced a team that 'soared high in Scotland's top flight, playing a brand of football that captivated the Black And White Army' (*Paisley Daily Express*, 2008), quietly went back to his physiotherapist's practice in 1983 and it was there, more than a quarter of a century later, during a break from attending to the aches and pains of patients, that he first spoke of his separation from Ferguson and the latter's coolness towards him.

If it was distressing, he betrayed little sign of it: more a sense of regret that the contributions to St Mirren's rise of players and others — not least Currie's successor as chairman, Willie Todd — had been overshadowed in Ferguson's memoirs.

Todd, indeed, was ruthlessly disparaged in the book, and perhaps that was understandable given the acrimonious build-up to Ferguson's departure in 1978 and the industrial tribunal case that followed, but McFarlane insisted that Todd was a good man who 'was kind to Alex and did a lot for him'. That, however, is best considered in the context of chronology.

Ferguson had been at the club almost a year by the time McFarlane joined St Mirren, having finally been persuaded after a chance meeting as Ferguson drove his car past a shop from which McFarlane was emerging.

When he had arrived, the furniture had included a remarkable character called Archibald 'Baldy' Lindsay – and Ferguson's autobiography denies Lindsay not a whit of credit for the identification and recruitment of young players. He calls Lindsay 'perhaps the most remarkable of the countless scouts that I have used during my career in management' and speaks of him movingly, never more so than in relating how, after a long spell of silence between them – if one felt the other was behaving like a fool, neither would suffer it gladly – Lindsay rang him at Aberdeen to recommend a youngster, Joe Miller, who happened to be his nephew. Miller went on to play for not only Aberdeen but Celtic and Scotland, although by then Lindsay, who had been ailing when he made the call, was long since dead.

Baldy Lindsay was a taxi-driver who had run a football club for youngsters. Nurturing talent was his passion and one of his favourites was Billy Stark, a polite young man who had trained as a schoolboy with Rangers and Dumbarton while playing for the Under-18 team of the noted amateur club Anniesland Waverley, where players had to report for matches in collars and ties.

Once a noted Argentine author was asked why his country had produced so many fine footballers (albeit mainly for export). 'It is simple,' he replied. 'Because all over Argentina, in every small town or village, there are unselfish men who see it as their role in life to teach children how to play properly.' The Scotland in which Ferguson grew up had been reminiscent of that; he paid fulsome tribute to Douglas Smith, the founder of Drumchapel Amateurs, and, a generation on,

Stark received the benefit of similar tuition at Anniesland.

Even after Stark left school to become a trainee draughtsman, he was pursued by Lindsay despite the scepticism of Ferguson, who thought the lanky lad a 'beanpole' liable to struggle with the demands of the senior game.

Many years later, having enjoyed a fine career and become manager of the Scotland Under-21 team, Stark chuckled at the recollection. 'Baldy would phone the house every night or turn up at the door to badger me into going to St Mirren. Eventually I did. I signed for Ferguson on the bus home from a pre-season friendly at Selkirk in the Borders. The strange thing was that I'd had a nightmare of a match, certainly in the first half – I improved to mediocre in the second. And Ferguson signed me. I was astonished.

'It was only the second time I'd met him. The first time had been the night I played at Love Street in a [specially arranged] game for Anniesland Waverley. All he said then was 'You did okay and we'll keep an eye on you.' Later it struck me that it wouldn't have mattered to him how well I did at Selkirk. He'd have been looking for specific things.'

And trusting Baldy Lindsay. Stark became an elegant and effective member of Ferguson's St Mirren team before also joining him at Aberdeen and winning a championship medal.

Ferguson never pretended to have initiated the St Mirren youth policy. Already secured were the midfielder Tony Fitzpatrick, whom Ferguson, after seeking Provan's opinion, promoted to the first team as captain at eighteen, and a central defender, Bobby Reid, who might have achieved greater things but for a knee injury. But Ferguson did make the system prolific.

'I was forced to do it,' he said later, 'because there was no money to buy players. But once you get used to working with young kids and seeing them come through to the first team you know it's a good way. It's a great source of satisfaction.'

'He's done it all his career,' remarked Stark, 'and it takes a brave man.'

There is a saying among managers that the problem with a youth policy is that your successors get the benefit of it after you have been sacked, and it applied to Ferguson at St Mirren. He brought in the striker Frank McGarvey after being tipped off by the Rangers scout Willie Thornton that he was 'no use to Rangers' (in other words, Roman Catholic). McGarvey went on to play for Scotland. As did the left-back Iain Munro and centre-forward Jimmy Bone. And the production line served Ferguson's successors such as Jim Clunie and McFarlane, whose sides included not only Fitzpatrick and other Paisley notables such as Lex Richardson and Billy Abercromby but a young Frank McAvennie and Peter Weir, yet another destined to play for his country.

When Stark arrived, the manager's first requirement had been met. For the 1975/6 season, Scottish football was being reorganised. In place of a First Division of 18 clubs and a Second of 20 there would be a Premier Division of 10 and a First and Second of 14 each. So Mirren's task was to get into the middle tier by finishing in the top six of the Second Division. Fitzpatrick's precocious craft and leadership proved the catalyst for an improvement that saw them win eight times in a row to qualify with a couple of matches to spare.

Stark Improvement

Billy Stark came into all this knowing Ferguson mainly as a player. He remembered having been taken to Rangers matches by his father and appreciating Ferguson's goals and 'his rumbustiousness, his aggression'. And how did he now like him as a manager? 'Well,' said Stark, 'I'd no one to compare him with, but "like" is not the term I would use. Anyway, would you find any manager a *nice* man? What you could certainly recognise in him was that drive, that almost manic desire which I think has played a big part in his success. I think he's unique in that way and you picked up on it straight away. He was thirty-three and still had that youthful enthusiasm. You thought it was his age but, of course, he's carried it through his career.

'Coming from Anniesland Waverley. I was used to discipline, but he was on to you for every tiny detail. Dress code, timekeeping – he was very big on those things. And he had an omnipresence. You always felt you were being watched by him, at or around the club.

'It was the same at Aberdeen. Even though by then he'd allow his assistant – Archie Knox, or whoever it was at the time – to take training and there'd be no sign of him and at first, knowing him, you'd think it strange, and then suddenly the Merc would pull into the car park. Sometimes he'd just watch from there. It was for effect – no doubt about it. You'd know he was there.

'It was something he tried to impose on you – that there was nothing you did that he didn't know about. That control thing has always been a part of him. Right from the start at St Mirren – the embryonic stage.'

The sharpness of Stark's observation was borne out many years later when Ferguson, discussing the degree of delegation that had helped him, he believed, to stay so long at Manchester United, recalled his first glimmer of understanding that it had its uses.

Archie Knox, whom he had made his assistant at Aberdeen – they were to have a long and cheerfully foul-mouthed association – was frustrated. 'I don't know why you brought me here,' he complained. Ferguson expressed bewilderment. 'I don't do anything,' said Knox. Ferguson replied that he looked after the players in the afternoons. 'I'm the fucking assistant manager,' Knox stormed on. 'And you still do all the training sessions! It's ridiculous.'

The only other person present was Teddy Scott, a long-serving member of the Pittodrie coaching staff to whom Ferguson always listened. Scott looked at Knox, then at Ferguson, and said: 'He's right.' The way Ferguson remembered it was that Scott continued: 'Why are you doing all the training sessions, barking and yelling and coaching all the time. You should be observing. You should be in control.'

That was when the penny dropped: when Ferguson heard the word 'control'.

The next day he told Knox he would 'give it a go'. Knox snorted. So he agreed to let Knox train the team on a permanent basis and Stark, when he arrived at Aberdeen in 1983, noticed the difference.

St Mirren under Ferguson had finished sixth out of fourteen in the new First Division and the next season, with McFarlane helping Ferguson to guide the first team, they achieved promotion as champions, giving Ferguson his first honour as a manager. Just as encouraging had been the presence in a Scotland Under-21 squad of four St Mirren players: Stark, McGarvey, Fitzpatrick and Reid.

By now the supporters were buoyant – they had provided the bulk of the £17,000 it cost to bring Jackie Copland, a strong and experienced defender, from Dundee United – although progress was not always smooth behind the scenes. Once Ferguson, furiously lecturing the players on the evils of drink after they had been caught in a pub, smashed a Coca-Cola bottle against a wall, showering them. 'The quickness of my temper and depth of my anger often worried me,' he recalled. Yet Stark, looking back, could see method in much of his madness.

'It could have you in turmoil,' Stark said, 'but it made a better player out of me. There were countless episodes, but the worst I personally suffered was when we played Celtic at Love Street and eventually lost 3-1. During the game, Celtic got a free-kick around halfway. I was playing right midfield and turned to jog back. They took it quick, played it over my head to someone who crossed and they scored.

'After the game, Ferguson went loopy. I was in a corner getting changed when suddenly he threw a boot at me. That's why I always have a laugh when people talk about the David

Beckham incident.' This right-sided midfielder escaped injury – while Beckham was to require a couple of stitches over an eye, Stark got away with a blow on a shoulder – but the memory remains vivid. 'I was distraught and yet it was a defining moment. I don't believe these incidents were off the cuff. Part of his method was to test players, to see if they had the stuff to go forward rather than buckle.

'I resolved to prove myself to him. I never again, in my career, turned my back on the ball. If he'd just had a quiet word with me, it might have been different. But the ferocity of the message embedded it. I was about nineteen at the time – and it saw me through another seventeen years.'

The 'hairdryer' treatment – as Mark Hughes was to describe it at Manchester United – was often in evidence. 'He'd come right up to players, bawling in their faces,' said Stark. 'But nobody ever challenged it. You just took it.' As Provan observed: 'Players in those days didn't answer back. He got through to them. And we were promoted.'

Among those taking notice was Ally MacLeod, by now at Aberdeen but preparing to take charge of the Scottish national squad. As Willie Cunningham had done at St Mirren, he asked Ferguson if he fancied being his successor at Pittodrie, but on this occasion Ferguson put his own interpretation on Jock Stein's advice. Although Aberdeen were a bigger club with room for expansion – under MacLeod they had finished third in the League and won the League Cup, and plans were already under way to develop their ground into a 23,000-capacity all-seater to take advantage of the North Sea oil boom – he told MacLeod he preferred to try to take St Mirren to the same level.

It was never going to happen. Although crowds had risen

at St Mirren, money remained tight and Ferguson's young team struggled in the Premier League, especially after Christmas, winning only four of their last eighteen matches (and losing twice to Billy McNeill's championship-challenging Aberdeen). The threat of relegation was kept at bay, but the atmosphere at the club became inimical to progress of the sort envisaged by Ferguson a year earlier.

A Nest of Vipers

Every account makes Love Street sound like a nest of vipers. Not least Ferguson's, which portrayed Willie Todd, the director who had taken over from Harold Currie as chairman, as an ego-driven megalomaniac meddler with a constant need to be put in his place. Todd's ally on a quarrelling board was John Corson, whom Ferguson dismissed as a footballing ignoramus unable to recognise Fitzpatrick when he was club captain. Michael Crick's book offers a balanced picture of Todd in quoting the former director Tom Moran: 'Bill Todd was one of those guys that, once you got on the wrong side of him, there was no dealing with him . . . he and Fergie were at each other's throats.'

So much for the office politics, which were to become so bitter that Ferguson's secretary, June Sullivan, was drawn into a conflict of loyalties that led to Ferguson first speaking sharply to her and then not speaking to her at all.

That the club, despite an increase in the average crowd from 2,000 to 11,000, had been unable to keep pace with Ferguson's ambitions was emphasised by reports speculating that he might succeed Jock Wallace at Rangers. Nor was he in any mood to disbelieve his own publicity. At one stage towards the end of that 1977/8 season, he demanded not only a Mercedes car but a salary of £25,000 which St Mirren clearly could not afford (to put it in perspective, at that time McNeill had Aberdeen challenging for the championship on £11,500 a year). Something must have told him he was in a position of strength and everyone who was at St Mirren then – except Ferguson – says it was an indication that Aberdeen would offer him McNeill's job when the former Celtic captain returned to Parkhead to take over from Jock Stein.

The exact sequence of events is hard to define. All that seems plain is the implausibility of Ferguson's claim, both to the industrial tribunal and in a subsequent book, *A Light in the North*, written while he was at Aberdeen, that the approach from Aberdeen came on the evening of the day on which St Mirren sacked him.

He writes in his autobiography of a 1-0 victory at Ayr that eased the club's relegation worries and adds: 'Willie Todd and I were no longer talking to each other and when Aberdeen made another approach to me there could be only one reaction.' The length of time between the Ayr match and the approach is not specified, but the match took place on 18 March and he was not sacked by St Mirren until 31 May – nearly eleven weeks later later and a full month after the end of the season.

Not only that: 'My position [in deciding how to receive Aberdeen's advances] was complicated by the fear that St Mirren might have enough of a contractual hold on me to encourage them to sue. So I foolishly delayed announcing my decision to leave and thus gave Todd a chance to implement his plans to get rid of me.' This last sentence removes any doubt that both Todd and Ferguson correctly believed the end was nigh before the ugly formality of dismissal confirmed it.

But for how long? Given the uncharacteristic vagueness of Ferguson's recollection, the best hope of precision went to the grave with Jim Rodger in 1997.

In *A Light in the North*, Ferguson wrote: 'This time contact was made with me through one of the most powerful and influential sports writers in Britain ([Rodger] . . . a man of the utmost integrity and one you can trust with your life.' In his autobiography, he calls Rodger 'an invaluable friend to me'. But Rodger was also a friend to Todd and St Mirren, whom he just as discreetly tipped off not only that Ferguson was planning to leave – and take the bright young Stark with him – but that Aberdeen were hoping to avoid paying St Mirren compensation for the three years left on Ferguson's contract.

So Todd did indeed start plotting and, on the last day of May 1978, Ferguson was summoned to Love Street, sacked, and read a list of thirteen supposed offences from a type-written sheet to which St Mirren were to allude in claiming that he had broken his contract. Ferguson laughed, saying the only reason to get rid of a manager was incompetence, but cleared his desk and the same evening was speaking to the Aberdeen chairman, Dick Donald, accepting his offer and promising to drive north the next morning. A whirlwind romance and no mistake.

The Paisley public, of course, and St Mirren squad were shocked but, said Stark, the players had little chance to dwell on the news because it came in the close season and the nation was preoccupied with Scotland's prospects at the forthcoming World Cup.

As Ferguson hit the road, his old mentor Ally MacLeod,

whose bullish prognostications about what the Scots could achieve in Argentina had caused much excitement in the land and curiosity farther afield, was supervising one of the last training sessions before the match against Peru that was to burst the bubble. Scotland lost 3-1 and, by way of complication, were obliged to send Willie Johnston home for failing a drugs test. Then they held Iran to 1-1 only with the help of an own goal. The final match was against mighty Holland and, with MacLeod's men requiring to win by three to reach the knockout stage, one wit famously asked: 'Where are we going to find three Dutchmen prepared to score own goals?'

At one stage, Scotland did in fact lead 3-1, Archie Gemmill's memorable solo providing false hope. The match ended 3-2. By then Ferguson was in the United States with the Aberdeen vice-chairman, Chris Anderson, 'studying the commercial initiatives associated with the North American Soccer League' (yes, the pace of life had certainly quickened since he encountered Aberdeen) before taking a family holiday in Malta.

Not that he forgot his farewells. Stark remembered taking a call from him.

St Mirren rose from eighth to sixth under Jim Clunie, then a heady third, then, under McFarlane, fourth, fifth and fifth again. But Aberdeen were always ahead of them; in the year St Mirren finished third, Ferguson's Aberdeen were champions. Nor did the Love Street crowds quite match the levels of the Ferguson era. Players were lost, some of them, such as Weir and Stark, to Ferguson. The dream had died — or moved to Aberdeen.

Rancour and Defeat

Behind was left rancour and bewilderment. Rumours often accompany the departure of a football manager and this was a classic case as the Scottish football community buzzed with talk of illicit payments and tax evasion that was, to an extent, borne out by the tribunal hearing a few months later.

Some of St Mirren's allegations against Ferguson were risible: that he had gone to the European Cup final, which was in London that year (Liverpool beat Bruges through a goal by Kenny Dalglish and, Ferguson pointed out, he saw it at his own expense); and allowed Love Street to be used free of charge for a Scottish Junior Cup semi-final (the club pettily argued that a fee might have been charged).

Others were dubious: that he had been paid for giving advice to a bookmaker (the man was an old friend); that he had taken £25 a week in expenses without the directors' knowledge (Ferguson later produced a letter contradicting this).

Further allegations, including those of unauthorised bonus offers to players, did indeed indicate an unacceptably cavalier attitude to relations with the board – and were to conspire in his painful defeat at the tribunal.

Ricky McFarlane was at his side throughout those final months at St Mirren. 'As someone who worked more closely with him than anyone,' he said, 'I would simply not countenance the idea of any serious financial irregularity. There were a few occasions when he did things without the authority of the board, with players and so on, but it was never to do with his own personal gain. I know him well enough to be utterly certain about that.'

But the rumour mill, McFarlane implied, had been even more unkind to Willie Todd, who was held responsible for undermining Ferguson – 'there were others on the board trying to do that' – and deserved better. 'Willie got a bad name and has had a bad name in Paisley ever since. I feel sorry for him and I think it is very sad, because Willie loved the club and put a lot of his own money into it, and did some super things for Alex.' Including sanction loans; more than £3,500 was owed to the club by Ferguson in accounts published, to Ferguson's mind mischievously, after his departure. 'Willie was good to Alex,' said McFarlane. 'And was a good man.'

In an interview with the *Guardian* in May 2008, Todd spoke of regret. 'Nobody at the club worked harder than Alex did,' he recalled, 'and everyone was grateful for what he achieved. I got on well with him at the time, we were good friends and I have seen him a few times since . . . But in 1978 it was a simple case of myself, as chairman, doing what was best for the football club. I had no option but to sack him in the end.

'Four days before he eventually left, I knew perfectly well that he had told all the staff that he was moving to Aberdeen . . . Jim Rodger told us that Alex had asked at least one member of the squad to go to Aberdeen with him. It was a clear breach of contract on his part. He was still under contract to St Mirren and Aberdeen had not contacted us to discuss compensation.

'There were various other stories at the time, such as Alex wanting players to receive tax-free expenses, but that was not the real issue. The issue was St Mirren being destabilised because the manager wanted to leave.' Hence the tribunal. 'I do regret it. As I said, we got on well. It was just a pity Aberdeen had not come out and said they wanted our manager because then we could have spoken about compensation and done things amicably.'

A year later, I asked Todd if he wanted to add to that. By now he was eighty-eight, but still a frequent attender at St Mirren's matches and proud of his status as the club's first honorary president; even Ferguson never disputed that Todd was a true fan. But it was not a welcome approach. 'I don't want to be bothered,' he said. 'I'm nearly ninety years of age and it was all a long time ago. We didn't want to do anything bad. But we had to do what the lawyers told us. If we hadn't taken their advice, maybe we'd have ended up with no compensation.

'When I say I regret it, I regret that mud had to be thrown at Alex's reputation. I don't regret getting compensation from Aberdeen.'

The Forgotten Man

While the dispute was raging, McFarlane stayed neutral. Because of what he knew, he declined to appear for either Ferguson or St Mirren at the tribunal.

This is not, of course, mentioned in Ferguson's autobiography, which simply says that, after being refused Jim McLean's permission to take Walter Smith from Dundee United as his assistant, he went for Pat Stanton, who had just ended his playing career at Aberdeen. 'He might deny that he wanted me to go,' said McFarlane, 'but it's the truth. He's that kind of person – you're either with him or you're not – but it would have been difficult for me to go to Aberdeen, for a lot of reasons.'

One was that the sums didn't add up. McFarlane had built a house in the new town of East Kilbride – near Ferguson, who had moved Cathy and the boys from the semi in Simshill – and it was a substantial detached residence, of the proportions required to accommodate a growing family (the McFarlanes ended up with five children). 'If I'd sold it,' he said, 'such were the house prices in Aberdeen at the time that I'd have got only a two-bed terrace for the same money. I was offered £6,000 a year to be Alex's assistant. When you've got a young family settled at school, that sort of money's not going to sway you. If it had been a huge salary like some people get in football now, it might have been different.

'I was at a dinner many years later and somebody mentioned that I'd turned down Fergie and Frank McGarvey said, "Aye, that was a bad mistake." But I wouldn't change the life I've had.' It enabled him to retain his philosophy. 'Football is more important than . . . than it should be, if you like.' Less important than life and death? He smiled. 'Yes, it is not true what Shanks said.'

One evening when McFarlane was manager of St Mirren, his eldest son was doing his homework. 'He used to ask me to help him and this was maths and it was a Friday night – I'll never forget it – and he came in with a piece of paper and said "Dad, can you do this?" And I just lost the plot. "You're talking to me on a Friday night about your stupid maths . . ." We had a match the next day and maybe we'd been under a bit of pressure. And I just saw his eyes opening wide and I thought, "What am I doing?"'

He had worked under Jim Clunie and, after a spell as caretaker, required persuasion by the board and players to take the manager's job. Later he had misgivings about taking charge of the Scotland Under-21s and after that, when Jock Stein offered to fix him up with another club job, asked the great man not to bother. McFarlane, by his own assertion, was not cut out for the hard and lonely and relentlessly driven world of management in which Ferguson thrived. But for the part he played in Ferguson's career to be overlooked was ludicrous.

His refusal to appear on Ferguson's behalf at the tribunal was crucial to the change in their relationship ('you're either with him or you're not') and McFarlane explained it by saying: 'There's actually a complexity of things that he doesn't know about. By the time he asked me to appear, certain things had been said to me by directors of the club and for me to go to the tribunal would not have been good for Alex because I would have been forced to say things [evidence was given under oath] that would not have been in his interests. So I told Alex I was not going to appear for either him or the directors.'

And did there follow thirty years – or more – of hurt? 'Not in any way at all,' said McFarlane. 'I don't feel hurt.' Or particularly estranged. He pointed out that during the World Cup of 1982 in Spain (from which Scotland were removed by the Soviet Union after Alan Hansen had collided with Ferguson's Aberdeen stalwart Willie Miller), they had met convivially. 'He and I went on a night out together. That was six years after St Mirren.' They would have encountered each other as fellow managers. 'We've also been to a couple of weddings of mutual friends and sat round the same table. A few years ago, he signed some autographs for me to give people. But I've never tried to make contact with him. Lots of people have gone down to see him and asked him to leave match tickets, but I'm not into all that. It's not my style.'

Nor to bear a grudge. 'Life's too short.' But Ferguson had never shared that philosophy. McFarlane smiled again. 'It's in his nature to take it to another level. Look at the BBC.'

If you did, if you had looked at BBC television between 2004, when a *Panorama* programme asked questions about the involvement of his son Jason in football as an agent, and 2009, when McFarlane was making his wry point (or, indeed if you had listened to BBC radio during the same period), you would not have heard an interview with Ferguson. As he told David Frost on ITV, he was waiting for the BBC to apologise. Then the slate would be wiped clean. It does not matter who you are. McFarlane's words resonate: 'You are either with him or you are not.'

St Mirren remained buoyant until in 1980 they reached the Uefa Cup, knocking out the Swedish club Elfsborg but losing to a St Etienne featuring the great Michel Platini (on precisely the same autumn nights, Ferguson's Aberdeen were being mauled 5–0 on aggregate by Liverpool in the equivalent of the Champions League).

The support never reached the levels of the Ferguson boom. There was a return to Europe under Alex Miller (assisted by Martin Ferguson) and even, in 1987, a Scottish Cup triumph under Alex Smith. In 1992, however, came relegation and the early part of the third millennium found St Mirren unsure whether they belonged at the first or second level of a Scottish game seeming to accept that never again could an Alex Ferguson – or Jim McLean – threaten the Old Firm.

It all serves to emphasise the magnitude of what Ferguson brought off at Aberdeen. 'In a strange way,' reflected McFarlane, 'my decision not to go may have helped him. He needed a year up there on his own initially, to fight his corner and make his own mind up about players.' David Provan, though Ferguson's affection for him was never to waver, was not invited, according to Ferguson, because he thought Aberdeen would consider one former Rangers player enough.

Nor was Provan to figure at Love Street. Instead, through a club director, he obtained a job as a whisky salesman. Later Scot Symon brought him back into football as second-team coach at Partick Thistle, working under Bertie Auld. The man who broke Provan's leg? 'Obviously there was animosity at the time of the injury,' said Provan, 'but . . .' Yes, life was too short. 'Bertie and I are still friends. I always remind him about the time he took a player off and played with ten men and explained that it was "for tactical reasons". Can you believe that? We always have a laugh about it.'

ABERDEEN

An Emotional Battering

Aberdeen, when Ferguson arrived, were already established as a club of some potency. They had finished second in the League in 1971 and 1972, won the League Cup under MacLeod in 1976/7 and in 1977/8, the sole season under McNeill that preceded Ferguson's arrival, had run Rangers close in both the League and Scottish Cup.

When they had played Ferguson's struggling St Mirren at Love Street in late March, the attendance had been 5,900; a month later, the clubs had met at Pittodrie in front of 17,250.

This was not a St Mirren. It was a club of harmony that could, once Ferguson had got going, be compared with Bobby Robson's Ipswich Town of the same era (when they met in the Uefa Cup in 1981, Ipswich were not only the holders of that trophy but English League leaders and in the midst of a five-match winning run in which their victims had included Liverpool and Manchester United, and Ferguson's Aberdeen still prevailed 4-2 on aggregate). It was a club with a vision at which Ferguson settled, a club with a brain. It was also a club with a budget and so Ferguson – he who had wanted a Mercedes and £25,000 from St Mirren – started on £12,000.

That was his basic pay. At St Mirren, he had been on £10,000 plus a £5,000 bonus for Premier League survival, and again there were incentives, albeit for winning trophies or finishing high in the League rather than merely remaining in it.

There were perks, too, and the car with which he started was not a Mercedes but a less racy Rover. Irresistibly we are drawn to the story of Ron Atkinson, Ferguson's extrovert predecessor at Manchester United, who, upon asking for a Mercedes at his interview, was told by the chairman, Martin Edwards, that the previous incumbent, Dave Sexton, had been happy with a Rover. 'I was hoping for a car,' growled Atkinson, 'not a dog.' Ferguson was more humble, or at least patient; he got his Mercedes in due course.

The deal also featured an interest-free loan of £18,000 towards the purchase of one of those expensive Aberdeen houses. He was glad of that; he had given up Fergie's towards the end of his time at St Mirren due to poor returns and unruly customers and, upon joining Aberdeen, tried to sell his half-share in Shaw's to Sam Falconer, only to find that his partner was in debt. The failure of the business was to be acknowledged by liquidation in 1980.

By then Ferguson was devoting all his attention to football and his family had happily settled in a new house in the village of Cults, just outside Aberdeen.

At first, however, Ferguson had shared a flat in the city centre with Pat Stanton and returned to East Kilbride after Saturday matches to spend the rest of the weekend with Cathy and the boys. It was not until early in 1979 that the family moved north.

The wife and bairns had been well out of Ferguson's first few months at Aberdeen. 'The early phase,' he volunteered, 'was a troubled time', not just in terms of his relationship with the players but personally. Some of the 'emotional battering' he took was, he confessed, self-inflicted through his determination to fight St Mirren, 'to humiliate them as they had me'.

Hence the tribunal case, foolishly pursued against the advice of both a lawyer recommended by the Scottish Professional Footballers' Association and his new club chairman, Dick Donald. With the help of another lawyer, Ferguson poured scorn on St Mirren's thirteen allegations and counter-claimed unfair dismissal, seeking £50,000 compensation for the three years left on his contract.

The most damaging allegation concerned his behaviour towards June Sullivan. He has always admitted swearing at her – 'don't you bloody do that again' – when she took Todd's side in a dispute over whether a player could be paid expenses tax-free but the club's account was that he continued to behave unreasonably, refusing to speak to her unless she apologised and generally carrying the either-with-him-or-against-him principle to ridiculous, even vindictive, lengths.

The rest of the evidence now appears little more than a laborious exchange of time-warped trivia – while the board questioned their manager's right to attend the European Cup final, the manager complained, dubiously, that the club were paying some players more than him – but the verdict of the tribunal chairman, William Courtney, and other members, one representing management and the other the trade unions, was unanimous: St Mirren, they concluded, 'were entitled to think that the deterioration in relations was likely to be irreversible . . . it was only a short, logical step to decide they had no choice but to dismiss, and in the Tribunal's view this was a conclusion reasonably arrived at'.

The blow to Ferguson and Cathy, who had supported his campaign, fell just before Christmas, when he was already under stress due to the terminal deterioration of his father's health.

He recalled it one May morning in 2008 at the Manchester United training ground. After dispensing champagne in plastic cups to journalists gathered to hear his reflections on the Champions League triumph over Chelsea in Moscow less than thirty-six hours earlier, he responded to a question on retirement by saying: 'The big fear is what you do with yourself. There are too many examples of people who retire and get buried in a box soon afterwards because they have lost the very thing that keeps them alive.' And then Ferguson became wistful.

'I remember when my dad had his sixty-fifth birthday,' he said. 'The Fairfields shipyard gave him a big dinner in Glasgow. There were three or four hundred of his fellow employees there and the bosses. It was a big night and I came down from Aberdeen. The following week, my mother phoned and said, "Your dad's going for an X-ray. He's got pains in his chest." I said, "It'll be the emotion." It was cancer. One week after his retirement. One week.'

His father continued to watch matches when he could and, although weak, was at Dens Park, Dundee, in mid-December 1978 to see Aberdeen beat Hibs 1-0 after extra time to reach the Scottish League Cup final. By the time they lost to Rangers at Hampden Park three months later, Alexander Ferguson was dead.

He died in hospital late in the afternoon of an Aberdeen match while his son, just a few miles away at Love Street, seethed in the away dugout; Aberdeen had led St Mirren 2-0 at half-time only to be held to a draw because of goals from McGarvey and Copland that briefly put Ferguson's former team on top of the League and demoted his current team from third to fourth.

Ferguson had spent most of the second half protesting to the referee as his team lost their grip on the match and had two men sent off and, according to one account, was angrily thumping on the door of the officials' dressing room afterwards while a St Mirren employee waited to break the news of his father. Ferguson denied this. He insisted that he had berated the referee only at half-time.

Immediately Ferguson went to the hospital. He had seen his father there the previous day and remembered his final words: 'It's just one of those things, Alex.' Martin was there; he had been there at the end. The funeral was on the Wednesday. After it, on the way back to Aberdeen, where his team were to play Partick Thistle that night, Ferguson pulled into a lay-by and cried. Aberdeen won 2-1.

Ferguson is Working

The death of Alexander Ferguson, a believer in the decency of socialism, occurred only a couple of months before the beginning of the end of Old Labour.

The elder of his sons was preparing Aberdeen for the League Cup final when James Callaghan's Government suffered a single-vote defeat in the House of Commons at the hands of a coalition of Conservatives, Liberals, Scottish Nationalists and Ulster Unionists. Five weeks later, a general election saw Margaret Thatcher become Britain's first female Prime Minister, to the increasing distaste of, among others, the manager of Aberdeen Football Club and later Manchester United, where the players were only too aware of his aversion to the bling culture caricaturing the ostentatious, consumptive society that survived Thatcher's leadership and pervaded the Blair and Brown years.

Oddly enough, the journalist and political commentator Andrew Marr reflected in 2007 in his riveting *A History of Modern Britain*, Margaret Thatcher had set out to foster things like neighbourliness and hard work – as I read it, I recognised the sort of principles Ferguson's parents liked to follow – not

A star is born: Ferguson hits the headlines with a hat-trick for St Johnstone against Rangers. Yet he spent the eve of the match under a cloud; thinking he would be playing for the reserve team at Perth, he feigned illness.

By joining Dunfermline Athletic, Ferguson (*front row, second from right*) took a step into full-time professionalism with an excellent side that had proved themselves in Europe. Ferguson's globe-trotting chum Willie Callaghan is back row, second from left.

They got the elbow: Scot Symon (*top left*) was sacked as Rangers manager shortly after Ferguson joined. Davie White (*top right*) got rid of Ferguson.

But not before those infamous elbows had taken a toll. Here Ferguson (*far right*) pleads innocence. However Billy McNeil (*right and below*) got the better, scoring for Celtic in a cup-final rout.

Fergie at Falkirk: as his career began to run down, Ferguson went to Falkirk and caught the coaching bug, encouraged by his old boss Willie Cunningham.

Family man: Ferguson with his wife, Cathy, and twins, Jason and Darren.

In his early months as Aberdeen manager, Ferguson fought his old club, St Mirren, at an industrial tribunal. Here he is seen outside a hearing with a smile that was to disappear as the verdict went against him.

Breaking the Old Firm: Aberdeen take their first Scottish title under Ferguson, seen in the middle of the celebrating throng.

And the trophies kept coming with Gordon Strachan showing his joy after scoring in the 1982 Scottish Cup final against Rangers.

The Glory of Gothenburg: Mark McGhee leads the Real Madrid defence a merry dance in the Cup-Winners' Cup final of 1983.

On the flight home, Ferguson made sure even the press shared the champagne – here the author (*left*) awaits his turn as Gordon Simpson and Gerry McNee raise the cup.

Union Street, Aberdeen's main thoroughfare, was often packed with joyous crowds during the Ferguson era. Here he shows the people the Cup-Winners' Cup. They never found out about the ensuing punch-up at Pittodrie.

Sobering experience: after the ecstasy of Gothenburg, Aberdeen still had work to do that season – and they completed it by winning the Scottish Cup. Yet Ferguson criticised his team in a TV interview, a mistake he later corrected by apologising to the team.

Two generations of greatness:
Ferguson with Jock Stein (*left*), a
friend and a hero. Stein died before
the 1986 World Cup and Ferguson
took the team, complete with
strangely designed shorts (*middle*),
to Mexico. A defeat to Denmark did
not put them out, but failure to beat
Uruguay, after Ferguson had dropped
Graeme Souness (*bottom*), saw them
head for home.

consumer credit or 'show-off wealth'. Marr noted: 'That is the thing about freedom. When you free people, you can never be sure what you are freeing them for.'

As the Saatchi-conceived posters that helped to win that momentous election – 'Labour Isn't Working' – began to peel, it became evident that Ferguson was working effectively.

The outcome of what you might call his transitional season at Aberdeen was satisfactory: true, the League position had slipped from second to fourth (Celtic, retrieving the title from Rangers in McNeill's first season, and Jim McLean's Dundee United had overtaken them), but after the League Cup final his team had overcome Celtic to reach the last four of the Scottish Cup. In Europe they were knocked out by Fortuna Düsseldorf after overcoming an obscure Bulgarian team, but this could be ascribed to the learning process.

Anyway, such disappointments as Ferguson was experiencing were being sustained at a higher level, which was the point of the exercise.

Indeed, his immediate aspiration had been to go as high as Scotland could offer, which entailed overcoming the fatalism ingrained in the footballing culture of this and other countries where, decade after decade, the same two or three clubs are to be found sharing the trophies. It meant, in other words, beating Rangers and Celtic on a regular basis.

This Ferguson was to do. Within two years he had made Aberdeen champions for only the second time in their existence and, by the time he had left for Manchester United after eight complete seasons, they had a total of four titles. Their number of Scottish Cup triumphs had been increased from two to six and League Cup successes from two to three. In addition they had won the European Cup-Winners' Cup.

They had been doing pretty well before he came and under Davie Halliday, whose long spell of management straddled the Second World War, they had won each of the main trophies once. But nothing had prepared the Granite City for the frequency of celebration that jammed its main thoroughfare, Union Street, during the Ferguson era.

It would not have been possible without an enlightened board. There were three directors: Dick Donald, the chairman and owner of local pleasure palaces – cinemas, bingo and dance halls – the energetic and enterprising Chris Anderson, and Charlie Forbes. All had played for Aberdeen at one level or another. (Donald's son Ian, who also became a director in Ferguson's time, had been signed by Manchester United as a teenager and made a few appearances before being let go by Tommy Docherty in order to find a more appropriate level. After brief spells with Partick Thistle and Arbroath, he retired unnoticed and later took a seat on the Aberdeen board, serving for twenty-four years, four of them as chairman.)

Encouraged by the air of prosperity created by North Sea oil, and in the knowledge that the club, its nearest rivals being the Dundee duo more than sixty miles down the coast, could appeal to not only the 210,000 citizens of Aberdeen but inhabitants of the agricultural hinterland and fishing ports – again the comparison with Ipswich holds good – Anderson and Dick Donald had arranged for the modernisation of Pittodrie.

In 1980 it became Britain's first all-seated and all-covered stadium, preceding the provisions of Lord Justice Taylor's report by a decade, and, although the capacity of 23,000 was seldom tested in the early years despite the team's achievements, the average had risen to a healthy 15,000 by the time Ferguson left.

With this Aberdeen could compete with Rangers and Celtic at the time. Football was less fashionable than now and even Glasgow's big two struggled to half-fill their stadiums except when playing each other.

The historical perspective as viewed in 1978 would nevertheless have daunted a lesser man than Ferguson.

From 1904 to the outbreak of the Second World War in 1939, only one club other than Rangers or Celtic had won the Scottish League (Motherwell in 1932). The official resumption of football in 1946 seemed to bring a more competitive environment, with Hibs taking three titles, their Edinburgh rivals Hearts two and Aberdeen one, but most observers thought those days had gone with the failures of Dundee and Kilmarnock to sustain their successes of 1962 and 1965 respectively.

For fifteen years, starting with the assembly of the Stein Machine at Celtic, the Old Firm had resumed their dominance. Ferguson and his old room-mate Jim McLean, by now firmly established at Dundee United and beginning to harvest the fruits of a youth policy similar to Ferguson's, set about breaking it.

Making Winners

Some great managers of the 1960s, notably Bill Shankly at Liverpool and Don Revie at Leeds United, had attempted to change their club's psychology by changing its strip. Naturally they had been influenced by the all white of Real Madrid, which Revie adopted exactly; Shankly sensibly retained Liverpool's red but extended it to the shorts and socks. Their idea, we supposed, was to have their teams look uncompromising and substantial.

Ferguson had tried a variation on it at East Stirling, suggesting that their wishy-washy black and white hoops should give way to bold white shirts, black shorts and red socks – and been firmly slapped down by an aged conservative on the board. At Aberdeen the job had already been done, in 1966, during Eddie Turnbull's management. The team played in all red, like Liverpool. At least they wore all red. The miracle would take a little longer.

The first tactical decision Ferguson made was to move the defensive line forward. The season before his arrival, Aberdeen had had the best defensive record in the Premier Division, but Ferguson felt the habit of defending deep, understandable

120

because the centre-backs, Willie Miller and Willie Garner (gradually to be replaced by Alex McLeish), were not the quickest, worked against his philosophy of going on the offensive against Rangers, Celtic or anyone else.

He also resolved to phase out the local hero. Joe Harper, the fellow striker with whom Ferguson had toured as a player on the 'Scotland' trip in 1967, had been taken to the World Cup in Argentina by MacLeod, appearing against Iran, but his chubby face did not fit with Ferguson, who disapproved of his drinking and general attitude to fitness.

Inevitably, Ferguson addressed youth development. 'My experience with St Mirren,' he was to say, 'strengthened my belief that youth was the way forward. At Aberdeen the likes of Willie Miller, Alex McLeish, John McMaster and Doug Rougvie had already come through the ranks so all I did was strengthen the scouting system. We scoured the country and found Neale Cooper, Neil Simpson, Eric Black, John Hewitt, Dougie Bell, Bryan Gunn and the rest.'

Almost mischievously, it seemed, he arranged for a satellite academy to be set up in Glasgow; in truth this was less a gesture of defiance to the Old Firm than a reflection of Ferguson's belief that West of Scotland youngsters tended to have more of the necessary devil in their make-up.

He worked closely with the chief scout, Bobby Calder, but went to see countless prospects for himself, sometimes more than once because he wanted to assess them in adversity – against a stronger side, say, or in wind and rain – as well as favourable conditions. He liked to meet the parents too, in order not merely to judge the boys' backgrounds but to estimate how much they might grow physically.

As well as the serene and thoughtful Pat Stanton, there was

the assistance in those challenging early days of Teddy Scott, a popular piece of the Pittodrie furniture who did far more than fulfil his basic function as reserve team coach – Ferguson called him 'indispensable' – and, of course, the highly supportive Dick Donald and Chris Anderson.

The chairman ran the club informally, doing much to foster its family atmosphere with his avuncular manner. Donald was always on hand to offer advice and Ferguson, relieved to be away from the strife of St Mirren, appreciated it. Some people even thought he had mellowed.

They were wrong. When he arrived, he had been thirty-six, only a few years older than some senior players, who were suspicious of him: quite naturally, for the club had been doing well under the previous regimes of MacLeod and McNeill. They objected not only to changes he made in training but the manner in which he demanded them and his explanations, which he admitted later could be ham-fisted in that he often compared players unflatteringly with former charges at St Mirren from whom, understandably, they felt they had little to learn.

There were men who had played for Scotland – Harper, the right-back Stuart Kennedy, the veteran goalkeeper Bobby Clark and Willie Miller, a leader from the back who, though only twenty-three, had been club captain for two years – and others who would go on to represent their country and earn even wider fame such as Gordon Strachan, Alex McLeish and Steve Archibald. There was also the goalkeeper Jim Leighton, who would succeed Clark and eventually be taken by Ferguson to a World Cup and then Manchester United, where his omission from an FA Cup final replay scarred him so deeply that a quarter of a century later he preferred to maintain a dignified silence about it.

Like Leighton, McLeish was on the fringes of the first team and once, when Ferguson directed a post-match tirade at the young defender, Miller brusquely intervened, asking why the manager didn't pick on someone senior. The ensuing exchange did nothing to dispel rumours of trouble between Ferguson and leading players – managers in such a position were later said to have 'lost the dressing room' – and it was certainly not the first row he had had with Miller.

Gradually they began to forge a relationship, Miller coming to accept that Ferguson was right to insist that he defended less cautiously, indeed expressing gratitude for the adjustment that turned a fine career into one of Scotland's most distinguished ever.

The relationship with Harper was never to improve. Ferguson thought the player unprofessional and tactically one-dimensional; Harper deemed the manager a finger-wagging bully. So it was natural for Ferguson to number the days of the one player who would never absorb his ideas. Whether or not Harper sensed this, he continued to score goals in that first Ferguson season, 1978/9. He had claimed eighteen in a mere twenty-three League matches when Ferguson made a striker his first purchase for Aberdeen. Mark McGhee arrived from Newcastle United and appeared in all eleven matches thereafter, scoring four times.

McGhee was nearly twenty-two and, although Newcastle's manager, Bill McGarry, had offered him the opportunity to stay, he chose a £70,000 move to Aberdeen instead because Ferguson had earlier tried to sign him for St Mirren. 'I was with Morton at the time,' McGhee said, 'and the fact that he'd now come back for me made up my mind, even though I didn't know much else about him and had never even been to Aberdeen, let alone played there.

'He was also different from other managers in that I wasn't asked any questions – I was told what *he* wanted from *me*. I almost signed the contract without seeing it. While I was listening to him, he slipped the pen into my hand. He was in total control.'

McGhee joined Aberdeen in the hotel near Glasgow Airport where they were preparing for the League Cup final against Rangers. It was late March, nine months into Ferguson's time as manager and a month after his father's death. Rangers won, giving John Greig his first trophy as manager, but Ferguson's team remained a work in steady progress.

By the time the next season began, he had changed the midfield, moving Strachan, a gifted but unfinished twenty-two-year-old, to the right-sided position he was to occupy for the remaining eighteen years of his career and temporarily introducing the steel of McLeish in the middle, to complement the passing technique of John McMaster.

Up front with Archibald in the early phase of that 1979/80 campaign was the familiar figure of Harper. He had made eleven League appearances, scoring three goals, when injury struck him down and beckoned McGhee back into the side, this time to stay. McGhee's time had come and Ferguson had been preparing him for it, developing the player whose potential had been discerned at Morton and Newcastle into the player he would become.

'I'd always been pretty much off the cuff,' McGhee recalled, 'and people had allowed it because I was good at getting the ball and taking people on. But I wasn't great at the more fundamental aspects of being a centre-forward. He taught me straight away that, even if I wasn't playing well, I could make a contribution.

'That wasn't the case before. If I wasn't playing brilliantly, I was no use whatsoever. He showed me that middle ground where I could contribute to the team by holding the ball up, winning headers and putting defenders under pressure. If I did that, I could do all the stuff I liked doing and it would be more effective. It changed me from being a 'nearly' player who could do the spectacular from time to time, beating three men and scoring a goal, to a proper team player.'

When Harper limped out of the 1979/80 season, giving McGhee his second chance, Aberdeen lay third, having lost five of their first fourteen League matches. They lost again at Morton in the new year and slipped to sixth – but suffered only two further defeats in the rest of the season. After McGhee had joined Archibald up front, they gained momentum, overtaking McNeill's Celtic in the last couple of weeks with the help of a 3-1 victory at Parkhead in which both McGhee and Archibald scored and striding on to bring the club its first championship since 1955.

In eight matches against the Old Firm, they had lost only an early season home encounter with Celtic. Rangers, managed by Ferguson's old friend Greig, had been beaten three times. Aberdeen under Ferguson had conquered 'provincial' Scottish football's endemic inferiority complex.

'Suddenly,' Gordon Strachan recalled, 'after eighteen months of working with Alex Ferguson, we'd seemed to explode. I don't know what happened in those eighteen months. The main thing I remember is suffering from incredible nerves in the last few games. I was always going to the toilet and people thought I was ill, but it was just the stress of realising we could win the League.'

They celebrated by winning with a flourish, 5-0 at Hibernian, in front of 10,000 of their supporters who had made the journey to Edinburgh. Not that Ferguson could let the day pass without a storm; for having insulted the referee at half-time he was to incur from the Scottish FA a second banishment to the stands of his Aberdeen career (the first had followed the scenes at St Mirren on the day of his father's death), thus maintaining the bad habits of his time at Love Street. But it was still a day of glorious sunshine.

Ferguson had earned the first major honour of his career – and more. He had won his battle for Pittodrie's hearts and minds. 'I finally had the players believing in me,' he said. And with the refashioning of McGhee he had shown they were in judicious hands. Ferguson was to describe McGhee as one of his three key signings for Aberdeen. And to conclude, as he analysed that first title triumph: 'Sadly it must be stated that the misfortune for Joe Harper brought a breakthrough for the team.'

Harper played one further League match for Aberdeen at the end of the 1980/81 season before becoming manager of Highland League club Peterhead for a season. He then became a newspaper columnist and broadcaster, a regular attender at Pittodrie, where he acted as host in the Legends Lounge.

Chastened by Liverpool

That to be champions of Scotland hardly equated to conquering the world was brought home to Ferguson and his players when they took part in the competition later known as the Champions League. The European Cup draw sent them first to Vienna, where a scoreless draw protected a single-goal lead McGhee had secured at Pittodrie, but then came a chastening experience at the hands of Liverpool.

Liverpool and Ferguson: their fortunes were destined to be intertwined. Just as Real Madrid had inspired his affection for attacking football on a broad front – in their 1960 final against Eintracht Frankfurt at Hampden Park, there had been dashing wing play from Canario and the lightning Gento on one side, Kress and Meier on the other – Liverpool had heightened his awareness of the game's power as theatre.

In 1977, as manager of St Mirren, he had been fortunate enough to visit Anfield on one of its greatest occasions and confessed himself intoxicated by the atmosphere of a European Cup quarter-final second leg in which St Etienne were eventually overcome by a goal from David 'Supersub' Fairclough. 'I didn't walk away from the ground after the game,' Ferguson remarked. 'I floated. I had been caught up in the most exciting football atmosphere.'

Liverpool went on to win the trophy that year. They beat Borussia Moenchengladbach 3-1 in Rome. It was the first of their four European triumphs in the space of eight years. The second Ferguson saw, albeit without St Mirren's permission, in 1978 at Wembley, where Bruges lost to a goal from Kenny Dalglish, one of three Scots who had been introduced to the team by Bob Paisley; the others were Graeme Souness and Alan Hansen and Ferguson was to have interesting relation-ships with them all.

But on the first of two visits to Anfield in the autumn of 1980 he just watched them from the stands. He came to the fortress where Liverpool had not lost a League match for nearly three years, where they had scored no fewer than ten goals on average for every one the opposition were brave or foolish enough to put past Ray Clemence, and watched Middlesbrough go the way of all flesh, albeit by a relatively creditable four goals to two.

Ferguson saw the match with Archie Knox, the former manager of Forfar Athletic, who had become his assistant during the summer when Pat Stanton went into management at Cowdenbeath. At Anfield they met Shankly, and Ferguson, in his autobiography, recalls the great man's greeting: 'Hello, Alex, good to see you – you are doing a terrific job up there.' He was uttering awe-struck gratitude when Shankly went on: 'So you're down to have a look at our great team?' Yes, said Ferguson, they were indeed. 'Aye,' said Shankly, 'they all try that.'

Ferguson's spying mission was in vain. Liverpool won at Pittodrie through a goal from Terry McDermott and tore the

Scots apart at Anfield, a Willie Miller own goal being the first of four without reply. The full-back Phil Neal quickly got the next. At half-time came the immortal rallying cry from Aberdeen's Drew Jarvie: 'Come on, lads – three quick goals and we're back in it.' He would not have been joking. Not with Ferguson present. At any rate, Dalglish struck next and finally even Hansen came up from the back to score.

It left Ferguson no happier than you might imagine, even though his team had been facing a side destined to become European champions again, this time by beating Real Madrid. 'He came in after the match,' McGhee recalled, 'and slaughtered us. *Slaughtered* us.'

McGhee then smiled. 'I always remember that the match was sponsored by KP, the snack foods company, and they had put a plastic bag on everybody's hook in the dressing room containing all these various nuts and cheesy crackers. After the manager had come in and had his go at us, we were all looking down and then we got quietly changed and climbed on the bus with our KP bags – nobody was leaving them behind – to go back to our hotel.'

It was Strachan who broke the silence. 'I asked if anyone wanted to swap their chocolate dippers for salt and vinegar crisps,' he recalled, 'or something like that.' Ferguson immediately snapped that, if he heard anyone laugh – then, or for the rest of the night – they were all fined a week's wages. 'So we're all like this,' said McGhee, pursing his lips, 'just about keeping it in.

'We leave Anfield for the city centre and at the hotel we get off the bus in our Aberdeen tracksuits with all the other bits and pieces you take to a match, plus our KP bags, when Graeme Souness arrives. He's with his wife and another woman, maybe her sister, and he's wearing a long, light-coloured rain-coat with a fur collar, draped over his shoulders. So he's got this style and swagger and two glamorous women – and we've got our KPs.

'We sit down to dinner in the hotel restaurant and Souness is at the next table. He greets us cheerfully but we're scared to have a laugh with him in case we get fined. So for Souness the champagne corks are popping and we're just sitting silently eating, with Fergie glaring over at us from time to time in case anyone laughs. We felt like a bunch of wee boys.'

Strachan and the Shankly Tapes

It was only six years after Aberdeen's Anfield spanking when Ferguson came down to Manchester to settle to the task of doing to Liverpool what he had done to the Old Firm. By then Aberdeen, having won a European trophy themselves, were big boys. In 1980 it had been just their bad luck to encounter the mighty Liverpool so early in a season that seemed never to recover.

In the summer they had lost Steve Archibald to Tottenham Hotspur; that is what happens to provincial Scottish clubs who win the championship, sad to say, though the £800,000 pleased Dick Donald, who always insisted on balancing the books. Though generous in spirit, he treated money in a manner that could be described as Aberdonian.

With injuries, notably to Strachan, causing further disruption, Aberdeen were beaten by Celtic to the title and won neither of the Cups. Maybe, like Dundee and Kilmarnock before them, they would prove one-hit wonders?

Not at all. Indeed, Ferguson, in that summer of 1981, was to make the second of the three signings he considered his most important for Aberdeen, giving the team a new dimension in the form of width. Peter Weir was more expensive than McGhee but proved a wise way of investing £300,000 of the Archibald money. Weir was twenty-three and had already played a few times for Scotland alongside Strachan, Miller and McLeish. Ferguson reckoned his skill and verve as a left-winger would balance the team and was emphatically vindicated.

'Weir was the one,' he later reflected. 'Weir made the team. Weir brought that left-sided thing that just opened it all up. Because wee Gordon Strachan, though he was doing well on the right, kept getting bogged down – he was always heavily marked. The minute we got Weir, the opposition could no longer concentrate on our right flank, because Weir would be away down the left. He was a very good player and would have been an absolute top, top one if he hadn't been such an intro-vert by nature.' He still won plenty: a Scottish Cup in his first season, and each of the seasons after that, two championships, a League Cup and the European Cup-Winners' Cup.

Strachan had been there from the start. He had begun at Dundee, where he became something of a teenage sensation in a friendly match against Arsenal after which he was sport-ingly applauded from the field by Alan Ball, a World Cup winner and England captain, who had been his direct oppo-nent. But some considered Strachan too small and slight for the rigours of Scottish football. Billy McNeill was not one of them. He took Strachan to Aberdeen in exchange for the more seasoned and powerful midfield player Jim Shirra and £50,000. But Strachan failed to find any sort of form and, having felt the scorn of the crowd, was dropped.

McNeill's departure, then, constituted relief and it was Ferguson under whom he thrived, Ferguson who discovered the position in which Strachan would be most effective. After various experiments, Ferguson placed him just in from the right touchline and there Strachan was not only to win titles north and south of the border but to represent Scotland in two World Cups.

All he knew of Ferguson, when McNeill's successor arrived at Pittodrie, was the St Mirren phenomenon: 'This incredible team. Where did these kids come from? Normally you hear of promising boys as they come through the school or youth ranks – but these seemed to come from nowhere. And they were so fit. I first came across them when I was at Dundee and they just used to run us off the pitch. But I'd never met Alex Ferguson.'

They got on well, the twenty-one-year-old and the boss fifteen years his senior. The reason was simple, said Strachan: 'He knew I loved football and was interested in anything to do with coaching and what made people tick.' So they travelled to night matches together in Ferguson's car.

Strachan recalled it in 2000, when he was managing Coventry City and Ferguson, having fallen out with him, was declining even to acknowledge his presence at matches between their clubs; he missed being able to talk about the old times.

'Going to those matches seemed natural,' he said. 'Like him, I couldn't get enough football. Rangers or Celtic, Arbroath or Montrose – I didn't mind. I used to be fascinated when, after fifteen minutes, he'd analyse a game and explain the differences between the ways the teams were playing. After a year or two, Archie Knox came as his assistant and took my place in the car. Anyway, we were playing so much European football by then that opportunities were not so frequent. I remember he used to play tapes of Bill Shankly talking. "Let's listen to Shankly", he'd say, and shove one in.' Less entertaining to Ferguson's passenger was 'a singer he liked, some awful Glaswegian singer who performed in pubs'.

Strachan observed Ferguson's gradual self-revelation to the players. 'At first,' he said, 'we didn't see the full extent of the drive, the aggressive will. But, when it emerged, I'd never seen anything like it in my life. My dad had got angry – but it was nothing like this.'

Argeş Piteşti was a case in point. The Romanian club were Aberdeen's next opponents after their remarkable Uefa Cup victory over Ipswich in 1981/2, when Bobby Robson's confident assertion after a 1-1 draw at Portman Road that Aberdeen could play no better on their own ground was spectacularly disproved, not least by a rampant Weir, who rounded off a 3-1 victory by teasing Mick Mills before scoring.

Aberdeen seemed assured of further progress when they beat Argeş Piteşti 3-0 at home, but the away leg began badly and Aberdeen were 2-0 down as half-time approached. Ferguson had switched from 4-4-2 to a single-striker system for the occasion, with a basic middle three supplemented by Strachan and Weir wide right and left respectively and McGhee up front. 'It's a great system if you've got the players,' said Strachan. 'But it was kind of thrown at us. We'd done just a day's training, if that, and my misfortune is that in the first half, while it was all going wrong, I was on the side nearest to the manager.

'He was on at me all the time, yelling at me to spin and link with Mark and all the other things, but I didn't know how to do it. Honestly, I wasn't being cheeky – I'd never played that way in my life. And then I did the silly thing. As Stuart Kennedy used to say, you should never be the one to shout back at him just before half-time. It's like a game of tig – *you're on*. So I knew I was in trouble when I told him to shut up or said something about the tactics or whatever it was.

'It was a long, dark tunnel at Piteşti and I was walking alone. We got into the dressing room and he hadn't arrived yet. In situations like this, the boys would keep their heads down. He would always be wearing these shiny black shoes and, sure enough, they appeared. They were moving about. And then they stopped – and they were pointing at me. I could feel the boys on either side of me edging away. And he came right up to me and slaughtered me.

'I stood up – I wasn't being brave, I just had to breathe – and he turned away and, with a hand, accidentally knocked a row of cups of tea in the direction of Willie Miller and Alex McLeish. He saw me smirking and that made him knock over this samovar. It was so big and iron-hard and must have been hot – it must have hurt.'

Ferguson's own account is that, yes, the samovar did hurt – 'nearly broke my hand' – but that only then did he disturb the cups of tea, hurling a tray of them against the wall above Strachan. He also noted with approval that Strachan 'obeyed instructions' in the rest of the match. Strachan's recollection is that Ferguson reverted to 4–4–2. Beyond doubt was that Aberdeen drew 2–2 on the night, winning comfortably on aggregate, after Strachan had converted a penalty. 'When it went in, all the guys came over and mobbed me, smothered me, because they knew I might do something stupid again. They were being good team-mates, looking after me, because I was so relieved I could have gone over and said something to him.

'I'd been so nervous walking up to the spot. Their goalie looked like the biggest in the world – as if he could tickle both posts at once — and I thought, "If I miss this pen, I'm a dead man."'

In the next round, Aberdeen were knocked out by a Hamburg team featuring Franz Beckenbauer. They were to resume their trophy-gathering with a 4–1 triumph over Rangers after extra time in the Scottish Cup final, but the championship again went to Celtic, albeit by a narrower margin with Aberdeen again runners-up.

The summer of 1982 indicated how Aberdeen had put themselves in football's forefront, Strachan and Miller taking part in Scotland's World Cup adventure (with their old friend Archibald) against such renowned players as Brazil's Zico, Socrates and Falcão and Oleg Blokhin of the Soviet Union, watched by a proud Ferguson. There was no disgrace in coming home early.

Fooling Bayern

Nor was there any drudgery for Gordon Strachan and Willie Miller in the return to work at Aberdeen. By now the players were getting used to Ferguson's ways: the nervous cough that was to recur for the rest of his career, often as the preliminary to a diatribe; the speech imperfection that caused him to say *bwuddy* when he meant bloody (as in hell); the rants that made 'Furious' a natural as well as alliterative nickname.

A former manager of Derby County and long-time aide to Kevin Keegan, Arthur Cox, once said he enjoyed the biographies of generals and had noticed that it did them no harm to be considered a little dotty by their men; Montgomery was mentioned. The men of Aberdeen were scarcely sold short in this respect. Yet they had the highest regard for Ferguson's management. They were inspired by him. He brought out their professionalism. They worked hard at the game and enjoyed it.

There was attention to detail in Ferguson's preparation for any match – even the humblest opponents would be watched and analysed at a team meeting – but it was the Old Firm he relished meeting most, as McGhee confirmed. 'Dominating them was a massive thing for him. And, since most of us had been brought up Rangers or Celtic supporters – apart from Gordon, who was a Hibs fan – we enjoyed it too.

'We used to talk about "first blood". I was under instruction, when the first ball went forward, to make contact. We were told to be physical. After I joined Celtic, Roy Aitken told me that, when we came to Parkhead and stood in the tunnel, he used to think we were on something. We looked *mental*. That's how much the big games meant to us.'

McGhee grinned. 'I remember someone living in Germany sent us a cutting from *Süddeutsche Zeitung* after we'd played Bayern Munich in the Cup-Winners' Cup winning season of 1982/3. There was a quote from their substitute goalkeeper at the time, Jean-Marie Pfaff, which the fellow had translated, and Pfaff was saying they knew they were in for a hard game when they looked at us in the tunnel and saw that hardly any of us had any teeth!'

That season, though, they went through the entire European campaign with just one yellow card; Ferguson's team did not thrive without discipline.

'We had incredible professionalism,' said Strachan, 'and imagination.' Once he and John McMaster bumped into each other during a match while trying to decide what to do with a free-kick and it gave them an idea that was to win the famous encounter with Bayern. 'It was pure acting. We pretended to bump into each other.' While faking remonstration with his team-mate, Strachan suddenly turned and chipped the free-kick to where he knew Alex McLeish would be waiting. 'It's hard to turn and hit a ball without looking at it, but I had to do it and big Alex headed a goal. In fact the ploy brought us two goals because almost immediately, before Bayern had recovered their composure, John Hewitt scored and the match was won.

'We'd practised the trick in training. We used to make up all sorts of things like that. We all joined in and I don't think it's a coincidence that so many people from that team have gone on to become managers [notably Strachan himself, McGhee, McLeish and Willie Miller]. At half-time we used to have eleven managers. We wouldn't be shy with suggestions. You don't get that so much in the game today. People are scared to upset each other. But in our dressing room there were eleven managers – only one boss, though.'

No one ever addressed Ferguson as anything other than 'Boss'. Only when out of earshot did he become 'Furious'.

The 1982/3 season saw another close call for the domestic title, which Dundee United took for the first time ever, Jim McLean's team sealing the achievement with victory over their local rivals Dundee on the concluding day. But Europe was thrilling enough for Ferguson as he and Aberdeen made history of their own in the Cup-Winners' Cup. It was only the third time a Scottish club had won a European trophy (Rangers had lifted the same trophy in 1972, five years after Celtic's European Cup triumph) and, as on the other occasions, the team consisted entirely of Scots.

Ferguson had fashioned his mainly by enhancing his inheritance, developing the home-produced Jim Leighton, Alex McLeish, Neil Simpson, Neale Cooper and Eric Black, adjusting the roles of Strachan and John McMaster and blending them all with the established Willie Miller and Stuart Kennedy. That Cup-Winners' Cup triumph took place five years after he had joined Aberdeen – yet, of the twelve players who appeared in the final, including the match-winning substitute John Hewitt, only McGhee and Weir had been bought.

They had been knocked out of the Scottish League Cup early by Dundee United, which did them no harm as the European campaign got serious. After an 11-1 aggregate win over Sion, of Switzerland, they squeezed less convincingly past Dinamo Tirana, Hewitt scoring the only goal at Pittodrie, then beat Lech Poznán 2-0 at home and 1-0 away.

The quarter-finals brought Bayern and again Ferguson's team kept a clean sheet in Germany, which was remarkable as their hosts, featuring Karl-Heinz Rummenigge and Paul Breitner, had put four goals past Tottenham Hotspur in the Olympic Stadium in the previous round. Reality seemed to hit Aberdeen early in the second leg when Klaus Augenthaler beat Leighton. Neil Simpson equalised, before Hans Pflügler, a left-back moved forward because the Bayern coach, Pál Csernai, thought his height would trouble Kennedy, restored Bayern's lead.

It looked as if Ferguson and Knox, for all the scouting trips they had undertaken before this pivotal match, would be outmanoeuvred. Then Ferguson sent on Hewitt, and the free-kick to which Strachan and McMaster applied their fiendish trick: 'We reckoned that, although our double act was well enough known in Scottish football by then, the Germans probably wouldn't have heard of it.' Even the Scottish tele-vision commentator was fooled as McLeish's header brought the sides level. Almost immediately the German goalkeeper, Manfred Müller, dropped a Black header at the feet of Hewitt, whose winner caused Pittodrie almost to explode. For many years to come, experienced locals recalled that moment as the most emotional the ground had ever known.

Müller recalled it ruefully, mentioning the speed and toughness of the match and the 'rather weak floodlights'. He could see enough, however, of Strachan: 'There was this small blond guy in midfield who made everything happen. It was obvious that he was a brilliant player.' He laughed when told of Pfaff's remark about Aberdeen's scary appearance, but agreed that they did have 'typically British' characteristics epitomised by the quick one-two that took them to the semi-finals.

Though Aberdeen lost 1-0 to Waterschei in Belgium in the second leg, they could afford it, having won 5-1 at home, and the return to Scotland was clouded only by an injury Kennedy had suffered that was to end his career.

Such was Ferguson's regard for Kennedy that he named him as a substitute for the final against Real Madrid in Gothenburg even though he was on crutches and unable to take the field even in an emergency. Many years later, Ferguson was to make apparently sentimental decisions in both the 2008 and 2009 finals of the Champions League, choosing first Paul Scholes for Moscow even before it was known that Manchester United would take on Chelsea, whom they beat on penalties, and then Park Ji-Sung in Rome against Barcelona, who utterly outplayed them.

Beating Real Madrid

Among the vessels used to take some 14,000 Aberdeen supporters to Sweden was a ferry, the *St Clair*. The official party went on a charter flight and a most distinguished guest, there at Ferguson's invitation, was Jock Stein.

By now Ferguson was rather more than a star pupil. He knew how to behave in the build-up to a match. If it were a routine fixture, he might affect anxiety in order to jolt his players out of any complacency. For this occasion, he instructed his entire staff not to betray a hint of nerves about the prospect of taking on Real Madrid, and himself avoided any praise of their players, even though, having flown from Belgium after Aberdeen's second leg to see Real complete their victory over Austria Vienna, he had deemed them distinctly beatable.

Stein, the professor of psychology, approved. He made a few suggestions of his own and one which Ferguson took up was to buy a bottle of good Scotch whisky for his counterpart, Alfredo Di Stéfano, upon whom he had first clapped awe-struck eyes during Real's dazzling victory over Eintracht Frankfurt in 1960. Stein's idea was to get over to the Real camp an impression that Aberdeen were honoured just to be in the final, thus, perhaps, putting the favourites off their guard.

A more likely factor in the outcome was the weather. It was extremely wet and Strachan, returning from the pitch after the players' loosening-up session with water dripping from his hair, found Ferguson advancing on him as the tension rose, anxiously demanding scissors with which to trim back his fringe; Strachan insisted on doing it himself. The pitch, made heavy by hour upon hour of rain, worked in Aberdeen's favour because, with the passage of time – and especially extra time – Aberdeen's stamina became influential.

'We were so fit,' said McGhee, 'that we would have been competitive in any era. Archie Knox is a very thorough coach and about twenty years later, when he came to work with me at Millwall and we decided to give the players a series of runs to build up stamina, we took their times and, just out of interest, compared them with those he had kept from our era at Aberdeen – my Millwall players were way behind us, even though all those years had gone by, with all the general improvements in fitness.'

The greasy, cloying conditions at the Ullevi Stadium helped Aberdeen to take the lead when McLeish, arriving to meet a corner kick Strachan had steered to the back of the penalty area, headed powerfully, the ball diverting off a defender to Black, who scored. Then they assisted Real to equalise. McLeish was short with a pass back to Jim Leighton, who brought down Carlos Santillana, conceding a penalty which Juanito converted. Yet, as McGhee recalled: 'Physically, we were too much for Real. I played against Camacho [José Antonio Camacho, a Spanish international on eighty-one occasions who went on to manage his country as well as, among others, Real] and beat him up most of the night. We had a great battle but eventually they took him off and someone else picked me up at a corner. He immediately punched me in the face. Wasted no time. Made no pretence. I had a lump on my jaw for about a year afterwards.'

The additional thirty minutes were under way. Hewitt had come on for the injured Black, but it was Weir who threatened Real most and suddenly, after a sequence of trickery that beat two opponents, he sent the ball up the left to McGhee, whose power and skill enabled him to plough on and measure a cross that Hewitt met with a diving header into the net. A split second before, Ferguson had been cursing Hewitt for having forgotten to 'bend' his run in order to avoid being caught offside or easily policed by the defence, but forgiveness was assured. The Cup-Winners' Cup was won.

Ferguson raced from the dugout, fell in a puddle and was trampled by Knox, thus losing the race to reach the players. Strachan was one of those who ran in the other direction, to Kennedy with his crutches. Although as a substitute Kennedy would receive a medal, his feelings were bound to be an uncomfortable mix. 'I'm sorry I can't help you, Stuart,' said Strachan. 'It's all right, Gordon,' he said. 'Just enjoy yourself.'

He did. Strachan even drank champagne at the party at the hotel; it was a night when even the light drinkers broke with habit and Ferguson did not get to bed until six in the morning. He and Cathy were among the last few revellers, although he came home swearing he had stayed sober because there was a match on the Saturday.

Flailing at Ferguson

Mark McGhee made no pretence at sobriety and, on the flight home from Gothenburg, the flow of champagne was maintained. Among the crew on the aircraft was McGhee's wife, Jackie, who made sure everyone who wanted topping-up was looked after. The Cup was filled with champagne and passed from seat to seat, players, staff, directors and even journalists taking turns for a toast.

An open-top bus greeted Ferguson and his players at Aberdeen Airport and the procession began. 'Union Street was jam-packed for its entire length,' Strachan recalled. It took two hours to reach Pittodrie, where a full house stood ready for the lap of honour.

McGhee was still drunk as he and the rest of the players got changed into their red club tracksuits. Not that anyone was complaining or finding the conditions in any way anomalous, Ferguson included. The players were standing in the tunnel waiting to run out with the Cup when someone mentioned that Ferguson and Willie Miller were missing. Club employees were sent in various directions to find them and, during the delay, McGhee noticed that the trophy was lying on its side on the tunnel floor. He bent down to stand it upright but, as he laid hands on it, Ferguson suddenly appeared from behind and wrenched it from his grasp, snarling: 'Willie's taking that out.'

Something in McGhee snapped. He had never had any intention of usurping the captain's place at the head of the team and was consumed by outrage. He seized Ferguson by the lapels and, before Knox or any startled team-mate could react, ran him back up the tunnel to the door of the boot room, which was half open and through which he propelled the manager before taking a first swing at him.

At that opportune moment, the peacemakers arrived to grab McGhee's arm just before his fist could connect and drag him away – though not before Ferguson had got in a retalia-tory blow (had he wished, the manager could have claimed both self-defence and, because the swing found its target, victory on points). A still seething McGhee was taken to the boardroom, where family members and the chairman, Dick Donald, helped to calm him down in time for the second lap of honour. He had missed the first and a photograph of it in a book commemorating the season records, by way of explana-tion, that McGhee had been 'too overcome by emotion' to join his team-mates at the outset.

He kept his distance from Ferguson for the rest of the day and woke the next morning at dawn. You can imagine his feelings as those bleary eyes opened: 'What have I done? Did I really do it? And what do I do now?' He decided it was best to face the music: to apologise and take whatever punishment was coming.

Knowing that Ferguson would be at Pittodrie before anyone else – a day off was out of the question, given that Hibs had to be faced the next day in the final League match of the season, one that could, given an unlikely combination of circumstances, end with Aberdeen champions – McGhee went straight to the ground to wait for him.

Although it was barely eight o'clock, the metal shutters on the main door were already open. McGhee walked through and there was Ferguson in the foyer. McGhee started to apologise, but Ferguson cut him short. 'It was my fault,' he said. 'I behaved badly.' McGhee continued down his own road of penitence, adding that he had been drunk and . . . 'Forget it,' said Ferguson. 'It's done. Now you and I are going down to the car ferry.'

And they did. Ferguson and McGee drove down to the harbour to meet the *St Clair* with its cargo of fans returning from Gothenburg and brandished the Cup at them as they lined the decks. Ferguson had promised to do that and there he was on the quayside, he and McGhee with a hand each on the ears of the trophy. It was as if nothing had happened between them. The tunnel episode was to remain inside Pittodrie's walls.

McGhee respected Ferguson more than ever. Far from losing credibility, the manager had surprised his men once again, and pleasantly.

Great Stuff, Lads

Yet Ferguson contrived to fill them with dismay only ten days after the glory of Gothenburg. They still had to play the Scottish Cup final against Rangers, which they won, through a goal from Eric Black in extra time, but hardly graced. 'There was nothing fresh about us,' said Strachan. 'Even the build-up to the final had been dead. We'd won the Cup-Winners' Cup but lost the League and now we had to go again – it was one game too many for our minds and bodies.' Ferguson seemed not to understand. He stood on the pitch at Hampden Park and told a television interviewer that the performance had been 'disgraceful' and his team, with the exceptions of Willie Miller and Alex McLeish, were 'the luckiest in the world'.

He was even more scathing in the dressing room, after ordering Strachan to stop trying to open a bottle of champagne as the tirade began. In his autobiography Ferguson said he had tried to 'bully and cajole' a performance from the players. For once it had not worked and the reaction was 'foolish'.

The sullen silence he had created had been broken only

by the late arrival of McLeish, who, unprepared, gave vent to a celebratory roar of 'Great stuff, lads!' As winning a Cup usually is.

Perhaps the most noted instance – and there are not many – of a manager criticising a trophy-winning display occurred when Bill Nicholson lamented the manner in which his great Tottenham team had completed the Double by beating Leicester City 2-0 at Wembley in 1961. But Nicholson made his point in a measured way. Ferguson went too far and an apology was inadequate; the players, upon hearing it the next day, metaphorically shrugged. He had truly hurt them, Strachan said, because they would never have let him down on purpose.

They had left Hampden for the reception at St Andrews, a congenial stop on the journey from Glasgow to Aberdeen, without their wives and girlfriends – the irate Ferguson had broken with custom by making the women travel separately – and the journey needed the levity provided by John McMaster when he teased Miller and McLeish about their having been exonerated by Ferguson: 'Maybe we'd better cancel the open-top bus – you two can just ride along Union Street on a tandem.'

Miller and McLeish were already embarrassed; they had even seen fit to plead on their team-mates' behalf to Ferguson, pointing out that, as central defenders, they could let play come to them, rather than make it, which demanded more mental and physical energy.

The reception was, Strachan said, 'more like a wake', and he and his wife Lesley walked out. He was later fined £250 by Ferguson.

The rants went on. The following season, in which Aberdeen picked up the European Super Cup with a 2-0 aggregate win over Hamburg (as Cup-Winners' Cup holders, they had taken on the European Cup holders), they began the defence of their trophy by overcoming Akranes, of Iceland, and Belgium, before travelling to meet Újpest Dózsa in Budapest in the quarter-finals. They lost 2-0 and, said McGhee: 'I missed a chance. It was a horrible muddy night. Gordon had a shot, the goal-keeper punched it on to the bar and it came down and stuck in the mud about two yards out. The goalie's fallen back and got tangled in the net and I'm following up for a tap-in. I'm already turning away to celebrate when the goalie somehow sticks out an arm and stops the ball on the line. Then, as I turn back to try to nudge it over the line, he flips it away. It's a terrible miss and sure enough I get the treatment from the boss. "That's the worst fucking miss . . ." It's not so much a hairdryer as a pyrocrastic blast [as in the gases coming out of a volcano]. He was actually touching me as he roared.'

Back at Pittodrie a McGhee hat-trick sent Aberdeen through on a 3-2 aggregate. Who knows if the volcanic blast helped? But most players got it at some stage or another, even the mountainous Doug Rougvie. Once Ferguson, after thrusting his face up at the defender's and delivering the customary abuse, let Rougvie leave before winking at Strachan. 'If he ever hits me,' he said, 'I'm dead.'

Ferguson behaved as if aggressive behaviour was just another tool of management, to be used for effect and not taken person-ally. McGhee remembers getting it at half-time in a match which Aberdeen were winning by three or four goals. 'It was against my old club Morton and I'd been tearing them to shreds, dribbling and beating people and laying on goals. And yet he slaughtered me, calling me greedy and selfish and asking, "Who do you think you are?"

'I put it to Archie and he came up with a theory about not wanting me to think I could do it in the harder games and so on. But I was still livid when I walked into the tearoom at Pittodrie to meet my wife and she told me Ferguson had just come up to her and Lesley Strachan and asked them out for a Chinese meal that night with Gordon and me and another couple of people. So he would disarm you. He'd knock you down and pick you up again.'

And they would respond. In the 1983/4 season, they took the League leadership in late October and never relinquished it, losing only one of eight matches to the Old Firm and only one of four to Dundee United, from whom they wrested back the title. They also won the Scottish Cup, beating Celtic 2–1 after extra time in the final.

There was a disappointment in the European semi-final in that they lost to Porto, but to be champions again and triumphant in a third consecutive Cup emphasised Aberdeen's predominance in the Scottish game. Ferguson had reduced Rangers and Celtic to the status of also-rans. He was not finished with them either. And that he was not to be deflected from his mission in the north had been underlined by two refusals to leave for Rangers to take up a post in which his friend John Greig, after five years without a championship, was struggling to live up to expectations.

After Strachan and McGhee

The first call had come from a Rangers director a few days after the triumph in Gothenburg. Ferguson said he would have nothing to do with any 'ousting' of Greig. Two months into the following season, Greig resigned and soon he received a call from Ferguson. 'He obviously felt for me,' said Greig. 'He said they had offered him the job. He didn't want me to hear from someone else and think he'd gone behind my back. He asked if he could speak to me for fifteen minutes. "On you go," I said, "but don't ask me if you should take the job or not – you'll have to decide that for yourself." And so we had a conversation and, at the end of it, he said he wanted me to be the first to know – he wouldn't be taking the job.'

In his autobiography, Ferguson talked of being 'reluctant to expose my family to a risk of a recurrence of the bigotry I had encountered at Ibrox in my playing days', and of being suspicious of the continuing boardroom politics (he had taken the advice of, among others, Scot Symon, who had encouraged him to take the job, but with this caveat). 'There was a battle for power,' said Greig, 'and Fergie had such a great chairman in Dick Donald at Aberdeen.' A chairman, moreover, who increased his salary to £60,000 a year, or about twice as much as the club's best-paid players.

So he stayed, also rebuffing overtures from England, and dealt with players who wanted to better themselves, or at least their own bank balances. One was Strachan, another McGhee. Both were to go in the summer of 1984, to Manchester United and Hamburg respectively. Doug Rougvie also left, for Chelsea. And yet the ensuing season saw Aberdeen retain the championship with a slightly improved points total.

Ferguson had done it by judicious replacement – Billy Stark and Frank MacDougall for Strachan and McGhee as he continued to plunder his former club St Mirren, from whom he had already taken Weir, the midfielder Doug Bell and the striker Steve Cowan – and brilliant squad management, in the process proving himself more influential on a club's fortunes than any individual footballer could be. Even the footballer he had himself aspired to be, in those boyhood daydreams of bulging nets for Rangers. It was a point that may or may not have entered his mind at the time, although he certainly became aware of his worth when he did it all over again with Manchester United.

New faces, meanwhile, kept coming through the Pittodrie ranks. 'Aberdeen's young players continue to thrive,' remarked *Rothmans Football Yearbook*, 'and to show a class which must give Alex Ferguson much satisfaction.' Satisfaction? Not quite. He grumbled that an injury to MacDougall, whose first season had brought twenty-two goals in the League alone, caused Aberdeen to lose to Dundee United in the Scottish Cup semi-finals and thus miss an opportunity of a fourth successive triumph in that competition, a feat not even Rangers or Celtic had ever attained.

Again they made little impression on the European Cup, losing their first-round tie to Dinamo Berlin on penalties, but retention of the domestic title had earned them another tilt.

Early in the season, Aberdeen had lost 2-1 at Celtic Park. Billy Stark had missed a penalty and in training the following week Ferguson mentioned it. 'Quite casually,' said Stark, 'he said to me, "I hope that doesn't cost us the League." It wasn't a conversation – he just walked on. And it was a while before the significance hit me. But it was quite a dramatic thing to say to a player. I went on to have my best season [from midfield, Stark scored twenty goals, fifteen of them in the League] and we won the championship. Maybe he was giving me that wee bit extra impetus.'

His wiles were never far from the surface. Ferguson used the 'West of Scotland press' to wind his players up, said Stark. 'He told us they wanted to see us get beat because they were all Rangers and Celtic supporters.' And referees? 'I don't remember him telling us the referees were against us. It was just the press. I think he preferred to deal with the referees himself! I remember way back at St Mirren, when we'd easily won a Cup tie against Alloa, he was banging on the referee's door afterwards. I don't think it was about the game. I think he was lodging something in the referee's mind for further on. He went on to do it in England as well with the wee sound bites and so on.'

Stark, like McGhee, had been recruited unceremoniously – 'he just told me the money I was getting and that was it' – but he did notice significant modifications in Ferguson since St Mirren. One was that he let Knox do training. Another was more subtle. 'I think the biggest compliment you can pay Alex Ferguson,' Stark said, 'is that, for all the changes that have taken place in football, he has always adapted. There were signs of that when I got to Aberdeen. He hadn't changed in terms of volatility or drive. But I noticed in the first day's training that he was learning how to manage international players.

'At St Mirren he'd expected nothing less than flat out from everybody. So I watched Willie Miller . . . and then I looked at Fergie. And there was nothing. And that was significant. Because Willie was the worst trainer in the world. Fantastic player, consistent, second to none. But he just didn't train at all and Fergie seemed willing to accept that because of what he did in matches. He was kind of on a pedestal along with Alex McLeish and maybe even Jim Leighton. That's not to say he wouldn't criticise them – but not to the degree that the rest of us got. Including the likes of Strachan and McGhee.'

Absent friends encountered mixed fortunes. Doug Rougvie became something of a cult figure at Chelsea but was eventually transferred to Brighton and Hove Albion, who had just been relegated to the Third Division, for less than half the £150,000 Aberdeen had received. McGhee, after scoring seven goals in thirty Bundesliga matches, returned to Scotland to join Celtic for £150,000. Strachan, however, was an instant hit at Old Trafford. Not only did seven penalties help him to become United's second highest League scorer on fifteen goals, just one behind Mark Hughes, as Ron Atkinson's team finished fourth in the League; he won an FA Cup winners' medal when United beat the champions, Everton, with a goal from Norman Whiteside at Wembley. Among Strachan's guests that day was Alex Ferguson. So much for talk of bad blood between them; the time for that had still to arrive.

Doing Deals

Ferguson had seen Strachan's departure coming – it was not too difficult, given the player's habit of expressing weariness with the battles against the same Old Firm faces, which were so often contorted with a rage against his trickery – to the extent that after the 1983 Cup final, when Strachan came into Pittodrie to hear he was being fined for his abrupt departure from St Andrews, he met Billy Stark in the lobby. Correctly deducing that Stark was to be his replacement, he mentioned it to Ferguson and indicated that he would like to see out the final year of his contract.

In those pre-Bosman days (before the 1995 court case in which a Belgian footballer earned his profession greater freedom of movement), a club would still receive a transfer fee for an out-of-contract player, but it would be governed by his market value only if he stayed in Britain. If he went to a European club, a formula for compensation would come into play which took account of the player's final salary.

Given that Strachan was on a basic £15,000 a year, which, even with the bonuses paid for success in Europe in the historic season of 1982/3, did not rise to more than £35,000, Aberdeen

156

would receive considerably less than £200,000 for him from Europe. They hoped to treble or even quadruple that in England and Ferguson's account is that he, personally, tried to arrange a transfer with various clubs south of the border before settling on a £500,000 deal with Manchester United that was presented to Strachan as a *fait accompli*. What he did not know was that Strachan had already signed a letter of intent to join Cologne in Germany.

Ferguson goes on to say that when he became aware of it he was aghast, Strachan, too, began to acknowledge that a terrible mistake had been made, and that there was general relief when Aberdeen were advised that the Cologne letter had no legal validity, after which Strachan signed for United.

Strachan recalled approaching his future from a different direction. 'I had a simple choice,' he said. 'There was Cologne and the Italian club Verona [who were to win the Italian championship the following season for the only time in their history]. I felt all alone. I had no agent. I was on £300 a week basic and I had a mortgage. I was twenty-seven and it was time to give my family some security before I got a broken leg or something. I had to sign for somebody. So I signed this piece of paper saying I'd go to Cologne, who were offering £1,600 a week [or £80,000 a year, more than twice as much as he could ever hope to earn from Aberdeen]. Then Manchester United came in and I had to explain to Alex that I wanted to go there instead.'

The transfer was held up for several weeks after Cologne complained to Uefa and a deal was reached in which Aberdeen would make them a payment and United travel to Germany to play a friendly match for their financial benefit. It never took place.

The signing of the letter had been arranged by Bernd Killat, an agent based in Germany who had arranged pre-season tours for Aberdeen and done work for Ferguson. When Aberdeen renewed their agreement with the kit manufacturer Adidas, for example. 'I negotiated a new deal for Ferguson with Adidas at the same time,' said Killat. 'It was for a lot of money.' He and Ferguson got on so well, he added, that on one occasion he stayed for a fortnight at the Fergusons' house in Cults.

For bringing together Strachan and Cologne, he was due to receive the *Deutschmark* equivalent of £40,000. It was a lot of money: even at Aberdeen prices, he could have bought a small house with that. But when the deal broke down he got nothing. Killat held 'the influence of Ferguson' responsible. Certainly Ferguson seemed happy enough with the outcome. 'When I eventually went to sign for United,' said Strachan, 'Alex came with me. I've never heard of a manager doing that.' It was indeed unusual to find a manager so proud to be selling a top player. Except in the case of Ferguson, who had also turned up at Tottenham with Archibald in 1980.

'And less than a year later,' said Strachan, 'he was my guest at Wembley. He rang me on the morning of the Cup final, to encourage me and tell me that fortune favoured the brave and all that, and then came to the United reception afterwards. In fact, Gary Bailey [the United goalkeeper] thought he was my dad, because he was sitting with me all night.'

McGhee's departure, arranged by Killat, was less complicated. It was known that he would go to Hamburg at the end of the 1983/4 season and the deal brought in £300,000, or a profit of £230,000 on the outlay to Newcastle, emphasising how Ferguson, with his skill in developing players, was more than funding his salary increases. McGhee left with as much goodwill as Ferguson could summon and later they became friends for a time.

Snubbing McGhee

McGhee, after his German sojourn, played for Celtic and Newcastle again and in 1991, when he became player/manager of Reading, it was on the recommendation of Ferguson. Thus Ferguson did for McGhee what Ally MacLeod had done for him – and McGhee was soon climbing the ladder.

In his second full season, Reading were promoted from the Third Division as champions and McGhee had them challenging for another promotion when, in December 1994, he was approached by the struggling Premier League club Leicester City. Though under contract, McGhee quit. Unable to keep Leicester up, he again walked out to join Wolverhampton Wanderers a year later, thereby acquiring a reputation for disloyalty that was to stick.

Wolves were in the same division as Leicester – and at the bottom of it. But under McGhee they avoided relegation and the next season they finished third, reaching the promotion play-offs, in which they lost over two legs to Crystal Palace, the eventual qualifiers for the Premier League. Their midfield sometimes included Darren Ferguson. His father, however, was no longer speaking to McGhee.

Darren had made a few dozen appearances for Manchester United before joining Wolves, then managed by Graham Turner, in January 1994. Turner soon gave way to Graham Taylor. And then came McGhee. Up to that point, McGhee recalled, he had either rung Ferguson or been rung by him every two or three weeks. Early in 1995, shortly after he had taken his new Leicester charges to play Ferguson's champions at Old Trafford and come away with an eyebrow-raising 1-1 draw, the phone rang in his office.

'Cole or Collymore?' asked Ferguson.

'Collymore,' replied McGhee.

It was the wrong answer, for Ferguson was about to break the British transfer record by signing Andy Cole from Newcastle for £7 million (including the value of the winger Keith Gillespie, assessed at £1 million, who went the other way). In fact Ferguson would clearly have been happy with either centre-forward for, after initially being rebuffed by Kevin Keegan when he tried for Cole, he made strenuous efforts to persuade Frank Clark, then manager of Nottingham Forest, to part with Stan Collymore.

McGhee went on: 'He explained that, if United had been a counter-attacking team, he'd definitely have gone for Collymore but that, because they tended to spend a lot of time in and around the opposition's penalty area, Cole, being a predator, was probably the better choice. I listened, as always. "Oh well," he added, "if I'm going to spend £7 million, I may as well get on with it." And the next day I read that he'd bid for Cole. Those were the sort of intimate conversations we'd have.

'In fact, he was the one who talked me into walking out of Leicester. After I'd done it, when I got home, I actually felt physically sick. But I had done it. I was going to Wolves. And then – bang! – nothing. He had slammed the door shut. The calls stopped. And to this day I cannot be sure why.

'People thought it might have been something to do with Darren, but I never had a problem with Darren. I often think that, when he advised me to go to Wolves, the idea was that, if I did well there, the next step was Manchester United. At least he made me feel that. And maybe he didn't think I had done well at Wolves.' But McGhee's first eighteen months had been promising enough. And as he said: 'It was from the day I joined Wolves that the calls stopped.'

In the end McGhee became just one more manager not to get Wolves back to the top division. He was dismissed in November 1998. 'I always remember that, the weekend after I got the sack, Mick McCarthy [McCarthy was manager of the Republic of Ireland squad at the time] asked me to go to a match at Blackburn and watch a couple of the Irish lads who were playing. And Alex Ferguson was there. He was standing by a door when Tom Finn, who was the club secretary at Blackburn, said, 'Your mate's here' and motioned me towards him. And he walked right past me. And he's hardly spoken to me since, except when it's been absolutely necessary, at an Aberdeen function or something. I've phoned him a couple of times to ask about things, but there's no relationship.'

McGhee was speaking early in 2009, when he was in charge of Motherwell. That summer he became the tenth manager to try to fill Ferguson's shiny black shoes at Aberdeen. His first competitive match was at home to the Czech club Sigma Olomouc. In the first qualifying round of the Uefa Cup at Pittodrie, on the turf where Bayern Munich had once quaked, the Czechs won 5–1.

Scottish teams no longer caused a stir in Europe. The times

when Ferguson (and Jim McLean) strode out in Jock Stein's footsteps were history. And no longer was there any domestic challenge to the Old Firm. Ferguson had left all that behind. He was a quarter of a century on. His Manchester United had reached the Champions League final of 2009, and won the one before that. From nowhere could the scale of his achievements be seen in such stark relief as Aberdeen.

For a time it was widely believed that McGhee might be the next outstanding manager to come from West Central Scotland, after Busby, Shankly, Stein, Ferguson and George Graham, who was winning English titles with Arsenal in 1989 and 1991 while Ferguson still sought his Old Trafford formula.

McGhee's Wolverhampton experience put paid to such talk. After nearly two years out of the game – with the blessing of Ferguson, whose recommendations were frequently sought by prospective employers, he would have been unlikely to manage that – he turned up at Millwall and, with Archie Knox at his side, seemed to conjure the old magic. The east London club were promoted from what is now League One as champions and finished fourth in the equivalent of the Championship. Defeat by Birmingham City in the play-off semi-finals closed the door to the Premier League, however, and again McGhee was to lose his job, after three years, which also proved the case at Brighton.

Back in Scotland, he did well enough at Motherwell to be a strong candidate for the post of national team manager (it went to George Burley) and then came the return to Pittodrie, where thirty years earlier his engagement to replace Joe Harper had put the Ferguson stamp on Aberdeen. The North Sea still roared at the back of the Beach End stand but inside lay a different, less exciting and optimistic, world.

Life and Death with Big Jock

It was at the start of the 1984/5 season that Ferguson received the call to combine his Aberdeen duties with assistance to Jock Stein, by now national team manger after his ousting at Celtic and a brief stay at Leeds United. His previous aide, Jim McLean, had quit in order to concentrate on Dundee United, but Ferguson, while aware of the hazards of a dual role, was never going to pass up an opportunity to learn at close quarters from this 'one-man university' of management.

Although he had become a friend of Stein's, there would always be an element of awe. Not that this constrained Ferguson from asking to be responsible for the preparation of training – a task he himself now delegated – and to be involved in picking the team. Stein was happy to agree to the first request but naturally suspicious of the second. He said he would do as he assumed Ferguson did at Aberdeen: in other words, listen with respect to the views of his assistant (Knox had by now left to manage Dundee and been replaced by the retired central defender Willie Garner) but pick his own team.

In a friendly against Yugoslavia at Hampden Park, Scotland won 6-1 with outstanding performances from Kenny Dalglish and Graeme Souness, who a year earlier, in their Liverpool shirts, had been instrumental in the disposal from the European Cup of Ferguson's Aberdeen. Ferguson was impressed by a close view of Souness, whose professionalism amended the image that may have been conveyed by those popping champagne corks in the Liverpool hotel.

There was so much talent available to Scotland at the time that Stein could afford to choose between the two young scamps, Charlie Nicholas and Mo Johnston, who, as Ferguson put it in his autobiography, graced as it was by the collaboration of Hugh McIlvanney, 'sometimes took the view that their quarters were inadequately furnished if they did not have a little female company'. The World Cup qualification began with a 3-0 home victory over Iceland in which Nicholas scored and continued with the 3-1 dispatch of Spain in which Johnston scored twice.

Early in 1985, however, the Scots lost the return match with Spain in Seville and also at home to Wales, a disappointment preceded by tension in the camp when Stein and Ferguson, seeking hints on how to combat the dangerous front pair of Ian Rush and Mark Hughes, met reticence from Rush's Liverpool clubmates Souness, Dalglish and Alan Hansen. Manchester United's Arthur Albiston obliged the management by discussing Hughes in detail, but still the Liverpool trio observed an *omerta*. Later Souness alone recognised his responsibilities by helping Stein and Ferguson in private. But the episode cannot have helped the spirit of the squad and may help to explain why only Souness went to Mexico with Ferguson for the tournament.

First, though, Scotland had to qualify. The loss to Wales meant that, even though they proceeded to win in Reykjavik through a goal from the midfielder Jim Bett, whom Ferguson was to bring back from Belgium to Aberdeen, survival depended on the securing of a point in the concluding group match against the Welsh in Cardiff.

It was a long and anxious summer for all Scots with a love of football. A victory in the then customary match against England had emphasised that this squad had the talent to compete at a high level. It would go to waste if the Welsh obtained revenge for the knockout at the Scots' hands eight years earlier that had been completed by a Dalglish header at Anfield after Don Masson's conversion of a dubious penalty for handling.

At least a point was needed to earn a play-off against Australia. Souness was to miss the match through suspension and Hansen because he cried off with an injury the day before. Stein muttered to Ferguson that the elegant defender had thereby blown his chances of going to Mexico if Scotland qualified. But, tragically, that was not to be a decision for Stein.

He looked as if he had a cold and Ferguson remembers his taking pills in his hotel room on the day of the match. It was 10 September 1985.

Things went badly for Scotland in the early stages. Hughes had put Wales in front, and deservedly so, at half-time, during which Stein berated Strachan. Strachan was upset and Ferguson tried to encourage him to lift his game and thus dissuade Stein from replacing him with the Rangers winger Davie Cooper. But it was another familiar face that more acutely dismayed Ferguson: that of Jim Leighton, who had been shaky in goal and, it transpired, had just told Stein he had lost a contact lens. Stein eyed Ferguson, who swore he had no idea

Leighton even used contact lenses. He later found that even the Aberdeen physiotherapist had been kept in ignorance by Leighton, on whose behalf a spare pair of lenses were henceforth taken to matches.

Suddenly, Stein having decided to send on Alan Rough in place of Leighton, the time for a team talk was over. The tension on the bench was severe and Ferguson asked the doctor, Stuart Hillis, to check on Stein, who by now was grey-faced and perspiring.

Stein went ahead with the envisaged change, Cooper replacing Strachan. At last Scotland were on top, but the possibility that an equaliser might elude them recurred in the mind of the manager, who kept emphasising to Ferguson the importance of maintaining their dignity, whatever the outcome. It was as if he knew he would not be around to see it.

With about ten minutes left, the ball bounced up and hit David Phillips on an arm and Scotland were awarded a penalty. It was a dubious decision by the Dutch referee and Neville Southall, Wales's excellent goalkeeper, nearly saved Cooper's kick, but it squeezed in. Stein impassively surveyed the vindication of his team adjustment.

As the seconds ticked slowly away, an intrepid photographer lay on the grass a few feet from Stein's bulky and hunched figure, directing his lens up at a portrait of stress. Stein rose from the bench, seized the photographer by the feet and, staggering, dragged him away. He sat down again, wordlessly. Then the referee blew for a free-kick and Stein, mistaking this for the final whistle, got up again to shake hands with his Welsh counterpart, Mike England. He stumbled and had to be supported by Ferguson and others until medical help arrived.

When the players returned to the dressing room, they knew of Stein's heart attack and were subdued. Ferguson left and encountered Souness by the closed door of the medical room. Souness was crying. Stein was dead.

The secretary of the Scottish FA, Ernie Walker, asked Ferguson to ring Stein's wife, Jean. She had gone to play bingo. She returned home to be told by her daughter Ray about the heart attack. But neither knew Stein's condition. In vain, Ray begged Ferguson not to tell them he was dead.

Next he went to address the players and staff. As they filed on to the bus outside Ninian Park, he kept remembering Stein's plea for dignity, and it was observed. Although thousands of supporters waited outside the ground, there was near-silence.

Aberdeen, Itchy Feet
and Scotland

Ferguson assumed responsibility for the job of completing
Scotland's qualification for the World Cup – he remained
part-time, on the understanding that he and the Scottish FA
would review the position after the finals, if Scotland duly got
to them – and they succeeded, beating Australia 2-0 at
Hampden Park with goals from Cooper and Frank McAvennie
in the first leg of the play-off and then drawing 0-0 in
Melbourne.

That was in early December. The 1985/6 season, the last
Ferguson was to complete in Scotland, was not quite halfway
through, but already Aberdeen had a trophy on the sideboard:
the League Cup, oddly their first under Ferguson. Two of the
goals in a 3-0 triumph over Hibs in the final came from Eric
Black. They were also to win the Scottish Cup, rounding matters
off with a 3-0 victory, this time over Hearts, as the national squad
prepared to head for Mexico, but by now Black was missing.

Rumours that he had been privately negotiating with over-
seas clubs had proved true; he had told Ferguson near the end
of the season that he was joining Metz in France. Ferguson's

reaction was to banish him from the squad and Billy Stark recalled coming in one afternoon for treatment: 'There was Eric sitting in the dressing room having done a full day's training while the rest of the players were away preparing for the final. He was doing his penance for having gone behind the manager's back.'

Ferguson later began to review his behaviour – he had been no gentler towards Black than Davie White had been towards him at Rangers – in the light of a realisation that his feet, too, had been getting itchier from the moment he joined Stein and started working with the likes of Souness and Dalglish. For the players, he recognised, it was mostly a question of money (none got as much as him). 'Looking back,' he said, 'the thing that changed things for Aberdeen was winning the Cup-Winners' Cup. Because the players got restless – Strachan, McGhee, Rougvie and then Black – and although at the time I was angry with them for wanting to leave the ship, so to speak, in fairness to them they weren't being paid what they were worth. Aberdeen couldn't afford it.' When he had accompanied Archibald to Tottenham in 1980, he had been shocked to discover that the player would receive nearly £100,000 a year.

Yet in that 1985/6 season Aberdeen remained a match for most. The defensive triangle of Leighton, McLeish and Miller seemed eternal, Stark and Weir remained on the flanks, MacDougall still scored goals and the midfield had been lent class by the third of Ferguson's favourite Pittodrie signings, Jim Bett.

Ferguson, who still clung to the belief that he could emulate Stein by bringing the European Cup back to Scotland, had seen his team dispatch Akranes, their old friends from Iceland,

and Servette of Switzerland to reach the quarter-finals, in which they drew IFK Gothenburg. Ferguson had made his first European appearance as a player in Gothenburg – and won his first European trophy as a manager there. 'I really did believe we could go on and take the big one,' he said. 'But, when we were 2–1 up in the first leg at home, Willie Miller, of all people, decided to beat men going up the pitch and lost the ball. It ended 2–2 and after a 0–0 over there we went out on away goals. We even hit a post in the last five minutes.' IFK went on to secure a 3–0 advantage over Barcelona in the semi-finals, only to lose it at Camp Nou and go out on penalties.

It's Barcelona or United

Barcelona were managed by Terry Venables and, at the Englishman's suggestion, joined a disparate list of clubs which had taken an interest in Ferguson. Around this time, when it was assumed that Venables would be moving on at the end of the season, officials of the Catalan club came to London to interview Ferguson along with Bobby Robson, by then in charge of England, and Howard Kendall, who had guided Everton to the first of two English titles in three years. In the event, Venables opted to stay at Camp Nou and his decision was accepted despite Barcelona's massive disappointment in that European Cup final, played on the familiar ground of Seville: a team featuring Steve Archibald, whom Venables had brought from Tottenham, lost on penalties to Steaua Bucharest.

Aberdeen were left with their two domestic Cups. Although they had been top of the League when Ferguson, Leighton, McLeish and Miller returned from Melbourne, they finished fourth after winning only eight of twenty matches. Before the start of the next season, he decided he needed a more assertive assistant than Willie Garner. He brought Knox back from

Dundee and, in recognition of the status acquired there, made him 'joint manager'.

Despite this, Aberdeen had slipped to fifth by the time Ferguson left for Manchester United three months into the season, taking Knox with him. They had also succumbed to an instant knockout from the Cup-Winners' Cup by Sion, their first victims on the road to Gothenburg in 1982/3. The first home match after Ferguson's departure was against St Mirren. The ground was half empty and there were no goals.

For two years he had been in a deepening rut. But the requests for his services had been coming in for longer than that. In 1981 he was offered £40,000 a year by Sheffield United, who had just been relegated to the Fourth Division. He took more seriously the advances of Wolves, partly because of their history – they had been champions three times in the post-war period and taken part in memorable, pioneering contests with top European clubs. They had also shown signs of renewed ambition after John Barnwell's arrival as manager. Barnwell had not only broken the British transfer record in signing Andy Gray from Aston Villa for £1.175 million but kept the true cost to (he gleefully calculated) a mere £25,000 by selling the relatively mundane midfield player Steve Daley to Manchester City.

Barnwell, though he nearly lost his life in a crash during which the rear-view mirror of his car became embedded in his skull, had recovered bravely enough to lead Wolves to victory over Brian Clough's Nottingham Forest in the League Cup final of 1979/80, Gray scoring the only goal. But he could not keep the club from the jaws of relegation and was obliged, in early 1982, to resign. He cleared his desk and went home and within a day had taken a telephone call from an erstwhile assistant who said that Alex Ferguson was in the stadium. Ferguson was not, however, being impressed either by what he saw at Molineux or the directors he met.

He had warned Dick Donald that he was going to talk to them – £50,000 a year was on offer – but flew back to Aberdeen more appreciative of his surroundings than ever. 'The secretary had picked me up at Birmingham Airport,' he said, 'and told me I was going to meet the board. I asked why. He said they wanted to interview me. "I'm not here for an interview," I said. "You've offered me the job." He said they just wanted me to answer a few questions. So I went. But the questions were unbelievable.'

Ferguson smiled at the recollection of how he was told a true story of a young player who had gone to a bank in Wolverhampton, borrowed several thousands of pounds using the club's name and gambled it away. 'They asked me how I'd deal with it! I said they should be asking themselves how something like that could happen.'

The final straw greeted him at the stadium. 'It was an afternoon and there was only one person working there – Jack Taylor, the former referee [a distinguished one, who handled the 1974 World Cup final in which West Germany beat the Netherlands], who was on the commercial side. The place was like a ghost town. I couldn't get on the plane quick enough.'

His second rejection of Rangers left him on £60,000 a year and he had little difficulty, a couple of months later, in turning down an opportunity to succeed Terry Neill at Arsenal, much though he admired the grandeur of that club. He then engaged in a more prolonged flirtation with their north London rivals, Tottenham Hotspur, whose chairman, Irving Scholar, he found all the more engaging for a passion for football trivia and quiz questions which Ferguson, of course, enthusiastically shared. Once again, however, he found it impossible to leave Dick Donald and a happy partnership in which one would address the other as 'Mr Chairman' and be accorded the mock-courtesy of 'Mr Ferguson' in return.

It might have been easier to move south if he had been given the five years he sought from Tottenham – after offering two, they stuck at three – but in the event the London club replaced Keith Burkinshaw, who had resigned, with the in-house appointment of Peter Shreeves and that appeared to have brought Pittodrie two years of stability. Not Ferguson, though. Not quite. Not in the recesses of his mind.

'Souness started biting my ear off, talking about Liverpool and English football and why I should be there,' he said. 'And big Jock, over dinner, when we were with the Scotland squad, kept asking, "How long are you going to stay at Aberdeen?" And I started to ask myself.'

It may have crossed Stein's mind that he himself had passed up an opportunity to move to a big English club – Sir Matt Busby had asked him to be his successor at Manchester United – because he preferred not to uproot his family and had then, several years later, gone south, to Leeds, at the wrong time. But Stein didn't talk a lot about himself.

Once, when Stein and Ferguson flew to watch Everton overcome Bayern Munich in a memorable Cup-Winners' Cup semi-final – just as Aberdeen had done two years earlier – they popped into Howard Kendall's office afterwards and stayed for hours, exchanging views with what Ferguson described as 'a *Who's Who* of modern football'. Sometimes he went to Liverpool and was invited to join the famous Boot Room chinwags. He became friendly with David Pleat, then forging a reputation at Luton Town, on a trip to France for the European Championship in 1984 organised by Adidas for their pet managers.

He had even been entertained by Ron Atkinson at Manchester United, for in 1985 he wrote, in *A Light in the North*: 'One English manager whom I have a lot of time for and who is very different from his media image is Ron Atkinson . . . Ron has always been first-class to deal with and always makes himself available when I call the training ground or the stadium. A lot of people tend to think of him only as a fancy dresser with a liking for champagne but those who know him will realise there is a lot more to the man . . . The main impression I get from Ron is that he's a football fanatic who will chat and argue about the game till the cows come home. He is authoritative and well informed about the game and the players in it and it wouldn't surprise me at all if Ron's Manchester United side become one of the great teams in the club's illustrious history.'

A year later, he was in Atkinson's job. He could not have suspected it at the time, for, at Christmas in the year his paean was published, that team of Atkinson's, featuring Bryan Robson and Mark Hughes and Norman Whiteside and Paul McGrath and, of course, Strachan, with whom Ferguson kept in touch by telephone, were on top of the League, where they were to stay until February and the beginnings of a slide to fourth. Even Ferguson could not see that coming as, juggling his two jobs, he commuted between Aberdeen and the great theatres of the English game, the circles into which he was being drawn.

There were other factors. Dick Donald was semi-retired by now and, with time on his hands, liked to spend chunks of it with Ferguson at Pittodrie in the afternoons. Much as Ferguson loved him, he preferred to work intensely. And still he did not hurry his departure. He rebuffed Aston Villa; that was a foregone conclusion because the chairman, Doug Ellis, was widely perceived as a meddler with whom working relationships could be strained. No Dick Donald, certainly.

Even when Don Howe stepped out of the Arsenal job in the spring of 1986, Ferguson refused to divert himself from preparing Donald's Aberdeen for Hampden Park and the departed Stein's Scotland for Mexico. But he was careful to accord Arsenal, like Barcelona, the courtesy of an interview; by now he would have known the Aberdeen–London flight times by heart.

Offered the Arsenal job with George Graham as his assistant, he promised them an answer after the World Cup but, amid rumours that they suspected his heart was at Manchester United (although there is no reason to believe any approach from Old Trafford had been made, he had been linked with Old Trafford in the press and at least one United director, Sir Bobby Charlton, had been monitoring his career), they gave the job to Graham instead. Ferguson heard the news at Scotland's training camp at Santa Fe, New Mexico, from where they moved to Los Angeles and then on to Mexico.

Just before he left, he had spoken of his restlessness to Donald, who had advised him to leave Pittodrie only for United. 'That's the biggest challenge in football,' said the chairman. Ferguson needed no telling. As the tournament approached, he spent time with Strachan, whose room was next to his own in the Scotland hotel and who recalled: 'He said he would leave Aberdeen for only one of two clubs – Barcelona or Manchester United.'

At the World Cup

But that would have to wait. Scotland had flown out for the World Cup without Hansen, a decision for which Ferguson was to be unfairly criticised for many years, certainly in England; the Liverpool defender, though a magnificent performer for his club, had withdrawn from too many squads to suggest anything other than that he would take unkindly to the likelihood that the consistency of Miller and McLeish would consign him to the substitutes' bench. Or, as Ferguson put in his autobiography: 'I simply felt that he did not deserve to go.' David Narey, of Dundee United, went instead.

Ferguson did, however, harbour concerns about the possible reaction of Hansen's friend Kenny Dalglish to his exclusion which were borne out by a telephone conversation shortly before the squad announcement. It was almost on the eve of the departure for Santa Fe that Ferguson lost Dalglish, too.

One of Scotland's finest players of all time, the holder of their records for caps won (102) and goals scored (thirty, shared with Denis Law), would miss what would have been his fourth World Cup because of a knee injury. Dalglish hotly denied that it had anything to do with the Hansen decision; he was merely taking the strong advice of a surgeon. So only Souness of the Liverpool trio was on duty when Scotland, drawn in a tough group with West Germany, Uruguay and Denmark, began by facing the Danes on the outskirts of Mexico City.

It had been a professional but enjoyable build-up. Ferguson had gratefully retained 'Steely' – Jimmy Steel, Stein's beloved tea-maker, impressionist, raconteur and all-round feel-good factor – to complement an impressive coaching team. Andy Roxburgh, Ferguson's old striking partner and by now highly regarded at the Scottish FA for his work with young players, had a limited role but Ferguson also brought in Craig Brown, then manager of Clyde, along with Archie Knox and Walter Smith. In time Brown was himself to take charge of the national team, after serving as assistant to Roxburgh, and to prove one of Scotland's most astute and successful managers. Smith, too, was to do the job before the lure of Rangers proved irresistible. So the coaching was serious. But there was fun, too, and Ferguson joined in the give and take at Santa Fe.

The players were in the main hotel building, the staff in log cabins, and once, Brown recalled, some players found their way into Ferguson's cabin and loosened all the light bulbs so that, upon his return at the end of an evening on which everyone had been allowed a few beers, none of the lights worked. 'Cursing, he came into my cabin to phone reception and then went back to his cabin to wait for the electrician. Somehow he found his way to the toilet, but the players had put cling-film over it so that, when he let go with a much-needed pee in the dark, it all splashed back on him. But he could take that sort of thing – he's always had a good sense of humour.'

Inevitably, given Ferguson's gift for quizzes and games such as Trivial Pursuit, there were plenty of those and Ferguson had to win. 'He'd obviously got a lot out of his education,' said Brown, 'and had a very broad knowledge. History, geography, politics – you name it. Even Dr Hillis, who was to become a professor, couldn't beat Fergie.'

There was golf, too, and a day at the races; a trotting track was nearby. But the training was earnest. 'After practice matches,' said Brown, 'he would take the players back and sit them down and they would all – not just Willie Miller and Alex McLeish but Anglos like Graeme Souness, too – be hanging on every word. There were none of the lapses of concentration some managers encounter. No one ever got fidgety.'

Though discipline was maintained with a light rein, everyone knew who was in charge. Once Steve Archibald reported a slight hamstring problem and said he would do his own warm-up before training the next day. 'You'll be getting up early then,' said Ferguson, 'because you'll be doing your own warm-up before you join our warm-up.' Which he did, of course, albeit after arriving, to Ferguson's mild irritation, in a stretch limo supplied by the team hotel.

And so to the football. Scotland played quite well against Denmark but missed chances and lost 1-0. Next they took on the Germans in Querétaro and, although again their football impressed neutrals, were defeated 2-1.

Ferguson and company were learning as they went along. The day before the match against the Germans, there had been special care to make the final training session in the stadium private. 'Alex had insisted on that,' said Brown, 'because there had been a doubt over Strachan's fitness and he didn't want Franz Beckenbauer and Berti Vogts to know his team. Yet later

Berti told me they'd known that Strachan would play. I asked him how. "Well," said Berti, "when we were barred from coming into the stadium to watch the session, I noticed a Coca-Cola man with his barrow arriving outside." The tournament was sponsored by Coca-Cola and the stuff was everywhere. "So," said Berti, "I gave this guy a Germany shirt or something and he let me borrow his white overalls and hat and I just pulled them on and wheeled the barrow into the stadium, where they were setting things up for the match.'"

Not that the Germans could prevent Strachan from giving Scotland the lead. Yet two German goals meant the Scots had to beat Uruguay in their final group match to stand any chance of remaining in the competition. It was back to Nezahualcoyotl, the sprawling shanty town not surprisingly known as Neza.

Ferguson dropped Souness, who was thirty-three and had been below his best in the heat, but Scotland seemed to acquire a massive advantage when José Batista was sent off in the first minute for a hideous foul on Strachan.

The decisiveness of the French referee, Joël Quiniou, should have eased the Scots' path to the knockout stages but instead they departed after a scoreless draw, bitterly complaining about the violence and sly gamesmanship of the Uruguayans.

According to Brown there was another reason for their departure: 'A player who gave the greatest individual perform-ance I have ever seen.' He referred to Enzo Francescoli, who, when playing for Olympique Marseille, became the ultimate hero to a boy called Zinedine Zidane. 'Francescoli played our entire back four on his own and, although we finally managed to put some pressure on the Uruguayans late in the game after Davie Cooper had come on, we were eliminated.' The

Scottish press blamed Ferguson for omitting Souness and everyone went home.

Privately, Ferguson blamed himself not only for leaving out Souness but for letting himself be distracted in the build-up to the Uruguay match by a row with Steve Archibald, who had been left out, and proceeding to do himself no justice with a lacklustre team talk.

And, when the Scottish FA reviewed matters on the squad's return, the idea that they might cheer up the nation by appointing Ferguson on a permanent basis appears not to have occurred.

Some managers seem more suited to the club milieu than the international game and neither Stein nor, with admittedly limited opportunity, Ferguson was able to lift Scotland as they had Celtic and Aberdeen respectively. It might have given pause for thought to the many Englishmen who had yearned for Brian Clough to be put in charge of the national team; without day-to-day control over the players, would he have been as successful as at Derby and Nottingham Forest?

At any rate, the job of filling Stein's seat in the Scotland dugout went to Ferguson's old acquaintance Andy Roxburgh and he did it well, guiding Scotland to qualification for a World Cup and a European Championship with the assistance of Craig Brown, who, upon succeeding him, also secured a place in one each of the major tournaments, coping even more impressively with a sharp decline in the quality of player available to Scotland managers.

Pittodrie Postscript

There was to be no rousing finale for Ferguson at Aberdeen. The League match destined to be his last with the club, against Dundee, was a win, but it left them fifth.

Under Ian Porterfield, Aberdeen finished the season fourth, but never at any stage got close to a trophy.

The joint management of Jocky Scott and Alex Smith brought a revival, with a Cup double and a near thing in the League in 1989/90, three years before Dick Donald died of Alzheimer's disease.

Under the management of Roy Aitken, an old foe of Aberdeen's from his belligerent Celtic days, there was a League Cup triumph in 1995/6, but club football in Scotland was, like the national team, in decline.

No one could threaten Celtic or Rangers – Tweedledum would enjoy a few years at the top, then Tweedledee take his turn – and an eerie fatalism had fallen over even Pittodrie long before the appointment as manager, in June 2009, of Mark McGhee, Ferguson's first signing.

MANCHESTER UNITED:
EARLY DAYS

A Chat with Bobby Charlton

If fate guided Ferguson to Manchester United, it was Sir Bobby Charlton who kept its fickle finger steady.

Having survived the Munich crash in February 1958 and won the World Cup with England eight years later, then become a European champion with United two years after that, Charlton was football's most famous Englishman, a distinction he was to retain until the rise of David Beckham.

He was not alone in identifying a prospective new Busby, for the Old Trafford chairman, Martin Edwards, had also been monitoring Ferguson's career. But Charlton was the first United director to make a semblance of an approach.

Ferguson mentions it in his book but, despite Ron Atkinson's suspicions, it fell short of the improper. It is understandable that Atkinson, who was to begin the next season in charge, should have felt miffed upon learning of it, but he himself had vaguely offered to go a few months earlier, towards the end of a season whose rich promise had faded dramatically; there was a succession issue to be addressed.

And all Charlton said to Ferguson, while attending a Scotland training session in Mexico as part of his duties as a television analyst during the World Cup of 1986, was that, if he ever fancied moving south, a call would be appreciated.

Charlton had always taken an interest in Scottish football; it was natural, he said, for one brought up only a few dozen miles from the border (he and his brother Jack came from the pit village of Ashington, County Durham). His understanding of what it had taken Ferguson to defeat the Old Firm was acute and he followed up his interest in conversations with the United defender Arthur Albiston at the Scots' training camp. 'I never thought much about it at the time,' said Albiston, 'but Bobby kept asking what the training was like and so on.'

Not that Edwards needed much convincing by Charlton; his opinion of Ferguson had only been enhanced by the manner in which the Aberdeen manager had done business over Strachan. 'There was a general agreement on the board that Alex was the outstanding candidate,' he said.

Edwards remembered being impressed when Ferguson criticised the Aberdeen players on television after they had won the Scottish Cup final. Although Ferguson regretted that, Edwards said: 'His fury showed the sort of standards he set. Just to win was not good enough. He wanted to win in style.' The Manchester United way? 'Well, we were to see plenty of it in his time with us.'

Edwards was no Dick Donald. Not only was he two years younger than Ferguson; the game he had preferred to play, as a consequence of his middle-class education, was rugby union. He had been on the board since 1970 and succeeded his father, Louis Edwards, as chairman in 1980. Louis had become wealthy through meat packaging but died after a hostile television programme about his business ethics which extended to

United and an alleged slush fund out of which the parents of promising youngsters were paid.

Martin, too, had his critics, mainly supporters who suspected his heart was not in the club. But his affection for United and its traditions was genuine.

Only a year into his chairmanship, an obligation fell upon him to oversee the dismissal of the manager, Dave Sexton, despite a sequence of seven consecutive wins that had left United in eighth place at the end of the season – the style of football was deemed unattractive, prompting the *Daily Express* to rename the stadium 'Cold Trafford' – and the search for a replacement proved embarrassing in that Lawrie McMenemy, Bobby Robson and Ron Saunders all publicly declined the job. Edwards learned from that and went about getting Ferguson more skilfully.

The idea of there being a vacancy had occurred only towards the end of the previous season, which Atkinson's side had begun as runaway League leaders, looking ready to dominate the English game. They won their first ten matches with Bryan Robson, Mark Hughes and Gordon Strachan to the fore, but were flattering to deceive. The slump was more dramatic than could be excused by injuries afflicting Robson and his midfield sidekick Remi Moses, plus Strachan and Jesper Olsen. United finished fourth.

Edwards and Atkinson agreed to give things another go but, as Arthur Albiston recalled, they went from bad to worse. Hughes had been sold to Barcelona. 'Also, in fairness to Ron,' said Albiston, 'a few of us had come back from the World Cup unfit. Including me – I ended up having a stomach operation after Alex Ferguson took over. And of course Robbo had put his shoulder out with England in Mexico.

'But we had a big enough squad to have coped better than we did. We were terrible. I remember playing Charlton Athletic and being up against a young Rob Lee. He knocked the ball past me and, feeling my stomach muscle, I took about ten minutes to turn and go after him. God almighty! I could hear the crowd gasping in horror.'

On Saturday 1st of November 1986, a home draw with Coventry left United nineteenth out of twenty-two clubs. It was relegation form.

On Tuesday the 4th, they went to Southampton for a League Cup replay and were beaten 4-1. The game was up. On the private flight back north, Edwards and his fellow director Mike Edelson resolved to replace Atkinson with Ferguson. The only other candidate mentioned was Terry Venables.

On Wednesday the 5th, Edwards gathered the other key board members — Charlton and the lawyer Maurice Watkins — and there was unanimity.

Edelson rang Aberdeen and, faking a Scottish accent, pretended to be Strachan's accountant in order to get through to Ferguson. He then handed the phone to Edwards, who gave Ferguson a Manchester number to ring. Was he interested? Yes. Could everyone meet that night in Scotland, somewhere safe from prying eyes? Yes. Ferguson would ring back in an hour.

Meanwhile, he spoke to Archie Knox and, with less relish, to Cathy, whom he knew would be upset at the thought of uprooting herself and the boys; she did not surprise him. He also rang his journalist confidant Jim Rodger for advice about handling media interest.

Then he gave Edwards the meeting place — and, fortunately for all concerned, no prying eyes were to swivel across the car park at Hamilton service station on the M74 south of

Glasgow at 7 p.m., when Edwards slipped out of his car into Ferguson's, leaving Edelson and Charlton to follow them to the home of Ferguson's sister-in-law in the Glasgow suburb of Bishopbriggs.

There, the questions became harder.

What was the salary? Disappointing. Less than he would make in a good year at Aberdeen. Less than those of most of the star players he had been hired to lead. A lot less than Robson's (and less, Ferguson would have known, than Strachan's). Less (though he could hardly have known this at the time) than the £80,000 Edwards got as chief executive. But enough to start with. There was no haggling.

Would he have a transfer budget? At a push, replied Edwards, a small amount might be found. If Ferguson had expected the promised land, he was disappointed. But he was never going to turn his back on Old Trafford.

Was there a drink problem among the squad? Yes, replied Edwards.

Ferguson had not plucked this question out of the air. He and Strachan had kept in touch and the curse of the working classes was, indeed, only too evident in the middle-class Cheshire villages where Atkinson's players tended to live. Bryan Robson played a captain's role, leading by example, though the enthusiasm of Paul McGrath and Norman Whiteside for a drinking session could never be questioned.

Ferguson was acutely aware of it. 'In the phone calls he made to me almost weekly,' he wrote in his autobiography, 'Gordon Strachan kept telling me the word in Manchester was that I would be the next manager. There was not the merest hint of an official approach to support these stories and I was left musing on some of Gordon's comments on how the great club was being run. He cited . . . the drinking that was going on among the players and the alleged indifference of Big Ron to its damaging effects.'

According to Strachan, it was usually Ferguson and not he who made the calls, but they were not sinister. 'We'd chat,' said Strachan. 'He'd ask me how I was getting on, what the training was like and about the players and so on. Later the word got about that I'd been a sort of spy for him.

'I do remember telling him that some of the lads, including Bryan Robson, liked a drink — but I would never have said that if I'd known he was coming down to be their manager. I was just talking to my ex-manager as a friend.'

Edwards confirmed Strachan's view at the meeting in Bishopbriggs and before that night of the 5th of November was over — remember, remember — and the bonfires turned to glowing ash, the negotiations became decidedly less professional.

We can only imagine how Edwards felt when Ferguson asked if United would buy his house in Cults to save him the trouble and possible financial loss involved in a quick sale, or if they would clear his debt to Aberdeen, which had risen to £40,000 (if he had been as astute a gambler on shares and horses as on footballers, it might have been different). In each case the answer was firmly negative and Ferguson can never have accepted defeat more philosophically. Hands were shaken.

On Thursday the 6th, Edwards and Maurice Watkins flew to Aberdeen to meet Dick Donald and his son Ian and compensation of £60,000 was agreed for the loss of Ferguson and Archie Knox, to whom Donald had vainly offered the opportunity to stay in sole charge. They told Ron Atkinson he had lost his job, and the press, who were then called to Old Trafford for the announcement of Ferguson's appointment.

Strictly speaking, United should have sacked Atkinson, approached Donald for permission to speak to Ferguson and only then made him an offer. But a football club, as United had discovered while trying to fill Dave Sexton's shoes, cannot function that way with dignity. 'So we broke the rules,' Edwards said, 'by a day.'

Drinking to the Past

The speed of the operation to recruit Ferguson left the players acutely inquisitive about the character of their new manager. 'They went to wee Gordon first,' said Arthur Albiston, 'and he kept shtum.' This was almost certainly mischievous; other players remember Strachan's expressions clearly hinting at imminent fireworks. 'So they asked me,' continued Albiston, 'because they knew I'd been with Scotland too. I was quite pleased by the appointment and told them so. I said he was very organised and very fair. If you crossed him, you were in trouble. If you tried your best, you'd have no problem.'

Strachan harboured a mixture of emotions: 'One, he was a top manager and just what the club needed at the time. There was so much potential – it just needed discipline and organisation. But I'd heard it all before. I'd worked with him for seven years. I was delighted for him, delighted for Manchester United – but not sure it was for me.'

Ferguson spent one last night in Aberdeen. As he turned his mind to his new players – he was to meet them the next day, the Friday – most of them partied. Even though their first match under his management, away to Oxford United in an elite division of which their membership was threatened, was to take place in less than forty-eight hours. They were in two groups. Some were invited to Atkinson's house. Others made their own arrangements.

The morning saw them gather in the gym at United's training ground, The Cliff, to be addressed by Ferguson. He was probably the most apprehensive man in the room. This was not St Mirren, or even Aberdeen. There were some big names facing him – and they included the biggest drinkers. It was his job to tell them they were selling themselves and the club short. Nice guys like Albiston wished him well.

Ferguson recalled: 'They must have thought I had little to say for myself and, if they supposed it was all a bit nerve-wracking for me, they were right.' They did notice. As Albiston said: 'He was more nervous than I'd seen him with Scotland. He just said he was disappointed – and surprised – that we were in such a lowly position.'

They were fourth from bottom. And they dropped one place after losing at Oxford. Albiston remembered travelling to the cramped Manor Ground and seeing more cameras than usual. United lost 2-0. 'Never got started,' said Albiston. 'And I think the manager was surprised that, in English football at that time, your Oxfords, Lutons and Wimbledons could give the likes of United a good game. In fact, I think it shocked him. It was harder for the bigger clubs than it might have looked from Scotland.'

He was dismayed by proof of his players' poor fitness and, fortified by righteous indignation, assembled them in the gym again for a more resonant message: they would have to change their ways, especially on the drinking front – 'because I wasn't going to change mine'.

The lesson in English football's egalitarianism was under-lined at Norwich, where a goalless draw left United a further place lower, one off the bottom, and before long a 1-0 loss at Wimbledon, whose direct, muscular and nakedly belligerent football was to win the FA Cup eighteen months later, removed from Ferguson's mind all doubt that his team lacked the height and power to meet such challenges.

At least they had picked up their first win under Ferguson, beating Queens Park Rangers in his first match at Old Trafford through a goal from John Sivebæk.

Ferguson had only three days to savour this before hearing news he had been dreading. When he made his daily tele-phone call to his mother in Glasgow, she did not answer and it transpired that she had been taken to hospital. A few months earlier, Lizzie Ferguson, a smoker since her early teens, had been diagnosed with lung cancer. Ferguson, after ringing Cathy in Aberdeen, flew to Glasgow, to be told by the specialist that his mother had days to live.

Her selfless courage was with her, Ferguson noted, to the end; as he and his brother Martin sat by her bed on the Friday evening, she told them to leave and get some rest before their matches the next day (United were to play at Wimbledon and St Mirren, where Martin was a part-time assistant to Alex Miller, were at home to Celtic).

Months after taking over at Aberdeen, Ferguson had lost his father. He had been at Manchester United less than three weeks and now, once again, he was alone with grief. Alone in a crowd of just over 12,000 at a ground even more modest than Oxford's; that very afternoon he was in the deep south-west of London, at Wimbledon's Plough Lane, again seeing his team defeated.

They lost at home to Norwich City just before his forty-fifth birthday on New Year's Eve, and they were to lose to Luton Town, and again to Wimbledon, before the end of the season. But other results were more reminiscent of United's in the pomp of Atkinson.

They beat Liverpool, the champions, home and away, and overcame Arsenal, who were on top of the League and had gone four months unbeaten under George Graham (the Highbury board were not regretting his appointment), at Old Trafford. Nor were they disgraced by a subsequent home draw with Everton, who had just taken over from Arsenal at the top of the table and were to retrieve the title from their Merseyside neighbours that season.

'Obviously the new manager was having an impact,' said Arthur Albiston, 'but what really helped our results to improve was players coming back.' The likes of Robson, Strachan and Whiteside had not become bad players overnight.

At first Ferguson, as at Aberdeen, had been relatively restrained. 'I'd sort of warned the lads to expect fireworks,' said Strachan, 'but after a few weeks they were giving me odd looks. Anger is his petrol, his fuel, and I think he was holding a bit back.' Nor was he immune to self-doubt. 'He was feeling his way,' said Edwards. 'He took a while to come to terms with English football.'

When he started to live up to his reputation, some of the players were shocked, said Albiston: 'They'd never had anybody speaking to them like that and, while I wouldn't say it ever got out of control, a few couldn't get their heads round the fact that he was trying to help them.

'I'd had an early glimpse of it in a reserve game. Some of the young lads couldn't believe what they were hearing. They were shell-shocked. But he was looking for a response and he usually got it. If he didn't, you were probably on your way.'

Six months after his arrival, towards the end of the season and with United safely in mid-table, they went to Tottenham for a lunchtime kick-off and the entire first team were sprayed with both barrels by an irate Ferguson. 'I'll never forget it,' said Albiston.

Spurs had a very good side in that single season they spent under Ferguson's friend David Pleat; they had taken Arsenal to a third match in the League Cup semi-finals and were to finish third in the League before losing 3-2 to Coventry City in one of the great FA Cup finals. So Ferguson had taken the trouble to analyse them in the most rigorous detail.

'His team talk,' said Albiston, a non-playing member of the squad that day, 'told us what was likely to happen and how Spurs would play and so on. Chris Waddle would turn this way and that before he put his crosses in — and we'd to watch out for Mitchell Thomas coming in from left-back. And we lost 4–0 — with Thomas scoring a couple from Waddle's crosses! When he came back to the dressing room afterwards, everybody got it. Robbo included. It was a case of "and you, and you — oh, and I almost forgot about you". Every warning he'd given us had come to fruition.'

Not for the first time, or the last, a mighty force was released by Ferguson's vindication. Some players were on their way out. Sivebæk never played for United again, but others' days were numbered: the strikers Frank Stapleton, Peter Davenport and Terry Gibson, the winger Peter Barnes, the defender Graeme Hogg.

Even the warrior Whiteside and the immensely gifted

McGrath were to go in time. But that was to do with the booze culture: Ferguson was embarking on a cultural revolution.

How bad was the drink problem at United? Not that bad in the context of 1986, argued Arthur Albiston. 'Things are a lot different now,' he said. 'The influx of foreign players – and foreign coaches – since the mid-1990s has helped to bring about a change in the way players socialise. I don't think our club in 1986 was very different to any other. You felt you had to let off a bit of steam after matches, especially if you'd been travelling a lot.

'We used to bump into other players from Manchester City – or Liverpool and Everton – in the areas where most of us socialised. We all got up to the same things. Possibly what we did got highlighted more because we were underachieving.'

Certainly Liverpool got away with quite a lot. Once, having celebrated a championship, they actually played an end-of-season match at Middlesbrough when drunk – and drew 0–0. 'We could smell it on their breath,' an opponent ruefully recalled, 'and still we couldn't beat them.'

So Albiston's is a fair description of the mood of the time. But Ferguson was ahead of his time. He had seen what fitness could do for a team at Aberdeen – and now seen what the opposite could do for United. 'While I was doing my recuperation from the stomach problem,' said Albiston, 'he told me he couldn't believe how many players were missing training because of injuries.' And he followed his instinct that it was inseparable from the drink problem most obvious in Robson – though the captain trained like a demon when he could, as if desperate to prove he could live with the habit – and Whiteside and McGrath.

Had the old regime been too soft? Albiston, while reluctant

to criticise Atkinson – 'I had a great regard for Ron and played probably my best football under him' – did concede: 'He was one of those guys whose attitude was that, if you did it for him on a Saturday, the rest was fine. But if you miss too much training it's bound to catch up with you sooner or later. It's very hard when you miss two or three days a week and then try to play.'

Such was the class of the main culprits that Ferguson tried to be patient, even as he fielded reports of their drinking sessions and, on one occasion, even saw Whiteside and McGrath the worse for wear while appearing as guests on a football magazine programme on Granada television; persistent injuries meant they had plenty of time in which to get up to such mischief.

Robson he considered a manageable risk: the least heavy drinker and a magnificent player. Whiteside was almost as gifted, lacking only pace, but less disciplined. McGrath once had to be sent off the training pitch because he was too hung-over to run. He was an alcoholic and a hopeless case. Or so it seemed until he was transferred to Aston Villa and, with the help of Graham Taylor and later Ron Atkinson (not to forget a succession of knee surgeons), played on to a very high standard for several years, appearing gigantically in two World Cups for the Republic of Ireland.

McGrath had been shipped out of Old Trafford in the same week as Whiteside went to Everton. Whiteside went without complaint or rancour. McGrath raged at Ferguson, claiming that he had at first been offered a retirement package rather than a move. But no one accused Ferguson of haste: he had managed Whiteside and McGrath for nearly three years.

How had he tracked their often mazy movements from

pub to pub? Well, some managers are born to surveillance and others have it thrust upon them and Ferguson was a bit of both. As he had been at Aberdeen, where he had quickly formed his dim view of Joe Harper. 'It was easier to control there,' said Albiston, 'because Aberdeen's a compact city. Here a manager's got a problem. There are more distractions, more places to go.' But that was also true of Glasgow and Ferguson had been well tutored by Stein in keeping tabs on his squad.

Disillusioned fans were only too willing to help by ringing him with sightings. 'Put it this way,' said Albiston, 'you always felt you were being watched.' And the culture slowly changed. 'Players started to be more enthusiastic about training. The senior ones realised how good he was – and how determined to turn it around.'

Turning Off the Fans

As Ferguson turned in for the nights in the three-bedroom suburban semi he shared with Archie Knox until Cathy and boys joined him in the summer of 1987, he must have been aware that his had not been a wildly popular appointment.

The letters column of the local *Football Pink*, a reliable indicator, was lukewarm at best about the latest pretender to the throne of Busby. Students of the game were aware that, while Scots made good managers, those who flourished at a high level south of the border tended to have been schooled in English football, like Busby and Shankly.

George Graham was to underline that point. While crowds rolled up to watch his renascent Arsenal, and Pleat's Tottenham, some 11 per cent of the United support turned their backs on Ferguson's side. Not only that: despite the rise from eleventh to second in the League the following season, there was a further fall of 3 per cent in attendances. The season after that, another 7 per cent stayed away, so that on average there were 20,000 empty spaces at the 56,000-capacity stadium for every home match.

United still vied with Liverpool to be the best supported

team in the land, but the landscape of English football was very different then. It was to be a lot richer and more colourful in the heyday of the Premier League, when all-seat stadiums were packed to see some of the world's brightest stars and television contracts bulged. Indeed, the final flourish of the Atkinson era, in which United began the 1985/6 season with ten straight wins, was not even seen by the wider public because the League treated as derisory a joint offer from the BBC and ITV of £4 million a year for the rights to show matches live as well as the customary highlights.

That the broadcasters, who said they would rather show films than increase the offer, were justified in believing the club chairmen overvalued their product at that time (even though within twenty years it was to bring in a hundred times more) was emphasised by the compromise that put football back on the screens early in the new year. The League got £1.3 million for the rest of the season. Not per club: this was for the entire First Division (later Premier League). The television people, under whom a rocket was to be placed by Sky when the Premier League got under way early in the next decade, had correctly judged the public's opinion of the game. Attendances had fallen from a peak of nearly 41.3 million in 1948/9 to an all-time low of fewer than 16.5 million and, while football made headlines, they were usually about hooliganism.

On the field, English clubs had been successful, at least until the Brussels riot that condemned them to years of exclusion from European competition. It had taken nine years, after Busby's United had made the breakthrough in 1968, for another English team to become champions of Europe, but Liverpool's triumph over Borussia Moenchengladbach in 1977 was the first of four by that club in an eight-year period during which

Nottingham Forest, twice, and Aston Villa also took that title.

Then Liverpool made their ill-fated return to the final in 1985. It was at the Heysel Stadium in Brussels, where thirty-nine mainly Italian supporters of Juventus died after a charge by Liverpool followers. The match went ahead in order to reduce the danger of further bloodshed and, in an eerie atmosphere, Juventus won through a penalty by Michel Platini.

The FA immediately withdrew all English clubs from Europe and Uefa followed up with an indefinite ban. Margaret Thatcher acknowledged the national sense of shame. English football was in disgrace and its exile from Europe contributed to the low esteem in which the game was held when Ferguson came south.

It seems a long time ago now; Mrs Thatcher had all but squeezed inflation, the bane of the 1970s, from the UK economy and Neil Kinnock was squeezing Labour's militant left with the help of a thirty-three-year-old Peter Mandelson, under whose direction the red flag was replaced by a red rose as the party's symbol at its annual conference.

The red half of Manchester's football was also undergoing a revolution. Maybe not a quiet revolution, but a gradual one. 'You didn't notice a big difference in the training until the next summer, when we returned for the pre-season,' said Albiston. 'It wasn't dramatically tougher. But it was more serious than in Ron's time.'

Another significant difference was that, while Atkinson had devoted all his attention to the first team, Ferguson insisted on knowing everything about the reserves and youth team. The pattern established at St Mirren and Aberdeen was being followed.

Youth Culture

Ferguson was growing United from the roots. After St Mirren and Aberdeen, he would not have had it any other way. At the meeting with Edwards, Charlton and Watkins in Bishopbriggs, he had pointedly asked them: 'Are you sure you know what you're getting?' Charlton, the former Busby Babe, was the first to reply, said Ferguson: 'He told me that was why they wanted me – United had to get back to developing their own players. It was important for me to know that, and for them to know it was not going to happen overnight, and, in fairness to Martin, he supported me.'

This was twenty years on. We were speaking in Ferguson's smart office at United's training ground on Carrington Moor, to which the staff and players had moved from the cramped and outdated Cliff in 1999, leaving behind the vantage points from which journalists and opposition spies could peer at them, and the outstretched arms of autograph hunters. More than ever, football managers and players craved privacy, and Ferguson was no exception. He had come to refer to Carrington as 'our fortress'.

Gazing through the window at his latest platoons – young

recruits and multi-million mercenaries, all filing cheerfully to the training fields – he reflected on his inheritance from Ron Atkinson. 'There was a void,' he said, 'between the youths and the older players at the club.' Atkinson had not been the first manager to have allowed that to happen, nor would he be the last; the demand for instant success caused many to despair of ever having the time to build a youth policy as Ferguson had done, or Arsène Wenger at Arsenal.

'So don't get me wrong about Ron,' said Ferguson. 'He was a terrific manager. He was the kind of manager I'd have liked to play for. He relaxed players. But he believed in experience and you can understand that with managers in danger of losing their jobs all the time. They prefer to play safe. I'm a bit more reckless. But I am what I am. I could do it the other way – if I had enough money – but I wouldn't enjoy it. There's nothing to beat the satisfaction of bringing through your own players and seeing them succeed. I think that's probably why I took my coaching badges at Largs all those years ago. I wanted to educate players, not just train them.'

Edwards backed him all the way. Not just philosophically but with hard cash. 'Everything I asked for to do with the youth team,' Ferguson recalled, 'I got. The system was changed and we took on eighteen extra scouts and that cost a lot of money, even though at first they were given expenses only. Later we took on the best and gave them salaries. For Martin it was never a problem. He was brilliant that way.'

Their relationship was not so smooth on other financial aspects, notably Ferguson's own salary, which he felt was on the mean side. He had been in the job little more than six months when he alluded to it. He and Edwards had gone to Glasgow to clinch one of his first signings. Needing an adequate replacement at centre-forward for Hughes, he had identified Brian McClair of Celtic. Before the trip, Edwards had mentioned having met almost all of United's 1948 FA Cup-winning team, with the notable exception of the centre-forward, Jimmy Delaney. Ferguson said he would put that right. 'So I phone the wee Jolly [Jim Rodger, his journalist fixer friend] and he phones Mrs Delaney and she says it's all right.

'After the signing we go to the Delaneys' house and you wouldn't believe it. The neighbours had all been baking and there was a long table with a nice cloth and on it, apple tarts, cream cakes, sandwiches, scones – fantastic. And afterwards Martin asked why Scottish people would put on such a spread just for afternoon tea.' Ferguson, his Scottishness rearing like a lion rampant, grinned and replied: 'Because they're no' bloody miserable like you, Martin – at your house there's never even a biscuit!'

Knowing of Ferguson's taste for football trivia, I reminded him that Jimmy Delaney had been unique in winning Cup medals in England, Scotland (with Celtic) and Northern Ireland (Derry City). 'Aye,' he said, and, in an almost absent-minded piece of one-upmanship, added: 'He got to the final of another cup, too, but his team lost.' It did indeed: Cork Athletic, of the Republic of Ireland. After leading 2-0 only thirteen minutes from the end of normal time. But I had to look that up. Ferguson had the answer on the tip of his tongue. The wrong answer, admittedly; he asserted that Delaney's near-miss had been during a spell with Bangor City in Wales which research showed to be non-existent. But he did like his facts and figures. So did Edwards. And Edwards's memory almost rivalled Ferguson's. So, except when discussing money, they got on just fine.

An element of the Dick Donald role in Ferguson's life was taken by Sir Matt Busby. 'I was very lucky,' he recalled, 'that Matt was still at the club.' Busby had ceased to be manager in 1969, a year after the European triumph that brought him a knighthood (he shouldered the burden again, briefly, after his protégé Wilf McGuinness had buckled under it), but remained as a director until 1982, when he became president. He retained a small office at Old Trafford.

Ferguson, though he mainly worked at The Cliff, also had a base at the stadium. 'I used to love going into Old Trafford,' he recalled, 'and, as soon as I walked through the door, I'd know if Matt was around because I could smell the pipe smoke. It was amazing – the smell got all over the building. And I'd go in and see him for half an hour, sometimes more. He was wonderful with me. As was Bobby [Charlton]. They were a great support system – there's no doubt about that.'

Busby lived to see the reincarnation of his United. When he succumbed to cancer at the age of eighty four in January 1994, Ferguson's team were on top of the Premier League, marching towards a second successive championship. They had also won the FA Cup and the European Cup-Winners' Cup. And, as if in additional deference to the Busby tradition, the youngsters were coming through, not only in numbers but of a standard that was to serve England as well as the club.

Who knows what Busby's Babes, above all Duncan Edwards, would have achieved had they survived Munich? But David Beckham, Paul Scholes, Gary and Phil Neville and Nicky Butt fared pretty well. As did Ryan Giggs, the first star to dazzle Ferguson's Old Trafford. Two days after Busby died, Everton came to Old Trafford for a match played in an atmosphere of reverence that encompassed the supporters of both sides. The only goal came from Giggs, who was just twenty. Beckham and company were not long out of the youth team, gracing the reserves, being prepared by Ferguson's coaches for careers that would bring them the club game's biggest prizes.

Ferguson had been at United for only a few months when he heard about Giggs. It was a steward at The Cliff, one Harold Wood, a jobsworth familiar to the journalists waiting outside the gates in the hope of a meaningless word with a departing player, who gave him the tip-off about a schoolboy training with Manchester City. The boy was thirteen, said Wood, and a United fan. His name was Ryan Wilson. He was a son of Danny Wilson, the Welsh stand-off half of Swinton rugby league club. On the break-up of Wilson's marriage to Lynne Giggs, Ryan was to take his mother's side, and her surname.

The scout Joe Brown, a former Burnley manager, was sent to watch Wilson and a trial hastily arranged at The Cliff. Ferguson remembered the sinewy kid scampering across the pitch like a puppy chasing paper in the wind. It was a nice simile, but short of footballing relevance. Then he added that young Wilson held his head high – a mark of quality – and looked relaxed and natural on the pitch.

Ferguson, Brown and Archie Knox became regular visitors at the Giggs home. Ryan started to train with United instead of City and from that moment, said the late Chris Muir, the City director with responsibility for an acclaimed youth development system, 'we knew we had a serious fight on our hands'.

Night after night Ferguson, with Knox and Brian Kidd and the astute scout Les Kershaw, would hold trials under the floodlights at Albert Park in Salford. No wonder that henceforth Muir referred to Ferguson as 'that bugger'. But as the years went by and it became apparent that cancer would claim another victim and Muir, a splendidly convivial Scot whom even the certainty of death seemed not to daunt, held a farewell party for his friends, Ferguson was prominent among them, his presence enhancing an unforgettable occasion.

United's efforts to identify and secure talent intensified in 1988 with the appointment as youth development officer of Brian Kidd, who had been a teenage goalscorer in the European Cup triumph over Benfica at Wembley twenty years earlier and gone on to play for City too; his brief was to concentrate on local kids, using scouts who supported United, and so successful was the policy that the Nevilles, Scholes and Butt, all of whom hailed, like Giggs, from Greater Manchester, became garlanded internationals, alongside Beckham, who had been enticed from London without too much difficulty because his father, Ted, was a United supporter to whom Bobby Charlton was such a hero that he had given David the middle name 'Robert'.

These represented the second wave of youth created by Ferguson. The first were a group of players already attached to the club when he arrived, proving that United had not been wholly inactive on the youth front; twice in Ron Atkinson's time, United had reached the final of the FA Youth Cup, while Mark Hughes had come through the ranks and David Platt been allowed to move to Crewe Alexandra before hitting the big time under Graham Taylor at Aston Villa.

Among those whom the press dubbed 'Fergie's Fledglings', after the Busby Babes, were Russell Beardsmore, David Wilson, Deiniol Graham and Tony Gill. Overall they were not in the same class as the generation that delivered Beckham and Scholes and, in some cases, they were unlucky with injuries: the defender Gill, for instance, had his career finished by a horrific leg break in a match against Nottingham Forest in the spring of 1989.

Lee Martin scored the goal that won United their first trophy under Ferguson, the FA Cup in 1990, before he, too, succumbed to fitness problems. 'But for injuries,' said Ferguson, 'Lee would have had a good career at left-back. Tony Gill would have made a decent player. And there was Mark Robins – a terrific finisher, maybe a wee bit short of some things that could have made him a better player, but a fantastic finisher who scored important goals for us.' Including the one supposed to have saved Ferguson's job; it gave United victory in the famous third-round FA Cup tie at Nottingham Forest. Robins also came on as a substitute in the semi-final replay against Oldham Athletic at Maine Road, Manchester City's old stadium, and got the winner. But he was never again more than a squad player and eventually left for Norwich City.

So, while Fergie's Fledglings refreshed the club, they could not lift it beyond the level achieved by Atkinson, under whom the FA Cup had been won twice. The task of making them contenders for a domestic championship last won in 1967 – or, as Ferguson more graphically put it, 'knocking Liverpool off their fucking perch' – called upon Ferguson to show his skill in the transfer market while building the long-term aspects of the club and, for all his complaints about Edwards's attention to the purse strings, money was spent.

Time, too, was allotted to Ferguson. He needed it.

Jousting with Graham

At the beginning of his first Mancunian summer, Ferguson told Edwards he required at least eight new players and Edwards quailed. He had, after all, warned Ferguson that funds were very limited. This was despite the sale of Mark Hughes to Barcelona a few months earlier for £2.3 million, the biggest fee United had ever received. Edwards, to his credit, often mentioned the desirability of keeping ticket prices as low as possible, while balancing the books.

Hence Ferguson lacked clout in attempting to secure Peter Beardsley, who joined Liverpool instead. But he had been covertly active in the transfer market long before Viv Anderson and Brian McClair joined the pre-season parade. According to George Graham, who chuckled at the recollection, Anderson had been approached months before the end of the season.

'We'd won the League Cup in our first season at Arsenal,' he said, 'and Viv was our right-back, but his contract was up in the summer and so I said I imagined he'd be signing a new one because it looked as if good times might be on the way. 'No,' he said. 'I don't think so.' We tried everything we could to make him stay, but he went to United. A couple of years later, one of our old players told me Viv had been leaving all along, even before we won the League Cup [that was in early April]. Alex had got someone in the England squad to sort it out. It goes on all the time, of course. You can laugh about it. Not at the time, though!'

Graham had long harboured a curiosity about Ferguson – and heard the rumours, which were accurate, that he had been sounded out about his own job. 'I'd never met him at that stage,' said Graham, 'but I was interested in successful people and what Alex had done to the Glasgow giants, and in Europe, with Aberdeen put him in that category. I wanted to know his philosophy, to pick his brains.' Yet their first meeting turned into an angry confrontation: the first tunnel row of several involving Arsenal and United in the Ferguson era.

Arsenal had come to Old Trafford as League leaders; the Graham effect on them had certainly been more dramatic than Ferguson's on United. But United won through goals from Strachan and Terry Gibson. It was a stormy match and, as the teams left the field, the managers clashed. 'I can't remember what the argument was about,' said Graham (it may have owed something to David Rocastle's dismissal for a retaliatory foul on Norman Whiteside), 'but there we were in the tunnel, typical Scots, at each other's throats – and we hadn't even had a drink!'

They soon became friends. So much so that once, when Ferguson was demanding a pay rise from Edwards, he suddenly brandished a copy of Graham's Arsenal wage slip.

'We were friendly,' said Graham. 'Except when our teams met.' And even then the final whistle was final. Perhaps the most notorious meeting of the clubs in Graham's time came in 1990, when a twenty-one-man brawl took place. An hour after the match, as the Old Trafford corridors crawled with journalists seeking reaction, recrimination and views on the likely punishment — I came across Ferguson and Graham chatting amiably in a quiet corner, as if at a cocktail party.

For Graham, who had been a member of Arsenal's Double-winning team in 1971, the wait to bring the club his first championship as manager was relatively short; he won it in his third season, 1988/9. Liverpool had been champions when Ferguson came south. Everton were next, in 1987. Liverpool took the title in 1988 and 1990, Arsenal in 1989 and 1991. Leeds United were to frustrate Ferguson in 1992 before he finally came out on top in 1993. Graham, asked if he had been conscious of the threat from his compatriot, said: 'Yes. From the moment I met him. It took longer than I expected — or he did, probably — but I knew he'd be successful.

'So did the people running the club. When people were saying he'd had enough time and they should get rid of him, I tried to find out why they seemed so happy with him. They could see the club growing. They could see him grabbing all the best kids, as usual.' Like Giggs. And Beckham, who had also been courted by Tottenham. But he needed to invest in mature players for the medium term and the early dividends did not impress many outside observers.

He had tried to get Beardsley, Gary Lineker's brilliant foil in the England team, from Newcastle but seen him join Kenny Dalglish at Liverpool instead. If that was a painful defeat, Ferguson also had to cope with the embarrassment of the own goal that cost him John Barnes. With Barnes and Beardsley lending more style than even Anfield had known, Ferguson's *bêtes noires* were to claim two more championships right under his nose. In that first summer, he had been offered Barnes by

Graham Taylor, then Watford's manager, for £900,000 and stalled fatally and later moaned that, as a newcomer to English football, he should have received better guidance from the United staff.

What – three years after the whole world had seen Barnes's wonder goal for England against Brazil in the Maracanã? It was an extraordinarily limp excuse.

With inherited players, by and large, Ferguson lifted United from eleventh to second in his first full season, 1987/8. There were only two newcomers and in each case the deal had pleased Edwards as well as Ferguson because the fees were tribunal-set and in line with United's valuation.

The wisdom of having Anderson approached on England duty was borne out by the relatively modest outlay of £250,000. Brian McClair, from Celtic, cost £850,000, but immediately gave excellent value. He had some qualities in common with the centre-forward, Mark McGhee, who had been Ferguson's first signing for Aberdeen: mobility, intelligence and a readiness to shoulder burdens for the team. But he also scored a lot of goals. Straight away he became the first United player since George Best to break the twenty barrier in a League season (in all he got twenty-four, including five penalties). Meanwhile, Anderson provided power and drive from the back – and effervescence in the dressing room.

Just before Christmas, an extremely significant signing was made when Steve Bruce came from Norwich City for £825,000. This proved quite a coup, for Bruce, though not quick or elegant, was a footballing centre-half with additional assets of leadership, leonine bravery and a knack of goalscoring whose memory was to be immortalised when his two goals won a thrilling match against Sheffield Wednesday in the run-in to the 1993 championship.

That Ferguson was beginning to settle became obvious on Boxing Day when United lost at Newcastle and Bryan Robson, a rare recipient of his ire, felt its full force. Gordon Strachan was there: 'I remember going home to my wife and saying I'd just seen a kid who was phenomenal. He played for Newcastle and his name was Paul Gascoigne and he had given Bryan Robson such a hard time that Fergie was yelling abuse at Bryan from the dugout.'

Ferguson resolved to buy Gascoigne and in the summer of 1988, after being rebuffed by Newcastle's manager, Willie McFaul, tried the direct route. Illicitly, of course. Just before he went abroad on holiday, Gascoigne rang to say he would be joining United. While in Malta, however, Ferguson discovered that Gazza had gone to Tottenham instead. But he did get Hughes back to Old Trafford and brought Jim Leighton from Aberdeen to keep goal.

It had been a pretty good season: a Ferguson sort of season in that it featured a characteristically one-eyed moan at Bobby Robson about there being an England friendly in Israel three days before United went to Arsenal in the FA Cup fifth round and lost 2-1. No member of either side featured in the international. Nor did Ferguson balance his remarks with a recognition that, as manager of Aberdeen and Scotland only two years earlier, he had squeezed two friendly internationals into a month in which his club played no fewer than six matches in twenty-two days. One of the internationals was, in fact, the annual unfriendly against England but the other took place in, of all places, Israel. He used Willie Miller and Alex McLeish in both friendlies, moreover, and Jim Bett in one of them.

Once again, his photographic memory was selecting its images.

There had been another Ferguson hallmark in the incident with Kenny Dalglish at Liverpool in the April of that 1987/8 season. The match had finished 3-3 and afterwards Ferguson gave a radio interview in which he implied, quite vividly – 'a lot of managers have to leave here choking on their own sick . . .' – that opponents and referees came under undue pressure at Anfield. Dalglish, walking past with a baby in his arms, told the interviewer: 'You might as well talk to my daughter – you'll get more sense out of her.'

For Ferguson to be irate about a draw at Anfield was a sign of progress; Liverpool were so markedly the finest team in England that nine days later, after they had beaten Nottingham Forest 5-0 at Anfield, the great Sir Tom Finney deemed their display as good as anything he had ever seen on a football pitch.

As it became obvious that the season would bring United no trophy, Ferguson addressed the future – and Arthur Albiston's would be elsewhere. 'I'd got my fitness back,' he recalled, 'and we won a few games, but then I got left out and didn't agree with that and told him so. "I understand your problem," he said. To be fair to him, he kept me involved and travelling with the squad. He knew that, having been in the team so long [Albiston had made almost five hundred appearances] I'd be hurting. From time to time, he'd ask me to have a word with one of the younger reserves. He treated me well and I've got nothing but respect for him.'

Ferguson had never screamed at the mild-mannered Albiston. Never? Well, hardly ever. 'The only time I can remember was when he and Archie Knox were playing head tennis in the gym. I was recuperating at the time and they started arguing about whether a ball was in or out. And he asked me what I thought and I said Archie was right. I got quite a blast for that. Just for giving an honest opinion!' Albiston smiled. 'I don't think I was the first.'

Soon Albiston was off to rejoin Atkinson at West Bromwich Albion. He was sorry to miss out on what seemed likely to be an exciting time at United. While they had never made Liverpool glance anxiously back on the road to the championship, a rise of nine places suggested serious progress.

The supporters, however, were not convinced. The last home crowd of the season was 28,040, to watch Wimbledon. Yet when Ferguson travelled with Bobby Charlton to Barcelona to seal the £1.8 million deal for Hughes his philosophy was one of near-boundless optimism. 'I'll never forget it,' he recalled. 'We looked around at those towering stands and, wistfully, Bobby said, "We should be like Barcelona". And I said, "Why aren't we?" And he said, "I don't know".' From then, Ferguson waged an intermittent campaign with the board to have the Old Trafford capacity increased. When Ferguson went to Barcelona for Hughes, it held 56,000 and Camp Nou nearly twice as many. Twenty years later, it held 76,000 and the gap had closed to 20,000. Old Trafford, moreover, seldom had an empty seat at a League match.

That was far from the case in 1988/9, when, despite Hughes and McClair – not to mention Robson – United struggled for goals, managing only forty-five in their thirty-eight League matches, and could attract only 23,368 when Wimbledon came in early May; fixtures against Coventry City and Everton pulled in few more.

Strachan Leaves the Nest

For Ferguson there was the pleasure of that first infusion of youth. It took place in the mid-winter of 1988/9. After Queens Park Rangers had drawn 0-0 at Old Trafford in the third round of the FA Cup, Ferguson decided to send a young team to west London for the replay: it would include Lee Martin, the ill-starred Tony Gill, Russell Beardsmore in Strachan's role on the right and the seventeen-year-old Lee Sharpe, whom Ferguson had travelled to Torquay to watch one rainy night and unhesitatingly signed (he went on to play for England but liked his nightlife and suffered from injuries and never quite fulfilled his potential).

'What I wanted to show,' said Ferguson, 'was a willingness to promote anyone who did well in the reserves. The worst thing for an older player is to lose his place to a younger man. It's the best competition you can ever get in a football club. There's no doubt about that.' There was no excuse for the displaced; it was not as if the manager, having bought a big name, needed to find a place for his expensive purchase. Accordingly Ferguson found it 'interesting' that Strachan, Robson and Whiteside expressed a wish to travel with the team to west London, even though they were injured. He mentioned it to Archie Knox, who said they were clearly concerned about the youngsters coming through. So he decided to take them.

They saw a thrilling match which United would have won 2-1 but for a late equaliser. United did go through anyway, with a 3-0 victory in a third match back at Old Trafford. They then overcame Oxford United and, after a replay, Bournemouth. Ferguson's team were in the quarter-finals, and again at home, albeit to a fine Nottingham Forest side who were about to win the League Cup. This proved the start of a slump. Not only did United fall from fifth to eleventh at the end of the season, they let their Cup hopes be dashed by Forest in a passive manner that angered their manager.

He would not have liked being beaten by Brian Clough anyway; he found Clough rude and had been snubbed by him at least once, when he and Edwards had called unannounced at Forest's City Ground only to be told that the manager was unavailable. Where, Ferguson asked, was the passion supposed to mark his teams? And yet seven of the side that day were Ferguson signings.

There were Leighton, Bruce, McClair, and Hughes. The utility player Mal Donaghy from Luton Town stood alongside Robson. There was the former Dundee United winger Ralph Milne, with whom Ferguson was unsuccessfully trying to replace Jesper Olsen (to think that it could have been John Barnes). And the teenage flier Sharpe.

The main conclusion to which Ferguson came, however, was that he had to get rid of Strachan, whom he felt had been intimidated by Stuart Pearce.

Two days later, Ferguson had an offer of £200,000 from Ron

Atkinson, now managing Sheffield Wednesday. He then rang Howard Wilkinson at Leeds United, whom he had promised to contact if Strachan ever became available, and asked for £300,000, which was agreed. Strachan made his Leeds debut at the weekend. He was thirty-two and dropping a division, but not for long. The following season Leeds were promoted as champions and Strachan received a letter of congratulation from Ferguson.

Two seasons after that, they were champions of all England. Strachan had beaten Ferguson to the honour. Leeds, with Gary McAllister, David Batty and Gary Speed joining Strachan in a wonderfully balanced midfield, had overtaken Ferguson's United in the closing stages of the race to the title. This time there was no letter.

Nor did the course of events imply that Ferguson had blundered in getting rid of Strachan. 'People said that,' reflected Strachan later, 'but he was right to sell.' The replacement Ferguson had in mind went elsewhere, for United could not match the salary Rangers offered Trevor Steven to leave Everton for Scotland (Ferguson's old club had become hugely and, as it turned out, overly ambitious). But the association was over. Strachan had become stale. The move to Elland Road revived him. He would never have been the same player under Ferguson at Old Trafford.

A consequence of the Old Trafford defeat that had sent him to Howard Wilkinson at Leeds was that United's season petered out. If only that had been all.

Forest strode on to play Liverpool in the semi-final at the neutral venue of Hillsborough, the home of Sheffield Wednesday, where, as the match kicked off, ninety-five people died in the crush at the Liverpool supporters' Leppings Lane

End. Among the first telephone calls taken by Kenny Dalglish was one from Ferguson.

When the abandoned match was played at Old Trafford three weeks later, Liverpool won 3-1. They proceeded to Wembley and beat Everton in the final. Dalglish's team, for all the strains of the mourning process, also kept winning in the League and would have taken the title as well but for the most dramatic transformation in the history of the competition.

Needing only to avoid a two-goal defeat by Arsenal at Anfield in the final match to fend off the challenge of George Graham's men, they trailed by one until the ninety-fourth and concluding minute, when Michael Thomas struck. Ferguson, watching on television, celebrated like an Arsenal supporter. 'I don't think I've ever been so delighted in my life to see anyone score a goal,' he said. 'You have to bear in mind that I had a fear of Liverpool when I came down.' And he believed this rough displacement from their perch could only assist him, even though his own team had finished ten places and twenty-five points behind the champions.

Welcome to Hell

For United – no matter what happened to Liverpool – things had to get better. And they did, but only after they had got worse. The season 1989/90 was to be Ferguson's most hellish and yet there was a glimpse of heaven at the end, with his first trophy. It was a season that had everything, including the most bizarre pre-match entertainment, provided by one Michael Knighton.

The background was that Martin Edwards, having sunk himself £1 million into debt to buy a 50.2 per cent stake in United (his father had left him only 16 per cent), wanted to sell. He had earlier entertained advances from Robert Maxwell – the entrepreneur, media mogul and owner of Oxford United – whose crooked business dealings were later revealed. Edwards had become deeply unpopular with United's fans in the process. But now United, as well as Edwards, needed money because of Hillsborough and the Taylor Report. The redevelopment of Old Trafford's Stretford End, a project close to Edwards's heart, would cost £10 million which the club did not have. Edwards had already told Ferguson he would sell to anyone who paid for the Stretford End and gave him a further £10 million for his shares.

And then Knighton appeared on the scene. An affable man, slightly chubbier than you would expect from a thirty-seven-year-old whom only injury, we gathered, had denied a career with Coventry City, he met Edwards in the summer of 1989 through an intermediary. Explaining that he had made a lot of money in property, he offered to meet Edwards's twin terms. Edwards, unaware that football would boom so spectacularly that massively richer pickings could be made, thought his dreams had come true – and shook hands on the deal.

When his fellow directors found out, there was dismay – they suspected that Knighton, despite the Scottish castle in which he had entertained Edwards, might have difficulty raising the scale of resources required – and embarrassment, which went only too public on the first day of the new season.

An hour before the match between United and Arsenal, the new champions, Ferguson and George Graham were having a cup of tea when the kit man, Norman Davies, said Knighton had asked for a United strip to wear. Ferguson laughed and agreed but joked that the team had already been picked.

Soon Davies reappeared and what he said caused Ferguson to turn on a television monitor that showed the pitch. There was Knighton, introducing himself to the fans who thought he was buying their club by trotting out to the centre circle in his strip and juggling the ball all the way to the goal at the Stretford End, where he whacked it into the empty net. 'I was starting to have a terrible gut feeling,' said Ferguson, 'about my new chairman.' It was magnificent showmanship nonetheless, and the 4-1 victory over Graham's champions that followed only enhanced the fans' good humour.

One of the goals came from the newcomer Neil Webb, from Nottingham Forest. The side also featured Michael Phelan, just arrived from Burnley, and soon there would be more signings.

Did Ferguson try to bring McLeish south from Aberdeen to partner Bruce? His autobiography makes no mention of it. Yet McLeish many years later, speaking in the build-up to a match between his Birmingham City and Ferguson's United, remained under the impression that a bid had been made. He told a long and amusing story about his old boss.

It went back to 1984, when McLeish, though due to sign a new contract with Aberdeen before the summer holiday, heard of interest from Tottenham and told a reporter he had 'an open mind'. Ferguson read this and called him in. McLeish said the signing could wait until after the holiday, but Ferguson insisted.

'So I go to see him,' said McLeish, 'and, as I'm getting out of the car I'm saying to Gill [his wife] I'm going to tell him it's time for a change. But I didn't have an agent. It's much easier now because players just take a back seat and let the agent knock on a manager's door. I told Gill I'd be back in five minutes because I predicted he'd go mad and throw me out of his office.

'And then I tap on the door, and I hear that cough, and my legs go.

'"Hi, boss," I says.

'"What's all this shit in the papers?"

'"Well, boss, I'd like to test myself down there."

'"This is about money, isn't it?"

'"Well," I says, "I wasn't that happy with the offer . . ."

'"You and Willie Miller are bleeding this club dry," he says. "I'll give you another fiver a week."

'And I go "Okay".

'I know – ridiculous. But he could be very persuasive. When I went out to the car, Gill asked if we were packing our bags and I said I'd just signed a new three-year contract and she said she knew I would.'

The contract had a year to run when Ferguson left Aberdeen. He told McLeish he would return to take him to United. 'He phoned me to say he had an agreement with the chairman that allowed him to come back for a few of us – Jim Leighton, Willie Miller, myself. But, when it came to bidding for me, he felt Aberdeen were asking too much.'

McLeish was thirty by then. Whatever the bid was supposed to be, the £2.4 million Ferguson instead gave Middlesbrough for the twenty-four-year-old Gary Pallister dwarfed it. It was the biggest fee a British club had ever paid.

Paul Ince was recruited from West Ham United and Danny Wallace from Southampton. The fees for Webb, Phelan, Pallister, Ince and Wallace added up to £8.25 million. Edwards had loosened the purse strings as never before – the assumption that he would soon be handing over the purse to Knighton may have conspired in this sudden extravagance – and Ferguson was taking full advantage.

Four of the five signings were in the team in early October, when Edwards took his fellow directors' advice and pulled out of the agreement with Knighton, whose money had turned out to be a loan from the Bank of Scotland. Webb had been lost to the side through a serious injury suffered when playing for England and missed a shocking 5-1 defeat in a derby at Manchester City. There were other disappointments and, by the time winter's chill had set in, the sunny disposition of the 47,245 who had revelled in the triumph over Arsenal had turned to scorn.

It was audibly worse, Edwards recalled, than at any time under Atkinson.

United, for all their spending, had been knocked out of the League Cup by Tottenham at Old Trafford and went into December lying tenth. By Ferguson's forty-eighth birthday at the end of a month during which they had taken just two points from six matches, they were fifteenth out of twenty. During a home defeat by Crystal Palace, a banner was unfurled telling Ferguson it was time to go. 'It was a terrible month for me.' He could not bring himself to speak to anyone about the depths of it, not even Knox, and presented a defiantly nonchalant face to the family.

'Dad never brought his work home,' his son Darren told the *Sunday Times* in 2009, when he was manager of Peterborough United. 'I remember him coming home the evening United were beaten 5-1 by City. He just laughed, not because he didn't care but because it was just one of those things that happen in football, things you don't see coming and can't do much to avert.'

So inwardly, through that long cold winter, Alex Ferguson questioned his methods, his routines, everything. Was he just another successful manager in Scotland who couldn't make it down south? And then came the FA Cup draw. 'Nottingham Forest, arguably the best Cup team in the land – away. Fucking hell! So that night Bob Cass phoned me [Cass, of the *Mail On Sunday*, was one of his favourite journalists] to get my reaction to the draw. What could I say? We go there with great optimism!'

This was many years later and he could laugh about it, but Ferguson was grateful for Edwards's words on the way to Nottingham: 'Whatever happens, you're staying.' He appreciated what he saw as an attempt to raise his morale, but Ferguson was too low to respond fully. 'Everyone's got their pride,' he was to reflect, 'and everyone's got a sensibility in respect of what people think of you, what your players think of you, and what people are writing about you.'

He was never one of those managers who claimed not to read the papers. 'The person who helped me most at that time,' he recalled, 'was Paul Doherty.' Doherty knew a bit about football and the media. The son of Peter Doherty, a brilliant footballer who had gone on to manage his native Northern Ireland, most notably at the World Cup in 1958, he was head of sport at Granada television, a big and affable fellow, confident enough habitually to refer to Ferguson as 'young man'.

One day he came to offer Ferguson a bit of advice and Ferguson listened. 'I liked Paul,' he said. 'He was a straight-shooter. He began by saying I was probably getting more advice than I wanted but that, as a media man, he could help me. I said, "What?" He said that, when I went into a press confer-ence after a match, I'd not to hurry but give myself a good half-hour to regroup my thoughts. No matter the result. "Because these guys," he said, "are looking to kill you. Week after week, they're waiting for you to crack."'

Ferguson didn't – at least not for another couple of years, by which time, having won trophies, he was in a position of relative strength. It was when United were striving to over-take Leeds at the top of the League late in the 1991/2 season. They visited West Ham, who were already relegated, and lost to a side whose efforts Ferguson described as almost 'obscene' (he later acknowledged this as a slight on the east London club's pride in adversity). The hint of paranoia was noted.

But by then, according to Edwards, the feeling in the board-room was that the wait for the title would not last much longer.

The picture of an inexorable process was not visible to Ferguson in the depths of his 1989/90 winter. He arrived at Nottingham Forest's City Ground on 7 January without the injured Robson, Webb, Ince, Sharpe and Wallace, but in the second half, as he records in his autobiography, 'a Mark Hughes pass set Robins up for the goal that settled the match'.

The goal credited, however mythically, with having saved Ferguson's career at United deserves more detailed descrip-tion. As Forest try to work the ball to Toddy Örlygsson on their right flank, he is determinedly challenged by Lee Martin, who just keeps the ball in play and knocks it inside to Hughes. This is when the goal is made. An ordinary player might have tried to find Mark Robins with an orthodox right-footed cross from the left. But Hughes did not fancy little Robins's chances in a straightforward aerial challenge. So, using the outside of his right foot, he bent his pass round Forest's central defenders, Des Walker and Steve Chettle, the spin on the ball making it break sharply back into the goalmouth so Robins could stay just ahead of Stuart Pearce and, as it bounced up off the muddy pitch, head it past Steve Sutton.

Forest had what they claimed as an equaliser correctly disallowed for a foul on Leighton before the final whistle sounded. 'United are through,' sighed Barry Davies on BBC television. 'Some joy at last for Alex Ferguson.'

Whoever deserved any thanks that were going, neither Hughes nor Robins got them. Indeed, as Robins mentioned in 2009, when he was manager of Barnsley and Ferguson brought United to Oakwell for a League Cup tie, his old boss had joked that he scored only because Pearce had given him a shove in the back: 'Excellent. So did I save his job? Yes, I did! He never thanked me, but he was a brilliant manager to work for. People said the pressure was on him but, as a young player trying to get into his side, I was oblivious to anything going on around him.'

A closer view of Ferguson's travails, which continued long after the win at Forest, was available to his son Darren, by now a United trainee and soon to be joined by Ryan Wilson (later Giggs). The list of associated schoolboys discovered by Kidd and the scouts makes for an even more impressive small-print read in retrospect. It featured not only Beckham, Scholes, Butt and Gary Neville but Ben Thornley and Chris Casper, who were to have promising careers ruined by injury, and Keith Gillespie, who was to go to Newcastle and onwards, becoming a seasoned Northern Ireland international, and Robbie Savage, who was likewise allowed to ply his energetic trade at Leicester, Blackburn and elsewhere, becoming an important player for Wales. 'This was part of the reason we had such faith in Alex,' said Edwards. 'The quality of young players coming through was startling.

However: 'The fans were still very unhappy. All they could see was that we had made five big signings and things seemed to be getting worse.'

You Bastard!

Even as United kept winning Cup ties – 1-0 at Hereford, 3-2 at Newcastle, 1-0 at Sheffield United – their League form remained grim and it was not until late March that they embarked on the run of victories over Southampton, QPR, Coventry and Aston Villa that lifted the threat of relegation. Robins scored in the first three of these matches after coming on as a substitute and rewarded Ferguson for starting him in the fourth with both goals in the 2-0 win over Villa. He also had a further contribution to make to the Cup run.

In early April, when Ferguson took his players across Manchester for their semi-final against Oldham Athletic, a vibrant Cup side under Joe Royle, Robins came off the bench but did not score in a 3-3 draw; it was quite a day for goals, because in the other semi-final Steve Coppell's Crystal Palace, despite the injury to Ian Wright that disrupted his renowned striking partnership with Mark Bright, beat Liverpool 4-3.

Three days later, Ferguson again had Robins on the bench. Again he used him in place of Lee Martin. And this time it worked. Robins took a pass from Phelan and expertly steered a low shot away from the Oldham goalkeeper, Jon Hallworth. United were at Wembley.

They remained a work in progress; their modest League position emphasised that. But Ferguson had brought down the age of the side with the promotion of Martin and Robins and the signings of Ince (twenty-one), Pallister (twenty-four), Wallace (twenty-five), Webb (twenty-six) and even the twenty-seven-year-old Phelan.

There were still problems. Though the arrival of the tall and pacy Pallister to complement the commanding Bruce had, after the horrendous early setback at Manchester City, given Ferguson the makings of a new Miller/McLeish partnership to protect Leighton, as at Aberdeen, the goalkeeper's form had been troubling him. Ferguson had even considered leaving Leighton out of the semi-final against Oldham, only to be dissuaded by Archie Knox, who said it would further erode Leighton's confidence.

So he stayed in for the final. But it had been obvious from Palace's triumph over Liverpool that their aerial threat at set pieces would be significant and so the plan was that Leighton would come for the ball only if certain he would get it. Palace nevertheless went ahead when their big central defender Gary O'Reilly scored from a free-kick. Robson equalised, Hughes put United ahead but, when Wright appeared as a substitute to equalise, a thrilling match in sapping heat demanded extra time. Wright then scored again, as did Hughes. Another replay it would be.

For this, Ferguson dropped Leighton. He had noticed the goalkeeper with his head in his hands after the first Wembley occasion – 'Jim knew he had given another poor performance and I think he felt helpless' – and decided to use Les Sealey, a cocky Londoner he had borrowed from Luton. Not quite as good a goalkeeper as Leighton, but more assertive and, given the Scot's apparent state of mind, less liable to cost United the Cup. At least in Ferguson's opinion; Knox still disagreed.

On the eve of the replay, shortly before the players assembled to hear the manager name his team and outline how they would play, Ferguson had an individual meeting with Leighton, who was so upset by the decision that he not only declined to listen to the manager's explanation and left the room but thereafter had little time for Ferguson until, after spells on loan at Arsenal and Sheffield United, the lugubrious keeper returned to Scotland in February 1992 to join Dundee, moving from there to Hibernian and back to Aberdeen and recovering so well that in 1998, when just short of his fortieth birthday, he went to the World Cup in France.

With Sealey between the posts, but well protected, United survived some hair-rising Palace tackles and won the FA Cup through a second-half goal from Lee Martin, whose shot on the half-volley flashed between Nigel Martyn and the near post after Webb, with a fine angled pass, had rewarded the twenty-one-year-old left-back's enterprising run from the back. It had taken three and a half years, but Ferguson's United had a trophy.

In the Wembley dressing room afterwards, the celebrations were diluted by Leighton's tears. So plainly upset was he that Sealey offered his medal as consolation. At the reception in the banqueting suite, Leighton's wife glared at Ferguson, who stared back: an unwise decision, for Mrs Leighton, far from backing down, kept her contemptuous eye on him while raising two fingers in a gesture unlikely to have been referring to United's victory.

Because of Leighton's long-held silence on the matter, we may never know if Ferguson had received the treatment he had given the Dunfermline manager, Willie Cunningham, in 1965: 'You bastard!' To give Ferguson his due, he had at least accorded Leighton the courtesy of being informed in advance. Not that Mrs Leighton was in any mood to appreciate the distinction.

At any rate, Ferguson could now use that first trophy as a stick with which to beat those who had criticised him. Not that he had been too reticent before. I had taken a bit, even though I had tried to be balanced in reporting his perceived crisis. Any notion that this, or a long acquaintance with Ferguson — on the way back to Aberdeen from Gothenburg in 1983, I had quaffed my share of champagne from the Cup-Winners' Cup — would be taken into account was proved misguided when he told me to fuck off shortly before the original semi-final against Oldham.

The main stand at Maine Road had an internal layout that journalists enjoyed, because through the large lobby passed all classes of people, including directors, players and managers. And, surprisingly — for few clubs could bear to countenance members of the press at close quarters, even then — us.

Ferguson had been addressing his troops in the dressing room below, preparing them for battle, when he walked past me, delivering his waspish advice as he went. I knew how Ferguson and other members of the Scottish football community talked. Four-letter words could often be used as terms of endearment. This was not such a case.

While I gaped, he said it again, adding, with a stab of a finger, that I was a cunt, and strode on. On the Monday, I rang his office. The phone went straight down. I left messages that were not returned. I wanted to ask him why he'd gone public when a private word, however blunt, would have done, but most of all I was curious to know what had annoyed him. The assumption that an article had caused offence left me bewildered; I was a wholehearted Ferguson admirer at that time, often in the face of scepticism from journalistic colleagues who underrated his achievements in Scotland or doubted that he could replicate them on the bigger stage. But he clearly had no wish to waste any further energy in explaining.

A few weeks later, as the League season drew to a close and United turned their thoughts to Wembley, I arrived at Elland Road for a midweek Leeds match, looking forward to watching Strachan, McAllister and the rest and assessing their chances in the top division the following season, and walked straight into Ferguson, Knox and Brian Kidd. Again the red mist descended – but on me! From somewhere came the temerity to tell Ferguson he owed at least the courtesy of a reply. 'After all the times I've supported you!' I even swore, albeit adjectivally, before flouncing away from the startled trio and their silent faces.

The point was made. But as the summer came and wore on – it was the Pavarotti summer of 'Nessun dorma' and Gazza left the World Cup in tears – it dawned on me that Ferguson's first trophy had given United a place in Europe, which had reopened its competitions to the English, and when they were drawn against the Hungarian club Pécsi Munkás in the Cup-Winners' Cup my paper asked me to travel to Budapest for the second leg. We were in the team hotel the evening before the match and, upon hearing that Ferguson was heading for the bar, I drank with a curiosity verging on nervousness.

In came Ferguson, grinning, greeting everyone in sight and,

when it came to my turn, asking what I was having. Once a row with Ferguson was over, it tended to be forgotten, as long as neither side had done something naughty. And telling a cunt to fuck off certainly didn't come into that category.

What had riled him? Someone suggested I consult a particular article I'd written for the *Independent*. It included a passage to the effect that 'matters at Old Trafford' had been 'ebbing out of Ferguson's control'. Of course! To question Ferguson's control; that would have been unacceptable.

UNITED:
STEPS TO GREATNESS

Beating Barcelona

A couple of months before Ferguson's first trophy, United engaged Michael 'Ned' Kelly, a former SAS man who had built up a security company. One of his duties was to arrange, through his network of stewards, the exclusion from Old Trafford's bars and lounges of unauthorised ex-players and other freeloaders. Another was to act as 'minder' to the manager on match days. There were plenty of fans who still wanted Ferguson out and they could become quite heated, especially when United lost.

Nor was the tension in the air totally dispelled by the FA Cup triumph. According to Ned Kelly, a lingering insecurity impelled Ferguson, upon hearing rumours that Bryan Robson was being lined up to succeed him, to summon the captain, who looked him very steadily in the eye while intimating that, if it had been true, he would have been the first to know. So the battle for hearts and minds went on. There had to be another trophy and it turned out to be the Cup-Winners' Cup: United followed in Aberdeen's footsteps by beating one of the Spanish giants, in this case Barcelona, in the final.

Wrexham, like Pécsi Munkás, had been beaten home and

away, and after drawing 1-1 at Old Trafford with a Montpellier team featuring Laurent Blanc, United won 2-0 in France, Bryan Robson delivering a masterclass in leadership. The final was reached with a comfortable 4-2 aggregate victory over Legia Warsaw and the ensuing triumph, with Hughes outstanding against his former club, testified to momentum. 'By then we knew,' said Martin Edwards, 'that a special team would be created. It was just a matter of time.'

Bruce, Pallister, Hughes and Ince were joined in that 1990/91 season by Denis Irwin, an understated but highly accomplished full-back who had impressed Ferguson with his performances for Oldham and cost a mere £650,000 and was to become a champion of England – seven times – and Europe with United before leaving at the age of thirty-six on a free transfer. At Wolverhampton, he was to enjoy promotion and a further season in the Premier League during which Old Trafford gave him a standing ovation. At left-back was Clayton Blackmore, another of those who had come through the ranks in the Atkinson era, making the most of young Martin's back problems, having perhaps the best season of a career that owed much to versatility.

Attendances generally edged up, assisted by hooliganism's abatement, and United led the way with an average of nearly 45,000. The board's confidence in Ferguson was expressed with a new four-year contract and a £50,000-a-year pay rise. Among the manager's other pleasures was the League debut he gave to his son: Darren came on as substitute for Bryan Robson at Sheffield United and was to start a couple of matches as well. Another morsel of food for thought, during the mid-season victory over Tottenham at White Hart Lane, was the dismissal of Gascoigne after a foul-mouthed outburst at the referee.

A few weeks earlier, Ferguson had noted the resignation as Prime Minister and Conservative leader of Margaret Thatcher. Having been undermined by a challenge from the pro-European Michael Heseltine, she gave her support to John Major and it was he who took the keys to 10 Downing Street. Major had been Chancellor of the Exchequer. He was keen on sport, above all cricket, and his sympathy for football (he supported Chelsea) may have conspired in tax relief that helped clubs to rebuild their stadiums after Hillsborough.

Another football enthusiast was climbing the political ladder. Tony Blair had been adopted as Labour candidate for the safe seat of Sedgefield in County Durham, where he had spent part of his upbringing and developed an allegiance to Newcastle United, after a meeting on the night Ferguson's Aberdeen won the Cup-Winners' Cup; the selection committee had insisted he sit down and watch the match before his interview, and he had been happy to comply. Blair was a member of the Campaign for Nuclear Disarmament and a proudly declared socialist but, being young and good on television, found himself being nudged by Peter Mandelson to the forefront of the Labour reformation. On the night Ferguson's United won the Cup Winners' Cup, he was in the Shadow Cabinet, red rose having replaced red flag. Those eight years had been put to good effect and only another five were to pass before Blair became Prime Minister at the age of forty-three.

Over the League season, United rose from thirteenth to sixth. But there was plenty of stuttering along the way. They lost 4–0 at Liverpool and 1–0 at home to Arsenal in the match recalled less for Anders Limpar's goal than that twenty-one-man brawl (only David Seaman, the Arsenal goalkeeper, was not involved as either an aggressor or peacemaker), which prompted the FA to dock Arsenal two points and United one. The ultimate League position of neither club was affected. Arsenal took their second title under Graham, having lost only one of thirty-eight matches. Among those above United were Manchester City. Leeds came fourth and Gordon Strachan was Footballer of the Year.

At least Liverpool and Dalglish had slipped off their perch – even if Arsenal and Graham now temporarily occupied it. The recession of Dalglish's powers was not as Ferguson would have wanted. Their managerial relationship had never been as bad as the baby incident made it look and they went back a long way, to when Dalglish was a kid hanging around Ibrox and being teased by the professionals; later they even played against each other in an Old Firm reserve match when Dalglish was a Celtic teenager and Ferguson out of favour with Davie White. But gradually management had worn away at the happy-go-lucky personality of the younger man.

The burdens of Hillsborough had added to the stress of striving to maintain the most successful institution in a century of English club football. Skin rashes and irritability with his family were among Dalglish's symptoms and he decided to resign. This was before an FA Cup replay with Everton that ended 4-4; while Tony Cottee, an Everton substitute, scored twice, Dalglish made no changes. And the next morning he told the board he was going. The championship Liverpool had won under his management the previous season would be the last to come to the club for many years.

But United, still seeking the consistency with which Graham had endowed Arsenal, were successful only in Europe. Their hopes of retaining the FA Cup were dashed by Norwich and the most domestic excitement was caused by a run to the final of the League Cup in which Liverpool were beaten at Old Trafford and Arsenal thrashed 6-2 on their own ground, Lee Sharpe completing a hat-trick. Through Sharpe the width Ferguson craved was coming, at least on the left (and he was to obtain plenty from Andrei Kanchelskis on the right). United overcame Leeds in the semi-finals to earn a Wembley meeting with Sheffield Wednesday, managed by Ron Atkinson, but lost to a goal from the midfielder John Sheridan, a Mancunian and United fan.

By then they were heading for Rotterdam and another final in which a measure of the full fluency and swagger football had come to expect from United since the rise under Busby was displayed.

It was not the greatest of matches and the poor turnout by Barcelona supporters – the dank night and empty seats may have reminded Ferguson of Gothenburg eight years earlier – did nothing for the atmosphere. But United deserved to beat Johan Cruyff's team.

Steve Bruce scored nineteen goals in all competitions that season – an extraordinary total for a central defender, even if eleven were penalties – and it would have been twenty had Hughes not touched over the line his header from a Robson free-kick midway through the second half. Minutes later, Robson slipped Hughes through and, although in evading the sprawl of Barcelona's goalkeeper, Carlos Busquets, the Welshman appeared to give himself too demanding an angle for a shot, the force and accuracy with which he struck it left helpless the two defenders striving to cover.

With ten minutes left, a thirty-five-yard free-kick from Ronald Koeman went through the United wall and was touched by the diving Les Sealey against a post, from which it cannoned off the unlucky goalkeeper into the net. United held out – and partied for forty-eight hours, with Ferguson a keen participant. He had even been emboldened to cavort on the pitch, conducting the fans as they belted out a new anthem, Monty Python's 'Always Look on the Bright Side of Life'.

As Robson swigged champagne, Koeman swallowed disappointment. The Dutchman had only a year to await consolation, for at Wembley another of his renowned free-kicks beat Sampdoria's Gianluca Pagliuca to make Barcelona champions of Europe for the first time and earn Cruyff's players (including Pep Guardiola, who was to manage Barcelona against Ferguson's United in the 2009 final) membership of a celebrated 'dream team'.

Dreaming On

For Ferguson and United, the dream was about England and the title that had last been claimed in 1967. In the summer, Ferguson was dismayed to lose Archie Knox, who went to Rangers, but promoted Brian Kidd to assistant manager and received some benefit in the sense that his behaviour towards referees improved.

This, at least, was the recollection of David Elleray, a leading whistler who later served as chairman of the FA referees' committee. 'Brian did a lot to keep Alex out of trouble,' said Elleray. 'Once I saw him take Alex and drag him down the tunnel away from my dressing room. He knew Alex well enough to arrive just as Alex was waiting for you in the tunnel, ready to give you a volley of abuse, and get him out of the way.

'I remember once chatting to Brian and asking him where he liked to spend his summer holidays. "The other end of the world from Alex Ferguson," he replied. But he was good with Alex and I think Alex respected him. I think Alex is always better when he has a strong assistant.' Clearly Knox was strong. 'Yes,' said Elleray. So had Knox been able to moderate

Ferguson's behaviour? 'No,' said Elleray. 'He was as bad. In fact he was worse.'

With Kidd at Ferguson's side, the wait for the title seemed certain to end after a neat quarter-century, for the 1991/2 season saw United top for long periods. They collected another trophy, the League Cup, and yet it may have been their success in making themselves the hurdle over which Leeds fell in both that and the FA Cup that enabled the Yorkshire club to pip them at the post in the big race.

Again Ferguson had strengthened his team. Sealey had left the club (he was to die of a heart attack at forty-three) and the likes of Phelan and Blackmore become squad players, as specialists of true quality were brought in.

A right-winger of electric pace, only twenty-one years old, had been brought from the Ukrainian club Shakhtar Donetsk towards the end of the previous season and Andrei Kanchelskis was to prove a significant buy at £1.2 million rising to £3 million if he were sold at a profit (he went to Everton for £5 million eventually, being replaced by David Beckham).

Paul Parker, another quick player, an England defender who cost £2 million from Queens Park Rangers, would have been more significant but for injury problems that surfaced soon after his arrival.

But the biggest buy, in every sense but one (he cost just over £500,000), was the cheapest: Peter Schmeichel became a giant, a hero of the Ferguson revolution as well as his native Denmark and a worthy United captain on the night in 1999 when the club regained the European title.

Foreign players still verged on the exotic when Ferguson engaged Kanchelskis and Schmeichel; at the Premier League's inception (as the FA Premier League) a year later, there were

Welcome to Manchester: Ferguson is unveiled to the English media by Manchester United's chairman, Martin Edwards (*above*) who had confirmed to him that some players like a drink. Prominent among them were Bryan Robson (*right*), Norman Whiteside (*below left*) and Paul McGrath (*below right*).

Milestones: Mark Robins wheels away after scoring the goal often said to have saved Ferguson's job at United.

Lee Martin's half-volley wins the first trophy of the Ferguson era, the 1990 FA Cup.

Les Sealey, the beneficiary of Ferguson's decision to drop Jim Leighton for the final replay, hugs him.

First blood in Europe: United take the Cup-Winners' Cup in 1991. Mark Hughes making sure as he rounds Barcelona goalkeeper Carlos Busquets (whose son Sergio was in the Barcelona team who beat United in the Champions League final 18 years later). Hughes, whom United had brought back from Barcelona, celebrates (*below*).

Champions at last: Five of Ferguson's signings (*above, clockwise from left*, McClair, Bruce, Irwin, Hughes and Phelan) are so glad to get their hands on the new Premier League trophy that they happily wear those tracksuit tops.

Ooh aah: Eric Cantona (*left*) was recommended to Ferguson by Gérard Houllier.

The stars keep emerging as Paul Ince and Ryan Giggs congratulate Eric Cantona on a Wembley penalty conversion against Chelsea in 1994 (*right*).

Double Double: Eric Cantona seals the 1996 FA Cup victory over Liverpool that makes it two doubles in three seasons for Ferguson's United. Fortunately the boss has strong arms (*below*).

There's no substitute for class: Teddy Sheringham and Ole Gunnar Solskjær, the men thrown on by Ferguson as time ran out in the 1999 Champions League final, score the stoppage-time goals that confound Bayern Munich.

Football – bloody hell!: believe it or not, United have Europe's biggest prize. Sheringham celebrates with David Beckham and Ferguson helps to show off the trophy, unaware that in the stands Alastair Campbell is asking Cathy if he would accept a knighthood.

The Goldenballs Generation: the group of kids with whom Alan Hansen said United would win nothing included David Beckham.

He had gone blonde by the time Juan Sebastian Verón (*above*) arrived and then favoured a bewildering variety of styles as, after his marriage to Victoria "Posh Spice" Adams (*left*), he became a fashion icon, much to the distaste of Ferguson.

only about a dozen in it. Leeds had Cantona. Arsenal had the Swedish winger Anders Limpar and Sheffield Wednesday his compatriot the full-back Roland Nilsson. Schmeichel apart, Denmark was represented by another hero of the European Championship campaign, John Jensen, who joined George Graham's Arsenal. The Oldham right-back, Gunnar Halle, was Norwegian.

Quite a Scandinavian presence, you will notice – and it was the agent responsible for most of those moves, and more, who had helped Ferguson into the forefront of the English game's new internationalism. His name, Rune Hauge, was to become almost synonymous with the backhander or 'bung' habit which had been perennially discussed in the game but seldom proved.

In 1991, Ferguson recalled, Hauge had visited Old Trafford notionally representing a perimeter advertising company but had asked if he needed any players and, upon being told that something right-sided would be handy, sent a video of Kanchelskis. Ferguson and Martin Edwards saw the fleet, powerful winger play for the Soviet Union against Germany in Frankfurt and soon concluded negotiations with Kanchelskis's three agents.

One was German, another Swiss – 'We were beginning to think we were in a John le Carré novel,' said Ferguson – but the main one, Grigory Essaoulenko, was the most interesting, as Ferguson was to have confirmed in 1994 when, after Kanchelskis's contract had been generously renewed, the United manager received an unsolicited gift of £40,000. And rejected it. Ferguson also pointed out that Hauge, who had been 'peripheral' to the Frankfurt negotiations, only ever mentioned money to him once, and 'in a roundabout way', and never brought up the subject again.

George Graham found Hauge's generosity harder to resist and, also in 1994, was discovered to have received gifts of £425,000 in connection with Arsenal's recruitment of Jensen and the Norwegian defender Pål Lydersen. After a Premier League inquiry, Graham was sacked by Arsenal and banned from football for a year. He later managed Leeds United and Tottenham Hotspur and was generally regarded as having been unlucky in that, due to the diligence of the tax authorities in Norway and journalists both there and in England, he was caught. Because Hauge worked with quite a few clubs. By Ferguson's testimony, he was an excellent identifier and procurer of talent.

Nor was his gift lost to the game for long. An indefinite ban imposed by Fifa was reduced on appeal to two years and, short of putting up 'business as usual' signs, Hauge could hardly have appeared less devastated. It was less than two years, certainly, before another of his clients, a Norwegian forward, arrived at Old Trafford – and what a bargain Ole Gunnar Solskjær was to prove at £1.5 million.

Ferguson had been more hesitant in assessing Hauge's client Schmeichel than some others. Goalkeepers do not always adapt easily to the aerial buffetings of the English game and so Ferguson had him watched often by Alan Hodgkinson, the former Sheffield United and England goalkeeper who was his specialist coach at the time. 'We must have sent Alan over about ten times to watch him playing for Brøndby or Denmark,' said Ferguson. 'My fear was that he couldn't play in England. Alan said there was no doubt about it. He was a winner. He shouted and bawled at everybody. He was a real hungry bastard.' A glimmer of self-recognition always stimulated Ferguson's interest in a player. 'So I went over to his house in

Denmark and I could feel it in his handshake. He thrust out this massive hand. "You'll do me," I thought. And, after a few early problems adjusting, he was fine.'

Ferguson was speaking at The Cliff towards the end of Schmeichel's first season. United had just beaten Nottingham Forest 1–0 in a League Cup final whose quality, from both sides, had pleased him – whatever he thought of Clough as a person, he respected his footballing principles – and were firm favourites for the last League championship before the Premier League started. They led the table, as either they or Leeds had done since late August, with six matches to go and, at one stage in an interview I was conducting with Ferguson for the *Observer*, he actually talked about the title as if it were won.

Discussing squad rotation, an art of which he was about to become the arch-exponent, he looked at a chart on the wall of his office and started counting. He stopped at seventeen. 'Yes,' said Ferguson, 'seventeen players are going to get a League medal because they've played in fourteen matches or more.' There was a pause. 'If we win it, of course.' Not one of those players got a medal. Fourteen of Howard Wilkinson's Leeds players did. One was Strachan. But he inhabited United's past. Another was Eric Cantona and the enigmatic Frenchman, soon to transfer to Old Trafford, was to shape United's future more than any other player.

Cantona had arrived at Elland Road at an opportune moment. Some said he had carried Leeds over the finishing line with his fifteen appearances, nine as what Ferguson's old chum Craig Brown used to call a 'cheer sub' (a substitute who lifts the crowd, who in turn lift the players). But Ferguson's chairman had a more convincing explanation, one which the manager shared. 'Knocking Leeds out of both Cups lost us the League,' Edwards declared.

A trio of matches took place between the clubs in late December and early January, all at Elland Road with the inevitable high intensity, and, although Leeds won none (the points were shared in the League encounter), the outcome conspired to make the League Cup final the start of a season-concluding sequence of seven matches in twenty one days for Ferguson's men. Leeds, with a much less demanding programme, took the title with a match to spare.

Even Ferguson's rotational skills had not been enough to keep his men as fresh as Wilkinson's. But Ferguson had run by far his best campaign to date, the defence notably tightening as Pallister matured alongside Bruce and in front of the giant Schmeichel, and there was something approaching (but not, of course, reaching) satisfaction as he outlined his approach to squad management in the aftermath of the League Cup triumph.

'You use your experience,' he said, 'to decide who to rest and when.' For the September confrontation with Wimbledon, for instance, he had left out the young wingers Kanchelskis and Giggs and used Irwin only as a substitute. That had let in the dependable and combative veteran Mal Donaghy. 'You pick the ones who can handle it physically. So by doing something tactical like that you can rest people. You can combine the two.

'Sometimes you just pick the same team all the time. We had a spell like that in November and December [United were unbeaten in those months] when the players were at their peak, in full flow. Then you hit the Christmas and New Year period when the games come more frequently and the grounds change a little and you look to make changes. You check the younger players to see if there has been a draining effect on them.'

It all seemed to have worked. Since a 4-1 home defeat by Queens Park Rangers on New Year's Day – 'in among all those big matches against Leeds, it got lost, like an afterthought' – they had suffered only one further loss in the League, at Nottingham, and the mood in the squad was upbeat. Everyone wanted to play. The next match was at home to Southampton and Ferguson semi-jocularly confided: 'I've told eighteen players to report to Old Trafford – and I'm hoping at least one of them cries off.' Like most managers, he found telling people they were left out the least palatable part of the job.

In particular he hated disappointing Donaghy. It was on Ferguson's mind because Donaghy had just missed the League Cup final. 'He tends to miss out on the big games,' mused Ferguson. He had missed the FA Cup final in 1990 and, after taking part in every round up to the semi-finals, the Cup-Winners' Cup final in 1991. 'He's the odd-job man,' said Ferguson. 'If you need somebody to sort out the plumbing, he'll sort it. If you need somebody to fix the gas cooker, he'll fix it. He'll play anywhere you like and do a great job. But you can't keep bringing him in and out. You can't keep kicking him in the teeth.'

The trouble, Ferguson added, was the restorative property of the big match: 'When it comes to a Cup final, every bugger is fit.' It was the same now that United could almost reach out and touch the title. But he wasn't really angry that they were adding to his selection problems. 'It's an important time for the club and the pressure's on,' he said, 'and it's good that nobody wants to duck it.'

Donaghy was absent as they beat Southampton through a lone goal from Kanchelskis. Nor did he play two days later at his old club, Luton, where United drew 1-1. He came on as a substitute two days after that, replacing Neil Webb during the 2-1 home defeat by Nottingham Forest that let Leeds resume the League leadership for the sixth and last time and, as the matches kept coming thick and fast and the squad showed the strain, started at West Ham, where United lost 1-0, and Liverpool, where they went down 2-0 to a club, now managed by Graeme Souness, whose decline was to be masked by success in the FA Cup final against Sunderland.

Donaghy made his final appearance for United in a 3-1 home win over Tottenham while, over the Pennines, Leeds celebrated. In twenty League contributions that season, four as substitute, the Northern Irishman had worn six shirt numbers. Ferguson let him go to Chelsea – their manager was Ian Porterfield, who had replaced Ferguson at Aberdeen – and there Donaghy had two more Premier League seasons. Under Glenn Hoddle, who replaced Porterfield, he became marginal and missed yet another Cup final. But this was a good one to miss. Chelsea lost 4-0 to United, for whom two Cantona goals completed the Double.

Shortly after that Donaghy travelled to Miami with Northern Ireland for a friendly against Mexico and, having made his ninety-first international appearance, retired. He was nearly thirty-seven and it had been quite a career, featuring everything from two World Cups to the frustration that comes with a manager's need to make ruthless decisions. Donaghy went back across the Irish Sea and took charge of his country's Under-19 team. He had plenty of experience to pass on.

Darren's Hamstring

Mal Donaghy left United just as Ferguson's fulfilment approached. The club might have won only the League Cup – in the FA Cup, they were beaten on penalties by Southampton in a fourth-round replay at Old Trafford, while their attempt to keep the European Cup-Winners' Cup was ended in the second round by Atlético Madrid, for whom Paulo Futre scored twice in a 3-0 first-leg triumph – but the League campaign convinced most observers that Ferguson was getting there.

Indeed, two Fergusons seemed to be getting there. Young Darren was coming along quite nicely: in the reserves, mainly, though he had taken part in that end-of-season match against Tottenham. It was his ninth League appearance. He was never going to be a top player, mainly because of a lack of pace. 'Darren was like his dad in that way,' said a sage of the Scottish game. 'He had reasonable technique, too. But he wasn't as brave or aggressive as his dad.' And none the worse for that, maybe. 'His dad was aggressive to the point of being dirty.'

His dad also picked the Manchester United team at the start

of the fateful 1992/3 season. Alex Ferguson was never one to be embarrassed about selecting a family member. He had proved that by picking his eldest son, Mark, for Aberdeen reserves and he demonstrated it again by employing his own brother, Martin, as United's globetrotting scout. Darren's twin, Jason, had a season in the United youth ranks and it can safely be said that, had Cathy ever displayed a gift for the game or inclination to pursue a career in it, her husband would not have let the age-old prejudice against female participants thwart her, or him.

But Cathy had had enough to do in bringing up those three sons. Mark did his parents proud. At the European University in Paris he obtained an MBA and became fluent in French. He then worked as an investment-fund manager for Schroder's and Goldman Sachs, with whom he became a European champion in the same year as his father: in 1999 he was voted top European Fund Manager in the annual Reuters survey. Later he helped to found a firm whose chairman was Al Gore, the former United States Vice-President.

The twins chose football but, while Darren played the game, Jason inhabited its fringes. He went into television production with Sky and began so promisingly that he was tipped as the eventual successor to the head of sport, Vic Wakeling. In the event that distinction went in 2009 to Barney Francis, son of the journalist and broadcaster Tony Francis, a distinguished biographer of Brian Clough. Meanwhile, Jason Ferguson had been frying other fish. He had forsaken television to become a football agent – at least until unwelcome publicity caused United to sever their connections with the Elite Sports Agency, which he helped to run, in 2004. However, Jason continued to represent his father.

Darren, meanwhile, was coming to the end of a playing

career that had peaked early. He had begun the 1992/3 season as he ended the one before – in the first team. And what an exciting time it promised to be. He was twenty and (though it may have owed much to his father's falling out with Neil Webb towards the end of the previous season) in the side, deputising for Bryan Robson, no less. But it was hardly like for like.

United struggled to rediscover the momentum that had so nearly brought them the title. Lee Sharpe returned from injury and the team was reshuffled. Darren, having pulled a hamstring in a Scotland Under-21 match, never played again that season. In fact his days as a regular were over because the club, thanks to Cantona, made a growth spurt. By starting fifteen matches, however, Darren had done enough to earn a Premier League championship medal, even though United's form in those fifteen matches had been of anything but championship consistency.

An analysis of their results shows quite starkly what had happened. United had achieved defensive solidity the previous season. To ascribe it merely to Schmeichel's vociferous but splendidly defiant relationship with Bruce and Pallister, to state that Ferguson had reinvented his Aberdeen triangle of Leighton, McLeish and Miller, would be an over simplification and an injustice to the work of other team members, but the fact is that in 1991/2, Schmeichel's first season, the average number of goals conceded in a match fell from 1.19 in the previous League campaign to 0.79. It was to fall a little more in 1992/3. But the big difference was at the front. Here United had been getting worse. Their goal output had fallen sharply. Ferguson had not found his catalyst (his Peter Weir, as students of Aberdeen might have put it). And here luck came to the rescue of Ferguson's judgement.

Ah, Cantona . . .

Not for the first time, nor for the last, Ferguson had been casting his net wide in the transfer market, seeking a centre-forward hither and thither, trying one day for Alan Shearer, who preferred to leave Southampton for Kenny Dalglish's new adventure at Blackburn, and the next, it seemed, for the ill-fated David Hirst of Sheffield Wednesday, whom Trevor Francis refused to sell. Eventually, after inquiring about various others, he had settled for Dion Dublin from modest Cambridge United, whose resourceful manager, John Beck, had sent a video by which Ferguson, with remarkable candour, confessed to have been swayed.

Sad to say, Dublin broke a leg on only his sixth League appearance for United, in the midst of the run of wins that hoisted them to third. They had slipped back down the table, and been swiftly knocked out of the Uefa Cup by Torpedo Moscow on penalties, and been removed from the League Cup by Sheffield Wednesday, when Martin Edwards took the telephone call that was arguably the most important of Ferguson's career.

It was a Wednesday in November and Ferguson was in his

chairman's office, discussing the possibility of landing Peter Beardsley (a very different player from Dublin) from Everton. The phone rang and on the other end was Bill Fotherby, the Leeds director in charge of transfer deals, asking about Denis Irwin. After Fotherby had been rebuffed, Edwards continued to talk to him until Ferguson, apparently seized by an idea, handed over a scribbled note: 'Ask him about Eric Cantona'. Edwards complied and Fotherby, aware that Howard Wilkinson had clashed with the Frenchman on several occasions, said business might be possible. He added that he would speak to Wilkinson and call back within an hour.

In the thirty minutes before this momentous call came, Edwards asked Ferguson about Cantona's reputation for tempestuousness, which had been fostered by reports of fights with team-mates as well as angry gestures to fans and, only eleven months earlier, insults delivered to the faces of the French Football Federation officials who had disciplined him, after which he had announced his retirement from the game at the age of twenty-five. Ferguson replied that Gérard Houllier, the French national team manager at the time, had recently tipped him off about Cantona, stressing that he was a far easier professional to handle than those reports might suggest – and a talent worth making allowances for.

Houllier's word was good enough for Ferguson. And Ferguson's educated instinct was enough for Edwards. The deal was on and Edwards, having been asked by Fotherby for £1.3 million, worked hard to seal it for just over £1 million. Had Fotherby suspected what would ensue, he would have demanded a world record fee. Had Edwards and Ferguson known, they would have paid it. Without bothering to negotiate.

Cantona was to make United champions that very season.

He was to help them claim four titles in five seasons, two of which featured the League and FA Cup Double. So accustomed did they become to success that it was hard to credit that, when Cantona arrived, they had won only seven of seventeen League matches and lost interest in two cups.

His first League appearance was as a substitute in a derby against Manchester City, a 2-1 win at Old Trafford, and, although he neither scored nor shone, the effect he was to have on the team can be enumerated. In those seventeen matches pre-Cantona, they had scored eighteen goals. The remaining twenty-five brought forty-nine goals. At a stroke he had doubled United's scoring rate. The last barrier to their return to greatness under Ferguson had been removed. Or, if we are to relate the metaphor to Cantona, kicked away.

Eric was always a bit of a character. A bit like Ferguson in that he refused to let a decent background calm him down. He was born and brought up on the hillside outskirts of Marseilles and enjoyed, as Ferguson had done in Govan, an upbringing that was modest but comfortable in the context of its time (Zinedine Zidane, who grew up later in the city's Castellane district, had it much tougher). Cantona's turbulence, like Ferguson's, came from within.

He loved football but had to win. Whatever the game. Once, according to a fine biography by Philippe Auclair, the *enfant terrible* lost at table tennis and reacted by jumping on the table so forcefully that it broke (an anecdote that might persuade the Crystal Palace supporter at whom Cantona was infamously to launch himself studs first many years later to reflect that he was lucky to escape with a fright).

Cantona watched Olympique Marseille and, upon seeing them play Ajax, made an idol of Johan Cruyff. At fifteen he

was called to Auxerre by that club's great coach, Guy Roux –
one of the few who could be compared with Ferguson in terms
of one-club longevity and attention to the development of
youth – but made his life no easier while progressing to the
France Under-21s, who won the European Championship, and
then the full national team, for which he scored on his first
appearance, against West Germany.

Even in England, which was still relatively parochial, he was
noted as one of the most potent young footballers in Europe.
And those who had scrutinised him knew he had a physique
that could cope with the rigours of the English game. As
Auclair brilliantly put it: 'He was gifted the ideal body to
become himself.'

The arrogance with which he carried it was no lie either.
Transferred to Marseille, he ripped off his shirt and kicked the
ball into the crowd after being substituted – in a friendly. That
earned a month's ban. He was even banned from the national
team for a year for calling the manager, Henri Michel, a 'shitbag'
on television. He was loaned to Bordeaux and Montpellier
and then Nîmes, for whom he was playing when he threw the
ball at the referee. Summoned once more by the FFF, he was
handed another one-month ban which, after he had walked
up to each member of the disciplinary committee in turn and
called him an idiot, was doubled, prompting his retirement
from football.

To describe Cantona as complex would be fair. Not many
of football's stormier figures have nursed passions for classical
as well as rock music, for painting in both the passive and
active senses and for poetry. Nor is it mainstream in football
to take career guidance from one's psychoanalyst when an
agent is on hand. But it was he, the analyst, who advised

Cantona to forsake another sojourn at Marseille and try England when his suspension expired.

His international career had been thriving when he cut it short. Invited back into the fold by Michel's successor, Michel Platini, he formed a marvellous partnership with Jean-Pierre Papin. France went nineteen matches unbeaten, scoring forty-four goals, of which Papin got fourteen and Cantona eleven. It was after Cantona had scored twice in a victory over Iceland that was France's eighth in a row that he went to the FFF and blew up. By the time the French played next – at Wembley, where they lost 2-0 to Graham Taylor's England – he was a Leeds United player.

Platini had attempted to place him with Liverpool, only to have Graeme Souness decline the offer, and also asked Houllier, at that stage his assistant, to try his own contacts in England. Houllier rang the agent Dennis Roach, who arranged for Cantona to have a trial with Trevor Francis at Sheffield Wednesday. After a week Francis was not sure. He asked Cantona to stay for a further week and the response was predictable.

Wilkinson, at Leeds, got wind of Cantona's disenchantment and Houllier recalled: 'I was abroad but my secretary rang to say there was a Mr Wilkinson who appeared desperate to speak to me and had called several times. I took the number and Howard told me he thought there was an opening for him to sign Eric – what did I think? "Take him with your eyes closed," I said.'

Leeds paid Marseille £1 million. How significant a contributor Cantona was to their ensuing title triumph is hard to define, but, after a hat-trick in a 4-3 victory over Liverpool in the Charity Shield (later Community Shield) match, he scored six goals in the first twelve Premier League matches of the 1992/3 season and was firmly established in Elland Road's heart when Wilkinson concluded that the disciplinary baggage that came with him was too burdensome.

In the opening round of the Champions League, a bizarre error by the Stuttgart manager, Christoph Daum, who had allowed an ineligible substitute to figure against Leeds, dictated a play-off in Barcelona, where Wilkinson withdrew Cantona in favour of Carl Shutt and the substitute scored the winner. Next came Rangers in Glasgow. Again Cantona was taken off. 'And Eric went straight to the dressing room,' said Houllier. 'In France you can sometimes do that, but in England, or Britain, even if it's bitterly cold, a player is expected to join the others on the bench.

'Anyway, Howard invited me to the second leg. I went to the hotel where the team were staying and Howard took me to his room, where there was a TV and a recorder. He showed me the bit of the Glasgow match that came after the substitution and asked, "Where is Eric?" I said I assumed he was in the dressing room. Howard said he should have been on the bench.'

So they went to the match, at which Houllier found himself sitting near Ferguson. He knew Ferguson. They had met in Mexico during the 1986 World Cup. Houllier, who had guided Paris St-Germain to their first French title for half a century, was staying in the same hotel as Ferguson's Scotland party before the match against West Germany in Querétaro and they had encountered each other a few times since. Now they shook hands and settled down at Elland Road.

The match did not go well for Cantona, even though he obtained the empty consolation of a goal near the end of a second 2-1 defeat. 'I think Alex could sense my concern,' said Houllier. By then he was in charge of the French national team and Cantona's partnership with Papin was fundamental to their chances of qualifying for the next World Cup (or so Houllier was to believe until, after Cantona's sixth goal of the campaign had seemed to book France's place in the tournament, a wayward pass by David Ginola let Bulgaria break away and replace them).

The day after the Elland Road match, Houllier took a call from Cantona's agent, Jean-Jacques Bertrand. 'Eric didn't want to play for Leeds any more.' By Cantona's own account, he had requested a transfer by fax, putting his dissatisfaction thus: 'The salmon that idles its way downstream will never leap the waterfall.' It was not the only time he was to communicate by fish metaphor.

Straight away, Houllier was on the line. 'I immediately thought about Alex. I had his number and got through to him in his car, which was unusual in those days [it was November 1992]. I told him that a lot was said about Eric, and a lot of people were afraid of his personality, but that he was a nice guy and a very good professional – and a tremendous player. Alex said he would take him, but told me not to say anything to anyone.' Ferguson knew Leeds were interested in Denis Irwin. That was the bait. Leeds were given to misunderstand that an approach for Irwin might be entertained. Hence Fotherby's call to Martin Edwards.

It was, of course, not just the goodness of Houllier's nature but a duty to France that impelled him to find Cantona a more comfortable home at Old Trafford. The player's talent had been demonstrated to Ferguson on that very ground earlier in the season (and confirmed by Bruce and Pallister after the match) and Houllier offered assurance that reports of his disruptiveness had been exaggerated; that all he required was a firm, paternal and very careful hand. Houllier also gave Ferguson crucial advice that he responded to rigorous training; you can imagine Ferguson almost licking his lips in relish at that.

So Cantona came to Old Trafford. And United began to throb. They took the League leadership on their first outing of the new year, Cantona giving an inspired display in a 4-1 home win over Tottenham, and lost only twice more in the League (though Sheffield United removed them from the FA Cup). One defeat was at Ipswich and the other at Oldham, where Cantona was missing. By winning handsomely at Norwich, where Ryan Giggs, now nineteen and an acclaimed regular in the side, rivalled Cantona for brilliance, they established a slight advantage over Ron Atkinson's Aston Villa. They just had to win their last six matches and this time an almost luxurious thirty-one days stretched out in which to play them. United could only let fate slip through their fingers. This was the background against which Sheffield Wednesday came to Old Trafford on 10 April.

For sixty-five minutes, the match was goal-less, and then Old Trafford experienced terrible *déjà vu*. Only their Frenchman would not have recognised it, for he had been among the beneficiaries of their late fade the previous season. Was there to be another? The question crossed Old Trafford's mind as Chris Waddle drifted into the penalty area and, sensing that Paul Ince might injudiciously try a tackle, skilfully nudged the ball forward before falling under the inevitable impact. For the linesman, John Hilditch, who was refereeing because Michael Peck had limped off, it was an easy decision and John

Sheridan, the United fan whose goal had snatched the League Cup two seasons earlier, put the penalty away. Wednesday were in front.

Ferguson tried to think positively. He was glad he had been barking away at Hilditch before Peck's injury, reminding him that there had been so many stoppages for which time should be added. Then he sent on Bryan Robson, who had returned from yet another injury absence, for Paul Parker. The ensuing bombardment began to pay off with just five minutes of normal time to go, Bruce getting his head to a corner and beating both the Wednesday goalkeeper, Chris Woods, who made a valiant dive, and the defender by the relevant post, Phil King, who appeared to be day-dreaming and did not even try to intervene. Six minutes into stoppage time, Bruce headed past Woods again and the rest was pandemonium. Ferguson ran jubilant to the touchline. His assistant Brian Kidd sank to his knees on the pitch, glancing at the heavens, sure, like everyone else, that the title would be coming to Old Trafford at last.

The final whistle went. Ferguson, still speaking to the BBC in those days, composed his features. 'Well,' he said, 'we're a point clear . . .' That night at home he reran the match and calculated that the stoppage time was more than merited. Indeed, he thought there should have been twelve minutes. It was the first manifestation of an obsession with added time that would see him approach countless match officials, jabbing a finger at his watch – though never when United led.

That was it. Clean sheets helped United to win their next three matches and, meanwhile, Villa faltered, much as United had done the previous season, losing at Blackburn and then at home to Oldham, handing United the title. Ferguson was playing golf on that Sunday afternoon: out of nervousness rather than nonchalance. He was playing with his son Mark at Mottram Hall, near his Cheshire home, taking solace from the knowledge that, even if Villa had won, United could become champions by beating Blackburn at Old Trafford the following night. A stranger ran up with the good news. Father and son hugged, abandoned any thoughts of playing the final hole, rang Cathy and went home to find a throng of photographers which, for once, Ferguson thoroughly welcomed.

The celebrations were still going on when Blackburn arrived at Old Trafford, but United proved professional enough to win 3-1 before the long-coveted trophy was hoisted by the four arms of Robson and Bruce in recognition of the leadership each had supplied. United were even to beat Wimbledon in the final match of the campaign at Selhurst Park (which Wimbledon had shared with Crystal Palace since quitting Plough Lane in 1991). They were champions by a margin of six points. United occupied the perch. Liverpool were sixth, twenty-five points in arrears. They were never to crow on it again. Not in Ferguson's time.

Arsenal proved more resilient opponents, for, although they finished as low as tenth in 1993 and George Graham's days were numbered, Arsène Wenger was to arrive in England and give Ferguson the fight of his life.

In his autobiography, Ferguson dwells on a newspaper article in which Bryan Robson ascribed United's success to his – Ferguson's – development, saying that he had become more 'relaxed'. Ferguson wondered if it were more a case of his having stood back a little and observed individual players more closely. Anyway, he added, a massive contribution had also come from Cantona. This, from Ferguson, may have appeared becomingly modest. In truth it was not modest enough. Cantona had been the difference. Cantona had filled the team with more confidence than Ferguson ever had. Never before had English football seen such chemistry.

Never, to give Ferguson his due, had there been more skilful man-management. He learned from the breakdown of Wilkinson's relationship with Cantona at Leeds, once ringing Houllier to ask him to explain to his compatriot – 'naturally there was a language issue in the first year or so,' said Houllier – that he had replaced him in a match only to conserve his energies for a more important one.

Once Ferguson, asked why his battery of specialists at United did not include a psychologist, replied: 'I do that myself.' He had a more than satisfied patient in Cantona, who later said: 'He gave me freedom to be involved completely and not feel in jail. That's psychology – man to man.'

Ferguson also had the courage and wisdom to bend his own rules. On training, for instance. Having studied Cantona soon after his arrival, he was impressed by the newcomer's work but surprised to be asked by him afterwards if he could have two players to help with an additional half hour's practice of volleying. Ferguson allotted him three: two to deliver that ball from wide positions and a goalkeeper. The other players heard about this and such was their respect for Cantona that the next day several wanted to join in. Extra practice became part of the United routine and David Beckham was just one of those who flowered in such an environment.

What, Cantona apart, had it taken to bring United the title? The time the board had given Ferguson, clearly, and a lot of money. It had taken six and a half years and nearly £20 million for Ferguson to move United from fourth, where they had finished in the last full season under Ron Atkinson, to first.

By comparison, Brian Clough had taken eighteen months less to lift Derby County out of the Second Division and, in 1972, win the title – at a mere fraction of the cost. On Nottingham Forest the Clough effect had been even more startling. Less than three and a half years after taking over a team in the middle of the Second Division, he and Peter Taylor had made them champions of England in 1978. The cost? Less than £1 million.

When Clough started spending big, laying out nearly £1 million on Trevor Francis, Forest became champions of Europe a year later, and again a year after that. For Ferguson the interval between the English and European titles was to be six years. So Ferguson had worked no instant miracle. Clough, with Taylor, had done that. Clough, with Taylor, was a footballing genius. Ferguson's special gift would more fit the wry definition of genius usually ascribed to the Victorian Scottish essayist Thomas Carlyle: an infinite capacity for taking pains.

Seeing Red, Seeing Himself

By trial and error, Ferguson had built this team into which Robson still just squeezed from time to time, making only five starts in the first championship season but qualifying for a medal because of his substitute stints. He had to be replaced and Ferguson, as so often, used Manchester United's wealth and allure to make the obvious signing, breaking the all-British record to relieve Clough of Roy Keane, whom he had signed from the semi-professional Irish club Cobh Ramblers for £47,000 and for whom Forest now received £3.75 million.

This time Ferguson put one over on an irate Kenny Dalglish, who was by now at Blackburn and, having persuaded Alan Shearer to join him rather than Ferguson, moving the club upward to the extent that they had finished fourth.

Forest were relegated and Clough, prematurely aged by alcoholism, retired. Keane came on the market and Dalglish swiftly reached verbal agreement on a £4 million transfer but, a day before the paperwork was to be signed, Ferguson got in touch with first Clough's successor, Frank Clark, and then the twenty-one-year-old Irishman, whose change of mind cost Forest £250,000; United drove a harder bargain than a

266

Blackburn funded by Jack Walker, a Lancastrian made good, whose determination to buy his beloved Rovers the title was to bear fruit before long.

It was not the first time Ferguson had broken the transfer record between British clubs; he had done it in landing Gary Pallister. Nor was it the last. In Ferguson's first twenty years at Old Trafford, it was broken fourteen times, four times by Ferguson, who tried vainly to do it on other occasions.

Once he had come to terms with the English game, it was his turn to take the role of the Old Firm, using his financial muscle to relieve England's Aberdeens, such as Forest, of their assets, such as Webb and Keane (and he would have taken Stuart Pearce if he could). It was to culminate when he spent nearly £30 million on luring Rio Ferdinand from Leeds United in 2002, and £27 million on Wayne Rooney from Everton two years later; unlike his great rival Arsène Wenger at Arsenal, he was never reluctant to use his club's budget on the obvious signing. He had come a long way from Dick Donald and the parsimony of Aberdeen.

But after Keane there was no more hit-and-miss. A team had formed and, as at Aberdeen, the first title released a great surge of energy and ambition. The new man from Forest epitomised it. Robson, at thirty-six, had become peripheral and Keane, stepping into the boots of the almost inevitably injured club captain, joined Cantona in overturning a 2-0 derby deficit, scoring the winner against Manchester City after the Frenchman had struck twice.

That was in early November. United already had the leadership and would never relinquish it. Not this team. For the first time since Ferguson came to Old Trafford, it rolled off the tongue: Schmeichel; Parker, Pallister, Bruce, Irwin; Kanchelskis, Ince,

Keane, Giggs; Cantona, Hughes. At least that was the team which completed United's first Double by beating Chelsea at Wembley. Along the way there were plenty of matches for the adaptable McClair, and for Sharpe. The goals came from everywhere, not least the flanks: Giggs got thirteen in the League alone, Sharpe nine and Kanchelskis six.

As Bruce, the *de facto* captain, was later to observe: 'The manager had created a team that mirrored him in its fierce determination to win.' Ferguson never hid his relish for that aspect of Schmeichel, Bruce, Ince, Keane, Hughes and Cantona. 'I'm happy when I look out on the pitch and see myself,' he once said. So naturally, when that combustible mixture got stuck into the 1993/4 season, sparks flew and red was seen. At one stage even Ferguson became worried about the number of suspensions.

It started when Mark Hughes was sent off for kicking David Tuttle at Sheffield United in the third round of the FA Cup. In the fifth round, against Charlton Athletic at Old Trafford, Schmeichel went and this proved the first of four dismissals in five matches between 12 and 27 March. Cantona was next with an extraordinary two in four days, for stamping on John Moncur at Swindon ('that was deserved,' said Ferguson) and then clashing with Tony Adams at Arsenal ('I thought Adams made a meal of it') and finally Kanchelskis in the League Cup final for handling on the goal-line in the last minute of a 3-1 defeat by Aston Villa.

'We couldn't get out of the mire,' said Ferguson. 'So I called them all in. With Robson, as club captain, and Bruce. And I went round the lot of them. "One more fucking time and I'll . . ." And they were sitting there and you could tell. "Oh, aye," they were thinking. So I said, "From now on I'm going to fine you for everything. Two weeks for a sending-off. One week for a booking. Now off you go." And I can hear them walking down the stairs, giggling and laughing . . .'

By now Ferguson himself was laughing at the recollection. 'They knew I needed them. They knew I needed winners.' The kettles might also have found it amusing to be called black by such a notorious pot as Ferguson, the firebrand striker turned referee-baiting manager. But he did hope the message had got through. 'There's got to be a dividing line,' said the serial crosser of it, adding: 'We hardly had a problem after that talking-to I gave them. In fact our disciplinary record has been really good over the years considering that everyone's trying so hard against us in every game we play.'

Hardly a problem? Only a few months after his reading of the Riot Act came the incident at Selhurst Park in which Cantona, having been sent off for a foul on Crystal Palace's Richard Shaw, launched his kung-fu assault on a spectator. And only a few months after that it was Keane's turn to get nasty, stamping on Gareth Southgate in a 2-0 victory over Palace in the FA Cup semi-finals.

It was one of four occasions on which David Elleray dismissed Keane, who, while an infinitely more talented player than Ferguson had ever been, was perhaps the closest approximation of the manager temperamentally. And yet Elleray quite liked Keane: 'Everything he did was for all to see. You never got the elbow on the head when no one was looking. He once saw me before a match and said, "I expect you've got my name in the book already." And I said, "Yes, and I know what it'll be for. All I have to do is fill in the time." And he laughed. Well, half laughed. You couldn't really have a laugh with Keane.'

Although United's behaviour did gradually improve, their image was to be damaged by the vehemence of some players' protests to the referee Andy D'Urso in a match against Middlesbrough in January 2000.

He had awarded a penalty against the United defender Jaap Stam for fouling Juninho and was immediately confronted by a posse of five: Keane, Stam, David Beckham, Nicky Butt and Gary Neville. D'Urso kept saying 'Go away' but backpedalling – acknowledging his mistake later, he pointed out that he was new to the Premier League and refereeing his first match at Old Trafford – and the impression was of attempted bullying by a team who considered themselves above punishment on their home ground.

Even Ferguson could see the harm in that. 'I gave the players a lot of stick,' he said. 'It was a watershed.' Not that he could resist the temptation to indulge in a bit of special pleading. 'We continued to get silly sendings-off from time to time, of course, because at the end of the day we're judged differently from the rest.'

Back in 1993/4, temperamental issues did not prevent a side rated by Ferguson – and Bobby Charlton, and many outside observers – as up there with his greatest from completing the first Double in United's history. Despite the dismissals they conceded only three goals in seven FA Cup matches culminating in the 4-0 victory over Chelsea during which Elleray inadvertently helped them by giving a penalty without thinking. 'My whistle was in my mouth when Frank Sinclair challenged Andrei Kanchelskis,' the referee was candidly to admit much later, 'and instinct took over. I went up to get my medal feeling awful. I knew I'd made a mistake.' It was the second of two penalties converted by Cantona, and much debated – though not by Ferguson, who happily accepted it in the spirit of selective justice.

United also reached Wembley in the League Cup before succumbing to Atkinson's Villa. Only in Europe did the short fuses inflict self-damage. Back in the top competition for the first time in more than a quarter-century, United easily beat Kispest-Honvéd of Budapest before drawing 3-3 with Galatasary at Old Trafford and 0-0 in Istanbul and going out on away goals. Cantona was red-carded for dissent and took a whack from a police baton on the way off; it had been a stormy night for both United and their followers.

Fury was never far from the surface, even in the privacy of the dressing room. In mid-season Liverpool, by now clearly in decline, had managed to fight back from 3-0 down to draw with United at Anfield (Nigel Clough scored twice) and afterwards Ferguson was particularly scathing towards Schmeichel. The big Dane responded in kind, questioning Ferguson's qualities as both a manager and a person and feared Ferguson might well react by throwing a cup of tea in his face. Later Schmeichel apologised but Ferguson let him stew for a while, insisting he would have to be sold, before the incident was quietly forgotten amid the mourning for Sir Matt Busby, whose death in January 1994 was a reminder that lapses of dignity were not always a prerequisite of footballing success.

European Nights Off

The previous close season had been a deeply satisfying one for Ferguson. On the day that first United title had been clinched, he said, echoing his words on making a similar breakthrough at Aberdeen in 1980, he felt he had truly become manager of Manchester United and 'master of my own destiny'. He had then used what was to become a familiar ploy, challenging his players, telling them he had put in an envelope the names of six whom he feared might not reach the next level – and their response had been vibrant.

So what would he do for an encore? Conquer Europe, of course. It was the miracle that took a little longer. In fact, the 1994/5 season ended with United deposed as champions of England – by Dalglish's Blackburn – with neither domestic Cup as consolation. After a third-round defeat at Newcastle in the League Cup, in which Ferguson was sprinkling his team with gilded youth, they did go all the way to Wembley in the FA Cup but lost 1–0 to Everton.

The real disappointment was the Champions League. It began with a group stage. Indeed, for United it ended with the group stage. They beat IFK Gothenburg 4–2 at home, drew

0–0 away to Galatasary and drew 2-2 at home to Barcelona before visiting Camp Nou on 2 November for a chastening experience.

At that time Uefa had a rule that teams could field only three foreigners plus two 'assimilated' players (in other words, foreigners who had come through the youth ranks and played in the country for five years). Ferguson decided to sacrifice Schmeichel for an outfield player, giving the goalkeeper's jersey to the Englishman Gary Walsh. The likes of Pep Guardiola, Hristo Stoichkov and Romario were ruthless. Barcelona were 2–0 up at half-time when Ferguson called Ince a 'fucking bottler' and they had to be pulled apart. On the field, nothing changed. It ended 4-0. United then lost 3-1 in Gothenburg and a 4-0 trouncing of Galatasary proved academic.

The significance of the campaign had been in terms of youth opportunity. Likewise in the League Cup. The year before, the European exit at Galatasary's hands had convinced Ferguson of the need to rest first-teamers in the lesser of the domestic Cups, a habit that was to spread through the top level of the English game. So now he threw the kids in at Port Vale.

In the build-up to a League Cup final fourteen years later in which United, featuring young Darron Gibson and the even younger Danny Welbeck, were to beat Tottenham on penalties, he looked back in amusement to the trip to Burslem: 'The local MP complained about it in the House of Commons. He said the Potteries public were being denied the chance to see great players. He didn't realise they were getting the privilege of a look at even greater players! Because among the young ones I used that night were David Beckham, Paul Scholes, Gary Neville and Nicky Butt.' Two goals from Scholes gave United a 2-1 win.

In Europe, Butt had been a beneficiary of the nationality rule, appearing in every match. Beckham came in for the concluding home match against the Turks – and scored. Gary Neville, who also played in that match, was embarking on a prolonged run in the team. He and Butt were the first to establish themselves. Neville beat David May, a central defender or right-back for whom Ferguson had paid Blackburn £1.2 million, in the race to take over from the injury-afflicted Paul Parker. Butt deputised for Keane in midfield.

The other change in the team that season was enforced. Even before the Cantona incident, Ferguson had been considering a tweak at the front. Hughes was thirty-one and, for all his qualities, Ferguson felt a more penetrative player would make better use of Cantona's service.

The two at the top of his list were Stan Collymore and Andy Cole. That was when he rang his erstwhile centre-forward Mark McGhee and teasingly thought aloud before intimating that Cole it would be, for his predatory skills. Bang went the transfer record again. Cole left Newcastle for United and was soon playing alongside Hughes as Cantona took his involuntary leave of the game, being banned by United until the end of the season and the FA until the beginning of October and, having been hauled before Croydon magistrates for his kung-fu kick, given a two-week prison sentence that was replaced by 120 hours of community service on appeal.

That was when he talked of seagulls (journalists, we presumed) following trawlers (him) in the hope of being tossed sardines (tasty verbal morsels). He had always appeared much more troubled by separation from football than the prospect of a loss of liberty.

As for Ferguson, the manager was lucky in having failed to

sell Hughes to Everton to make way for Collymore or Cole. At least now he had a front pair capable of keeping the pressure on Blackburn. As United chipped away at their lead, Ferguson tried to add to that pressure, echoing the old Jock Stein trick by saying: 'Blackburn can only throw the League away now. We must hope they do a Devon Loch.' This was a reference to a racehorse that had mysteriously stopped while in the lead only yards from the winning post in the 1956 Grand National.

Blackburn did slow up a bit and had lost two matches out of four as they approached the final Sunday. If they lost or drew at Liverpool and United won at West Ham, Ferguson's team would be champions for the third time in succession. Blackburn lost, but United could only draw. Ferguson had been less than gracious to the new champions, saying he would not like to win the title playing as they did (they defended stoutly and attacked without ceremony, wingers repeatedly crossing for Alan Shearer). The central defender Colin Hendry had an apt reply. Had Blackburn not been a bit boring? 'I don't recall being bored,' he grinned. Ferguson took the FA Cup defeat with equal indignity, describing Everton as an 'ordinary' team.

And the end of that summer was a funny time, you might think, for Ferguson to demand another improved contract. Even though Arsenal had sacked Graham by now, he had been the highest paid manager in the country (even without Hauge's contributions) and that was what Ferguson thought he should be. Moreover, he wanted a six-year term, taking him to the age of sixty, and an understanding that he would be retained in some sort of advisory capacity beyond that, passing wisdom to his successor just as Sir Matt had helped him.

Edwards suggested he take this wish-list to the plc chairman,

Sir Roland Smith, who proved a formidable adversary, going straight on the attack with a claim that the directors were unconvinced by his recent performance as manager; Smith referred, among other things, to the loss of the popular Paul Ince to Internazionale of Milan, Andrei Kanchelskis to Everton and Hughes to Chelsea, all in the same summer. No, Smith told Ferguson, there would be no six-year deal, and no staying-on because it would cast a shadow over the new manager, just as Busby's presence had done to the likes of Wilf McGuinness and Frank O'Farrell. And that was that.

The decision to sell Ince had indeed surprised the directors and Edwards tried hard to change Ferguson's mind. But when one element of his management was threatened Ferguson seldom bent, and this was a case in point. 'I needed to be in control,' he said, 'of my team.' Ince had become too gung-ho tactically. Ferguson made this point in blaming him for Everton's goal in the FA Cup final; Ince resented it and told everyone who would listen that he was fed up with Ferguson. His £6 million departure for Italy made many fans question Ferguson's judgement afresh. Ferguson refused to accept any responsibility for Kanchelskis's departure, or even that of Hughes, despite his age and the fact that he had bought Cole to replace him.

Ideally, he would have liked to keep Kanchelskis, but the Ukrainian had manifested a restlessness which Ferguson ascribed to a clause in his contract of which the manager had not been aware guaranteeing the player a slice of any profit if he were sold; no wonder Essaoulenko could hardly contain his generosity.

The baggage that came with Kanchelskis had always been awkward. There had been that £40,000, for a start, concealed inside a samovar Essaoulenko had given Ferguson; why the money had been put in United's safe and not reported to the Premier League inquiry into 'bungs' which followed Graham's punishment was to become a pertinent question when the affair came to light in Ferguson's autobiography. But it was returned eventually, when Kanchelskis finally went to Everton, after another colourful episode when, according to Ferguson, Essaoulenko threatened Edwards and the United board decided to hurry the deal through.

Dirty deeds of another kind troubled Ferguson in the summer of 1995 according to Ned Kelly, who said Ferguson suspected the press were on to some aspects of his private and professional lives and ordered the former SAS man to organise a counter-surveillance sweep of his home and offices. While the Fairfields stage of the operation was going on, Kelly recalled – an expert from his army days was combing the rafters for bugging devices – Cathy made him a cup of tea. 'A true "lady" long before her husband was made a knight . . . here she was, going about her normal household chores, unaware of what was really going on.' In a parallel universe, football proceeded.

Towards the end of the domestic season there had been outings for Beckham, Paul Scholes and Neville's younger brother Phil. But in Europe it had been a case of evenings by the television, watching as Barcelona and Gothenburg went out in the quarter-finals to Paris St-Germain and Bayern Munich, who in turn were ousted by Milan and Ajax. Fabio Capello's Milan had won the previous year's final, beating Barcelona 4–0 with a performance hailed as one of the greatest ever given by a club side. But they could not overcome this young Ajax team of Louis van Gaal's.

In goal was Edwin van der Sar (later to win the Champions

League with United too). He was twenty-four. Among those in front of him were Michael Reizeger, Edgar Davids and Marc Overmars (all twenty-two) and Clarence Seedorf (nineteen). By the end of the final there had been significant performances as substitutes from the eighteen-year-olds Kanu and Patrick Kluivert, who scored the only goal against a defence featuring Paolo Maldini. Vienna hailed the new champions of Europe and never again, you might have thought, would we hear the words: 'You win nothing with kids.'

Yet that was what Alan Hansen said on the very first day of the next season.

UNITED:
APRÈS MOI LE TREBLE

Ted Beckham's Lad

'You win nothing with kids.'

The assertion, made on *Match of the Day* a few hours after Manchester United had lost 3-1 at Aston Villa, was to dog Alan Hansen for many years. While it was a reasonable enough statement of the sweeping kind for any pundit to make, it ignored not only what Ajax had done a couple of months before but the entire history of United in the pre-Munich era.

Matt Busby's team had been champions for two seasons when the tragedy occurred in February 1958. The team that might have brought the club its first Double in 1957 but for the injury inflicted on their goalkeeper, Ray Wood, by the Aston Villa forward Peter McParland in the FA Cup final (there were no substitutes) featured five players of twenty-two or under, including the nineteen-year-old Bobby Charlton. No fewer than eight had made their debuts as teenagers; it was a settled team, even though it contained only one player, John Berry, who was over thirty.

The team with which Ferguson started the 1995/6 season at Villa Park lacked Ryan Giggs, by now twenty-one, but still featured four players of twenty or under, including the eighteen-year-old Phil Neville. In addition two twenty-year-olds, David Beckham and John O'Kane, came on as substitutes. No fewer than seven of the thirteen had made their debuts as teenagers; most of them were to form the core of the modern equivalent of a settled team which, by the end of that season, had not only retrieved the League title from Blackburn but won the FA Cup.

In the space of less than a year, Ajax and Manchester United had proved that you win nothing with kids except the Champions League and the Double.

Before this, even Alan Hansen would have conceded that there was one competition you could win with kids: the FA Youth Cup. It began in 1953 and Busby's United won it in each of its first five seasons. The team lists make poignant reading. Eddie Colman and Duncan Edwards, each of whom played in the first three finals, died at Munich (in Edwards's case, fifteen days later). David Pegg played in two finals. In 1954 the team included three who were to perish, Colman, Edwards and Pegg, and two who were to survive, Charlton and Albert Scanlon. Charlton took part as late as 1956 and another survivor, Ken Morgans, in 1957.

Busby, while recovering from his own injuries, rebuilt the team as best he could, but while taking care not to turn his back on youth. By 1964, when United took the trophy again, the team run by Busby's esteemed assistant Jimmy Murphy had George Best, David Sadler and John Aston, all of whom were to play in the European triumph over Benfica in 1968, the excellent goalkeeper Jimmy Rimmer and Bobby Noble, a full-back of extraordinary talent which injury was to dim.

There were to be two defeats in finals in the 1980s, each supervised by Eric Harrison, whom Ferguson was so gratefully to inherit. Norman Whiteside, Mark Hughes and Clayton Blackmore played in the first. The second featured the group who were to become Fergie's Fledglings. The Manchester City team to which they lost – including Andy Hinchcliffe and David White, who were to represent England, and Paul Lake, who might have gone on to be an outstanding international but for injury – showed who were local top dogs in youth development. Until Ferguson took a hand. The snaffling of Giggs was only the start.

It was David Pleat, Ferguson's old friend, who proved more sage than Hansen. In 1992, when he was manager of Luton Town, someone mentioned that Manchester United seemed to be on the march under Ferguson and Pleat issued a further warning: 'This is only the start. Have you seen their youth team? These kids are capable of dominating English football for ten years.' So I went to see United's youth team. It was to win the Youth Cup that season and lose the next season's final to Leeds United and much detail of that first sight remains in the memory.

Except the score, that is; there are times when only the quality of the football matters and this was transcendental. The purity of United's passing style made it so.

The match was against Morecambe's reserves at The Cliff, on a dank Saturday morning. United had Kevin Pilkington in goal; a back four of John O'Kane, Gary Neville, Chris Casper and Steven Riley; a midfield of Keith Gillespie, David Beckham, Nicky Butt and Ben Thornley; then Paul Scholes lurking behind a centre-forward called Richard Irving, who, though he was one of the few not destined for the Premier League, did pretty well for himself in other areas, becoming an airline pilot – inspired by a visit to the flight deck on the way home from honeymoon in Mauritius – and setting up a property renovation company. Robbie Savage, whom Ferguson was always telling to get his hair cut, was among the substitutes.

Gillespie darted down one wing while Thornley plied the other with an elegant subtlety that reminded me of John Robertson, the Scot who had so wonderfully complemented the verve of Martin O'Neill in Brian Clough's Nottingham Forest teams (and who was to assist O'Neill in his managerial career). Scholes was a little magician. But the one who enthralled me was Beckham. He epitomised the style. Lean and upright, with floppy hair, he exuded the calm you seldom found in English footballers of even the highest class (the death of Bobby Moore in 1993 had been a reminder of that) and I had to tell someone about it, to share the excitement of the discovery.

There was only one other person. The car park at The Cliff, the only vantage point for those not allowed access to the pitch side where Harrison and the other coaches gathered (if Ferguson was watching, he would have been peering through the window of his office), offered a good elevated view and the fellow a few yards away was clearly accustomed to it. He had parked his big old-fashioned Rover and leant against the spare wheel strapped to the boot. I shuffled across, started a conversation and soon offered an opinion of the right-central midfield player who had my eye. 'That number eight – he'll get fifty caps for England,' I said. 'I hope so,' said Ted Beckham. 'He's my son.'

Three years later, David Beckham made his fifth League appearance for the United in that opening match at Villa Park. It was his tenth League appearance in all – Ferguson had sent him to Preston North End for a couple of toughening-up lower-division months – and he came on as a substitute for Phil Neville, scoring United's goal. Both Nevilles started, as had Butt and Scholes. O'Kane was the other substitute, replacing Pallister. With these kids United lost 3-1. With these kids they won the next five matches in a row. Then Cantona returned from exile after the kung-fu incident and, with these kids, took up where he had left off.

He was happily resettled in Manchester, with his wife in a little house that was startlingly unpretentious for a footballer. He felt loved again and Ferguson deserved a lot of credit for that, having flown to Paris to lift Cantona from the depths of his gloom at being cast out of the game in which he had finally felt at home. Cantona's lawyer arrived at Ferguson's hotel on a Harley-Davidson, handed him a helmet and drove him through backstreets to a restaurant where Ferguson and Cantona talked football like fans, delightedly raiding the fridges of their memories; the feast lasted beyond midnight and a unique manager/player relationship was strengthened.

Ferguson always made allowances for Cantona, wisely exempting him from the hairdryer treatment. He was the only exception. Once, the squad were invited to a reception at Manchester Town Hall and in advance Ferguson issued strict instructions about dress. Every player duly turned up immaculate in club blazer, trousers, collar and tie. Except Cantona. He wore a tracksuit and trainers. Any other player would have been sent home. Because it was Cantona, Ferguson pretended not to notice.

His sensitivity in handling Cantona had been noticed by Gérard Houllier. 'Not once during Eric's long suspension,' he said, 'did Alex criticise him. Never. Not a word. He showed loyalty. And every day, or two days at the most, he would call on him and have a coffee and a chat about what was going on at the club, while never mentioning the Selhurst Park incident.

That was top-class management. You show care. You show interest despite the fact that the boy cannot play for your team. In the art of management, it was a lesson from the master. And, when the boy came back, all that faith and support was repaid.'

As was to prove the case with David Beckham after the 1998 World Cup, when he was sent off against Argentina, and Cristiano Ronaldo, in 2006, when his sly wink after the dismissal of Wayne Rooney enraged the English media. Both were liberally to repay Ferguson for standing by them.

The impact of Cantona's return was not dramatic. Not at first, understandably. Indeed, there was a tricky spell leading to Christmas, when only three points were taken from five matches. But January and February found United recovering their momentum, closing on the leaders from the start, a Newcastle United invigorated by Kevin Keegan with Keith Gillespie, the makeweight in the deal that had taken Andy Cole to Old Trafford, looking much the better part of the bargain, and the glamorous David Ginola on the other wing; with Peter Beardsley and Les Ferdinand up front; and then, in the last third of the season, Faustino Asprilla, a Colombian of dazzling skills and infuriating individualism who, in the eyes of many observers, was to prove one egg too many for the good of the pudding.

Certainly Asprilla's arrival coincided with a dip in Newcastle's form, of which United took advantage by winning through a Cantona goal at St James Park in early March. That was in the midst of a six-match run in which Newcastle dropped fourteen points and United, dropping only two in eleven matches, overtook them. The stage was set for a remarkable piece of television on the night of 29 April.

I Will Love It . . . Love It

The star wore headphones. Kevin Keegan stood in an interview area at Elland Road, Leeds, after his team had defiantly won their third match in succession and told Andy Gray in the Sky studios: 'You've gotta send Alex Ferguson a tape of this game, haven't you? Isn't that what he asked for?' Ferguson had, of course, being playing mind games before Newcastle went to Leeds, goading Howard Wilkinson's home players, who were in mid-table, still nursing the wound of a League Cup final defeat by Aston Villa and drifting to the extent that they were to take only one point from their final seven League matches.

'Well,' said Gray, 'I'm sure if he [Ferguson] was watching it tonight there would have been no arguments about the way Leeds went about their job and really troubled your team.'

Keegan, emotion rising as he recalled Ferguson's complaints to the League fixture arrangers, went on: 'And we're playing Notts Forest on Thursday [three days later] and he objected to that! That was fixed up four months ago. I mean – that sort of stuff. We're bigger than that.'

Richard Keys, co-presenting alongside Gray, played devil's

advocate: 'But that's part of the psychology of battle, Kevin, isn't it?'

Gray: 'No, no . . .'

Keegan: 'No.'

By now he was emphasising his points with a stabbing finger. 'When you do that about footballers, like he said about Leeds, and when you do things like that about a man like Stuart Pearce [the England left-back and a member of the Nottingham Forest team who, having lost 5–0 to United at Old Trafford the previous day, were to hold Newcastle to a 1–1 draw at the City Ground later in the week] . . . I've kept really quiet, but I'll tell you something – he [Ferguson] went down in my estimation when he said that. We have not resorted to that. But I'll tell him now if he's watching it. We're still fighting for this title. And he's got to go to Middlesbrough and get something. And I'll tell you something – I will love it if we beat them, love it.'

This entered football's mythology as the rant that cost Newcastle the title. In fact, the title was all but United's as Keegan spoke. They had only that single match at Middlesbrough to play. It was their second in eight days and even a narrow victory would require Newcastle to win their concluding two by a combined margin of eight goals (in the event that would have been ten goals because United won 3–0 at Middlesbrough). The visit of Tottenham to St James Park would be Newcastle's third match in seven days; it was a minor reversal of the situation United had faced at the end of the season when Leeds beat them to the title. Now Newcastle ran out of steam, drawing with both Forest and Tottenham. But Andy Gray's little interjection on the side of Keegan as he had delivered his outburst stuck in the mind. Sometimes Ferguson's mind games were at the expense of the game's dignity. Yet he was to cross that line so often in the years to come that, in retrospect, Gray might seem almost puritan, a killjoy. Not that Ferguson was the only culprit. But it is fair to say that the standard of sportsmanship Gray was defending became a casualty of war in the Ferguson years.

As more than worthy champions nonetheless, United proceeded to Wembley, where Cantona, already Footballer of the Year, used immaculate technique in driving the only goal. The ball flew past a Liverpool goalkeeper, David James, who had been among the most fetching models of the off-white suits in which, to their eternal shame – and even now it is cited as evidence of the club's decline – a team now managed by Roy Evans had taken their pre-match stroll on the pitch.

Ferguson's side, by contrast, was built to last. The kids were barely out of their teens (or, in Phil Neville's case, still in them), Keane and Giggs were in their early twenties. There appeared plenty of mileage in Cantona and Irwin. Only the thirty-five-year-old Bruce, whose place went to David May in the Cup final, was deemed past his best and allowed to move to Birmingham City, dropping a division.

As the Double was celebrated, there were few toasts to absent friends – football is not like that – but it does seem extraordinary to reflect, at a distance, on the widespread belief that United had been reckless in jettisoning Hughes, Ince and Kanchelskis.

Ferguson had known that, with the kids, United would be all right. But he had thought some more ready for the fray than others. Beckham he had put in the latter category. He was not alone among the United staff, some of whom cited Beckham's apparent diffidence as evidence of a lack of fire inside. Ferguson even thought about buying another right-winger – and considered Darren Anderton and Marc Overmars – before replacing Kanchelskis's pace with youthful craft. Butt was to shoulder the central-midfield burden with the discipline Ince had lacked, forming a solid central axis with Keane. And this, with Beckham and Giggs on the outside and Cole ahead of Cantona, was to be the shape of things to come, a formation that, with the odd coming and going here and there, would win two more Doubles and the first Champions League of the Ferguson era.

That it was still not quite ready for Europe had, however, been emphasised by a first-round Uefa Cup knockout on away goals at the hands of the Russian club Rotor Volgograd. Even Raith Rovers did better than that, reaching the third round before succumbing to Bayern Munich.

Gordon Brown would have been proud of Raith. Born, like Ferguson, in Govan but brought up a son of the manse (child of a Church of Scotland minister) in Kirkcaldy, he had been a Stark's Park regular from boyhood to his election as MP for Dunfermline East in 1983, while Tony Blair was winning Sedgefield, and was never to waver in his affection for the little Fife club.

Blair would have been pleased to see his favourite club, Newcastle, challenging the best. Yet he was to go one better than Keegan and lift a most coveted trophy: the keys to 10 Downing Street.

He had been elected Labour leader in 1994, after the sudden death of John Smith, and was soon being praised by Lady Thatcher as probably the most formidable since Hugh Gaitskell. 'I see a lot of socialism behind their front bench,' she said, 'but not in Mr Blair. I think he genuinely has moved.'

Ferguson, for all his continuing protestations of allegiance to the traditional Labour cause, would have perfectly understood that. He had been introduced to Alastair Campbell by the ubiquitous Jim Rodger – both had worked on the *Daily Mirror*, Campbell as a political correspondent and Rodger as a chronicler of football's comings and goings – and formed a friendship with not only the power-in-waiting behind New Labour's throne but, in the run-up to the general election that was finally to oust the Conservatives, Blair himself.

In the summer of 1996, less than a year before the election, Ferguson sent a Cantona shirt to Campbell to auction at a dinner and, as Campbell recorded in his published diaries, it fetched £17,500.

That was the summer of Euro 96. The European Championship was held in England and 'Football's Coming Home' grated on the ears of those, like Ferguson, whose hearts favoured visiting teams. Ferguson did, however, dutifully approve Terry Venables's selection of Phil Neville, aged only nineteen, and his brother Gary for the England squad.

Scotland, under the management of Craig Brown, had qualified and been drawn in England's group. A memorable goal from Gascoigne, volleyed after a flick over Colin Henry, sealed their fate. Nor did the reigning champions from Denmark, with Schmeichel in goal, last long. Gary Neville was an ever-present for England until the semi-finals, in which they lost to Germany on penalties. The Germans beat the Czech Republic in the final and Ferguson, for whom I was ghosting a column in the *Sunday Telegraph*, identified the unsung hero as the midfield workhorse, the thirty-one-year-old and hitherto barely known Dieter Eilts, of Werder Bremen. But he had been quietly sizing up a couple of others for Manchester United.

The first indicated Ferguson's uncertainty about whether Beckham would settle on the right or in a central role. This was Karel Poborsky, a star of Euro 96, the scorer of a delicious goal for the Czechs against Portugal – having chipped the goalkeeper without breaking stride, he described his virtuosity afterwards as 'the easiest thing to do in the circumstances' – but destined to leave little impression on Old Trafford. The other was Jordi Cruyff, son of Johan, the Barcelona equivalent of Darren Ferguson and, likewise, to prove not good enough for United.

To think that Alex Ferguson could have had Zinedine Zidane – or at least made a more determined bid for him. Zidane, suffering the after-effects of a car crash in his final season with Bordeaux, was a pale shadow of himself at Euro 96. Juventus still had faith in him and, although Ferguson was to try to buy him from the Turin club for £10 million a year later, the boat had been spectacularly missed

Relatively inexpensive though they might have been, Poborsky and Cruyff were poor buys, lucky to end the season with League championship medals after making only twenty-six starts between them.

Ferguson obtained infinitely better value on the Norwegian market cornered by Rune Hauge. He got Ole Gunnar Solskjær, who immediately took over from Cantona as Ferguson's leading goalscorer. Not that Cantona minded: as a partner, he clearly preferred the intelligent Solksjær to Cole. At the back, Ferguson tried to replace Bruce with another Norwegian, Ronny Johnsen, a fine player who never seemed far from his next injury; though the same was true of Solskjær, both were to earn Champions League medals, in Solskjær's case unforgettably.

Putting on Spectacles

Perhaps the most significant development of 1996/7 was the emergence of Beckham as a major influence. He was given an England debut early in the season, being instantly called up by Venables's successor, Glenn Hoddle, to start the World Cup qualifying process in Moldova and, for his club, saw off the flimsy challenge of Poborsky and Cruyff for a place on the right, where Ferguson soon became convinced he was best suited with his wonderful gift for crossing.

Early exits from the domestic Cups focused midweek attention on Europe. This was a slightly better Champions League campaign, even though Ferguson, only too aware that United had never lost at home in Europe, was obliged to suffer the personal indignity of being the man in charge when they finally went down, 1–0, to Fenerbahçe of Istanbul. They were to lose by the same margin at home to Juventus and, in the semi-finals, Borussia Dortmund.

The home match against Borussia had brought about a change in Ferguson's appearance. 'It was after it that I started to wear glasses,' he was to recall. The subject of his memory had come up when I observed that, unlike many managers of the early twenty-first century, notably José Mourinho, he never took notes. 'I've a great memory,' he modestly explained. 'I rely on it. What I say at half-time is important and it has to be accurate. That's why I started wearing glasses after the Borussia game.' Lars Ricken scored for the Germans after seven minutes and, at half-time, Ferguson blamed Schmeichel for letting the shot in. Schmeichel defended himself on the grounds that it had taken a deflection. 'There was no fucking deflection,' said Ferguson. 'There was,' interjected Gary Pallister. 'It came off my leg.'

The spectacles Ferguson, then nearly fifty-five, had been given years before but never worn were brought out. 'You can't be wrong at half-time,' he said. Later he thought about having a screen in the dressing room on which incidents could be replayed. He discussed it with Carlos Queiroz, his assistant at the time, but decided against. 'You only have fifteen minutes at half-time and while you were showing something somebody had done wrong you'd be ignoring everybody else. A team talk is about everyone. Say Gary Neville's made a mistake – you don't want all the others sitting around watching it.'

So everything was logged mentally; there were no bullet points to consult. 'When I'm walking along the touchline, when I'm walking towards the dressing room, I'm thinking about the first thing I should say. Then, after seven or eight minutes, I take a break and my assistant comes in. And then I start working on the last thing to say before they go out for the second half. It's usually a summary of where they are and where they are going. Because there's always a road. And these next forty-five minutes are your last chance of reaching the destination. This is the time on which you're going to be judged.'

Trying to work out Ferguson's motivational principles was often difficult. For example, he rejected the screening of mistakes at half-time or the end of a match but would seldom hesitate to bawl out the offender or offenders in front of their team-mates. And his attitude towards the players' feelings during the week was different again, he stressed: 'I never criticise a player in a training session. When you're building towards a match, everything is geared towards going into it with confidence.'

Similarly, that last thing they would hear before rejoining the fray would be positive: about honesty of endeavour, about being part of Manchester United. 'And we don't under-emphasise their ability, put it that way. We *overplay* their ability. At our level, there's no point in being negative.' At one stage, if United were 1-0 up, he would say, 'You've won the game – now make sure you don't lose it.' Then he came to the conclusion that 'Now go out and kill them off' was a safer bet. But on the night they lost their semi-final to Borussia Dortmund, they were 1–0 down and, whatever directions Ferguson might have given them, could not find the road back.

Ferguson, it seemed at the time, had turned Old Trafford from a fortress into a haven. After forty years without a defeat there, United had incurred three in a season.

But there were consolations along the road to the last four, not least the class demonstrated by Beckham, who scored in open play against Rapid Vienna and Fenerbahçe away as United finished second in their group. After soundly beating Porto in the quarter-finals – all four goals came amid a coruscating performance in the first leg at Old Trafford – they avoided the favourites, Juventus.

Although United were to meet, in Borussia, even more formidable opposition, Juventus were the team regarded by Ferguson as the example to follow. 'All that skill,' he would say, 'and they work like beasts!' Gary Neville was listening. 'The manager was desperate to win the European Cup,' he recalled, 'and Juventus were the benchmark.' By now, Neville added, such a high priority was given to the European quest that Ferguson and Brian Kidd would prepare extra-meticulously. 'Sometimes they'd even set up the team for a League match on Saturday with the European game on Wednesday in mind.'

Ferguson admired none of his counterparts more than Marcello Lippi, who had led Juventus to the European title the previous year with victory on penalties over the still-powerful Ajax. 'That Lippi,' he had been in the habit of groaning, 'he's got us all beat.' Not Ottmar Hitzfeld he hadn't. Not the Hitzfeld whose Borussia put out United and went on to overcome Juventus – Zinedine Zidane, Didier Deschamps, Christian Vieri, Alen Bokšić and all – by 3–1 in the final.

Ferguson had obtained a formidable new rival and Hitzfeld, after moving to Munich, was even to recover from the shock of being beaten by Ferguson's United in the 1999 final and to lead Bayern back to the summit, where finally they planted their flag after a penalty contest with Valencia in 2001. Hitzfeld thus became only the second manager to win Europe's top prize with two clubs, after Ernst Happel, (Feyenoord 1970, and Hamburg 1983). Mourinho (Porto 2004, Internazionale 2010) was the third.

By the time United took their next European title in 2008, Hitzfeld was leading Bayern to one more Bundesliga title before taking charge of Switzerland, whom he guided to the 2010 World Cup. Lippi, in 2008, was once more the toast of the entire coaching fraternity, the man who had them all beat; his Italy were champions of the world, having triumphed in Germany two years earlier. All three of these men were standing the test of time.

New Labour:
His Part in its Victory

Back in that spring of 1997, Ferguson had been fighting on three fronts. Their order of importance to him was not known, though clearly he devoted most of his attention to United's domestic and European quests.

At home, Cole's return provided extra goals for a final spurt in which the challenges of Roy Evans's temporarily resurgent Liverpool and Arsenal under the new management of Arsène Wenger were seen off; it had been a strange season for United, especially in October, when they lost 5–0 at Newcastle. Attempts to ascribe this to the absence of Roy Keane, the cement of the team by now, were somewhat lamed by his presence in the next match at Southampton, where United went down 6–3.

The ship had steadied when Ferguson accepted his third challenge: that of helping New Labour to win the right to form the next Government.

On 30 January, Alastair Campbell's diaries of *The Blair Years* tell us, he had a chat with his chum Ferguson, whose team had just taken the League leadership for the first time that season. It was about the election campaign. Ferguson recommended attention to fitness, with a masseur on the battle bus (it was done) and the building of rest periods into the schedule. 'If you have physical fitness,' Ferguson told Campbell, 'you get mental fitness.'

On 25 February, three days after a whipped drive from Beckham had earned United a draw at Chelsea, Campbell again met Ferguson, whose view was that Labour looked like a team 2-0 up who just had to sit back and let their opponents make mistakes.

When Blair briefly joined the company of the two men, he, too, was given the benefit of Ferguson's advice. 'Alex felt tax was still a problem,' recalled Campbell.

Ferguson also said that Blair should be ready for 'stress levels' rising and should clear his mind by admitting only the most important matters. 'In positions of leadership, the appearance of calm was important and you had to work at it by cutting out everything that didn't matter.' And by delegating.

On 17 March, as Ferguson prepared to fly with United to Portugal for the second leg of the Champions League quarter-final, Campbell and Blair had time for reflection in which the party leader said he agreed with Ferguson that Labour could wait for John Major's Tories to slip up.

On 11 April, the night before United won 3-2 at Blackburn, Ferguson rang Campbell and said that 'we [Labour] were going okay, avoiding big mistakes'. He added that Blair looked 'strong and confident' and the Tories 'desperate'. Another tip Ferguson gave Campbell was to step 'outside the bubble and see the big picture from outside'.

On 20 April, the night after United had won 3-1 at Liverpool, Campbell and Blair were in Manchester and Ferguson came to their hotel for a drink. He asked how Blair felt; 'tired' was the answer. Ferguson told him to relax, believe in himself – 'you're here because you deserve to be' – and not be too aggressive towards Major, who, he felt, performed better under attack. Ferguson forecast a Labour majority of a hundred seats or more.

Anyone stepping outside the United bubble at that time would have seen that, while they looked a decent bet for the domestic title, Borussia had their measure in the Champions League. The second leg bore this out and the next day Cantona gave Ferguson another worry by telling him he intended to retire from football. A week later, on the election night of 1 May, Ferguson switched away from this and the strains of the title race by watching his political favourites romp home.

At one stage he picked up the phone and rang Campbell to say that the television cameras were filming him and Blair live through the curtains of the Labour leader's constituency home: 'I looked over,' wrote Campbell, 'and he said "yes, that one" and I went and closed the curtain.'

Ferguson had underestimated Labour's ascendancy. Their majority was 179, a party record.

The forecasting skills of David Pleat were to prove bolder and better. He had said an exceptional generation of kids would help United to dominate English football for a decade. Ferguson began to feed them into the team in 1994 and it was about ten years later, following the departure of Beckham to Real Madrid, that they were knocked off their perch, Wenger's Arsenal occupying it for one season and José Mourinho's Chelsea for two.

As for the forecast I gave Ted Beckham, at The Cliff, it was proved less than half right, errant on the side of pessimism: he hit the half-century of caps in England's opening match of the 2002 World Cup, against Sweden, and the century when Fabio Capello brought him back for a friendly against France in Paris in March 2008, and kept going, past Billy Wright's 105 and Bobby Charlton's 106 and Bobby Moore's 108 (albeit often with substitute appearances of short duration), until he became England's most capped outfield player of all time.

Arsenal on Top

The morning after the end of the 1996/7 season, Eric Cantona requested a meeting with Ferguson. He wasted no time in confirming his decision to leave football and Ferguson, though not wholly surprised – he had noticed both a dulling of the eye and a thickening of the waistline – asked the thirty-year-old to explain. He gave two reasons, both of which might have been puckishly designed to resonate with Ferguson.

One was that Cantona felt exploited by United's merchandising department. The other was that the club, when they brought in new players, were not ambitious enough (naturally Ferguson could have done with the freedom to offer even higher wages, to exceptional players, than could be paid under United's structure). Ferguson thought about all this and came up with the theory that plc status was partly responsible. He was nevertheless to break the British transfer record again (for Rio Ferdinand) before the Glazer family took United back into private hands in 2005.

Anyway, there was to be no change of mind. Football's loss was to be the cinema's gain. And Cantona was gone. It must have seemed an abrupt departure to the supporters who had idolised him – and yet it was marked by the style they had loved in him. There were no complaints. Old Trafford continued to echo to the 'Marseillaise'. The music would never die. Cantona, like Busby, was immortal.

Ferguson tried to replace him with Teddy Sheringham, who, though thirty-one, looked good value at £3.5 million from Tottenham. Sheringham was slow but extremely crafty and dangerous in the air. Nor did he let a personal distaste for Cole get in the way of their partnership – Sheringham scored fourteen goals in all competitions that first season, and Cole twenty-six – but the team could not dominate at home, let alone abroad. Arsenal were the team of that season. It was Arsenal who won the Double, and Arsenal who had the manager everyone was talking about.

United had been handicapped by the loss in late September of Roy Keane, who, in trying to foul Alfie Haaland at Leeds, succeeded only in injuring one of his own knees so badly that he missed the rest of the season. As he writhed in agony on the Elland Road turf, Haaland, thinking he could detect a familiar ploy used to avoid a yellow card, accused the Irishman of feigning (Keane never forgot the Norwegian's words and was to wreak a terrible vengeance years later, when Haaland was representing City in a Manchester derby).

Lacking Cantona, and now his successor as team leader, United were bound to feel the difference and it was testament to the structure Ferguson had built that they led the League until Easter. But after Arsène Wenger's Arsenal, who had beaten them 3–2 at Highbury, came to Old Trafford and won again through a goal by the near-unplayable Marc Overmars, it was clear that power had shifted south again.

Arsenal won both the League and the FA Cup and reached the semi-finals of the League Cup, from which United had beaten a hasty retreat at Ipswich, Ferguson's diluted side bearing evidence that the quality of the Beckham/Butt/Scholes/Neville generation was not to be repeated. Arsenal, moreover, had replaced Graham (not directly, for Bruce Rioch came in between) with a man who was changing the culture of the club, bringing it into direct competition with United in matters of both substance and style.

Nor was Europe of much encouragement to Ferguson. True, there had been a 3–2 victory over Juventus at the group stage; after Alessandro del Piero struck in the first minute, Sheringham, Scholes and Giggs retaliated and Zidane's gesture came too late. But in the quarter-finals a scoreless draw at Monaco proved insufficient because of David Trezeguet's early away goal, against which Solskjær's notional equaliser did not count.

Wenger had been at Monaco before the short spell in Japan that preceded his arrival at Arsenal. One of his star pupils had been Thierry Henry, who remembered the Old Trafford experience with glee. He already knew of Ferguson because the Cantona signing had put United in the spotlight in France. 'Their games were on TV,' said Henry, 'and there was lots of talk about Ferguson, what he had done at Aberdeen and now United, how he was a special character, very severe – in the right way – and very demanding of the players. Even though Cantona had gone, Ferguson was a big figure in the game.

'As a young player [Henry was twenty] I found it amazing that a team like Manchester United had so many youngsters in their squad. It was very unusual in Europe at the time, certainly at such a big club. Okay, you could say that Ferguson was given a great generation to work with, but he had to trust them. Another manager might not have done that. It takes a lot of courage and, as a youngster myself, I was impressed by that.'

Yet the Monaco kids, Trezeguet and Henry, were too good for United's on this occasion.

Juventus, meanwhile, marched on. They were to lose only to Real Madrid in what was their third Champions League final in a row. Guess who was to deny them a fourth. And guess who, at the same time, was to put Arsenal in their place. The most momentous of all Ferguson's seasons with United was almost upon us.

Le Déluge

In 2009, after France had qualified for the World Cup under the widely derided Raymond Domenech, Eric Cantona rather clumsily described him as 'the worst French coach since Louis XVI'. Clumsy it may have been, but its point survived.

Louis XVI was seen as a ditherer. He paid with his job come the Revolution in 1789 and was executed four years later. It may be that such terminally turbulent times for the French monarchy were what his late grandfather, Louis XV, had had in mind when he stated: '*Après moi, le déluge.*' After Cantona at Old Trafford, there had been a short, dry spell. And then came the flood. A flood of trophies. Including the most important one of all, the one Ferguson had dreamed of showing to Busby, the one for which – Cantona had implied it and Ferguson had taken the point – United's ambition had been insufficient.

There were changes on and off the field. The most significant was that Roy Keane returned from injury. But there were new faces, too. Ferguson had persuaded his supposedly skin-flint board to hand £10.6 million to PSV Eindhoven for Jaap

Stam, who thus became the most expensive defender ever (albeit pretty cheap in relation to Rio Ferdinand, who was to succeed the big and raw-boned but accomplished Dutchman). He had to pay Aston Villa £12.6 million for Dwight Yorke. But each was an immediate and spectacular success.

Another thing these purchases had in common was controversy. The Stam issue did not surface until, some years later, he wrote a book in which it was claimed that Ferguson had broken the transfer rules by approaching him – tapping him up, as the vernacular has it – before PSV. But the wrangling over Yorke was public. The Villa manager, John Gregory, refused all summer to let his star striker go unless United sent Andy Cole in the opposite direction. Ferguson clearly envisaged using them together. Impasse reigned until Yorke, selected for Villa's opening League match at Everton, gave an eloquently limp display. A week later he was playing for United at West Ham.

Yorke and Cole had an almost instant chemistry. Yorke, fleet of foot, technically deft and all the more refreshing for the grin that was his default expression, had been spotted by Graham Taylor on a Villa trip to Trinidad and Tobago. Yorke liked Cole as person. It was an achievement that had seemed beyond both Cantona and Sheringham.

Cole could be difficult. His attitude as a youngster had apparently persuaded George Graham to ship him out of Arsenal. But Kevin Keegan had coaxed lots of goals out of him at Newcastle and now Ferguson had seven million reasons, each of them a £1 coin, for getting the best out of him. Yorke was the key to that and their almost telepathic understanding led Thierry Henry to tell me in 2010 that he had never seen such a partnership in the Premier League.

Over the course of their first season together, they scored a total of fifty-three goals in all competitions. Yorke led the way with twenty-nine, of which eight came in the swashbuckling Champions League campaign that culminated in the glorious triumph over Hitzfeld's Bayern Munich in Barcelona. Though there could hardly have been a more extraordinary climax to any football match, it was somehow in keeping with the season that United's late, late goals should have come from substitutes, Sheringham and Solskjær. For this was a season in which everybody chipped in, very much a squad effort and proof that Ferguson had developed a rare insight into the art of chopping and changing.

Among those who filled in was yet another Norwegian. Henning Berg had come, like Sheringham, the previous summer, a £5 million buy from Blackburn, where he had won the title. He was to feature in two title triumphs with United. Like David May, who had also made the short journey from Ewood Park, he could play at right-back or in central defence. Gary Neville had similar versatility, as did the latest big talent to emerge from the youth ranks, Wes Brown, whom Ferguson expected to settle down at centre-back with both United and England. Phil Neville was challenging Irwin at left-back. Jesper Blomqvist, a Swedish left-winger who had done well against United for IFK Gothenburg, had bolstered the Scandinavian contingent and provided an alternative to Giggs.

Among the constants, the pillars alongside Schmeichel, Keane and Beckham, were the new boys. Whoever Ferguson stationed alongside Stam, the defence had the assurance once exuded by Bruce and Pallister. And up front Yorke had a devilish twinkle.

Only the League Cup eluded United. It would be more

convincing to say that United eluded the League Cup, for Ferguson, as was now his custom, used the second team in this. There were various advantages: he could give some action to fringe players such as Berg and the goalkeeper Raimond van der Gouw, assess the likes of young Jonathan Greening, who had come from York, and place in the shop window those who were not going to make the grade at Old Trafford, such as John Curtis, Philip Mulryne and Mark Wilson.

Ferguson's rejects had become a useful source of income to United. The youth ranks were producing players who, though not up to United's requirements, would have respectable careers elsewhere. John O'Kane had gone for £400,000 a couple of years back. Curtis was to fetch £1.5 million and Mulryne £500,000. Terry Cooke went for £1 million and Chris Casper, of the golden generation, £300,000. And so it was to go on: among the hopefuls at Old Trafford or on loan to Royal Antwerp, with whom United had an understanding, in the 1998/9 season were David Healy, Danny Higginbotham and Ronnie Wallwork, all of whom were to play in the Premier League for other clubs. Higginbotham went for £2 million and Healy £1.5 million (Wallwork took advantage of the Bosman ruling, let his contract expire and went for no fee) and several others raised tidy sums.

Ferguson's reserves got past Bury and Nottingham Forest before losing in the quarter-finals at Tottenham. The first team reacted to a slap in the face at Highbury, where Wenger's Arsenal won 3–0 in September, by losing only two more matches all season. Both were in the League. They lost at Sheffield Wednesday in November and at home to Middlesbrough just before Christmas. At that stage Villa had been leaders for most of the season, but Gregory's boys lost at Blackburn on Boxing

Day, conceding top spot to Chelsea, who were then overtaken by United at the end of January.

By now United were in the FA Cup's fifth round, having beaten Middlesbrough and Liverpool, each at Old Trafford and the latter in thrilling style, very late goals by Yorke and Solskjær outweighing an early one from Michael Owen. They were again drawn at home to Fulham, and then Chelsea, who forced a scoreless draw but were knocked out at Stamford Bridge, where Yorke scored twice without reply. This was on 10 March. The semi-final was to be against Arsenal – you could not accuse United of having it easy on this run – at Villa Park on 11 April. In the meantime, they had to deal with not only Newcastle, Everton and Wimbledon but two of Italy's leading clubs. This was getting serious.

The European campaign had begun quietly with a 2-0 aggregate win over ŁKS Łódź, of Poland (only the champions, Arsenal, were exempted from qualifying), and quickly become very exciting indeed. The opening group match was the first of two 3-3 draws with Barcelona, for whom Rivaldo was outstanding in both matches. The high-scoring theme was maintained against Schmeichel's old club, Brøndby, who were beaten 5-2 in Denmark and 5-0 at Old Trafford, and there were draws with Bayern, 2-2 in Munich and then, in the final group match, 1-1. By then Barcelona knew that their failure to win their home match with United meant no further progress, no chance of reaching the final at their own Camp Nou.

United then faced the first of their confrontations with the Italians. The wonderful flank play of Beckham and Giggs set up a 2-0 victory in the home leg against Inter, with Yorke again getting both goals, and the quality of the performance convinced Ferguson that his team were ready to cross the final frontier. Although Nicola Ventola pegged them back at San Siro, Paul Scholes's late goal relieved any anxieties that the match might go to extra time. Again United had been comfortable in coping with high-class opposition; the performances were stacking up. Then, just before the famous FA Cup semi-final, came the next stage of the Italian challenge.

To Ferguson it must have felt like a remake of *High Noon*: his team against Lippi's for a place in the final. Midway through the first half at Old Trafford, Antonio Conte struck and until the ninetieth minute it seemed the away goal would be the only one. Then Ryan Giggs gave United the encouragement they so desperately needed.

They had quickly to reset their minds to the FA Cup, for Villa Park loomed. There they drew goallessly with Arsenal, who had Nelson Vivas sent off, and so had to go back three days later.

With big matches coming thick and fast, Ferguson changed his team, starting with Sheringham and Solskjær up front and Jesper Blomqvist on the wing in place of Giggs, who sat with Yorke on the bench. Beckham, with a swerving drive, put United ahead, but the match seemed to be drifting away from them when first Dennis Bergkamp equalised and then Keane was shown a second yellow card and sent off. United held out until stoppage time, when Phil Neville brought down Ray Parlour, conceding a penalty. Bergkamp took it, Schmeichel saved. Still Arsenal appeared the likelier winners.

Then Patrick Vieira, with the most wayward of passes, inadvertently picked out Giggs, who was on for Blomqvist. It was the 110th minute but, for Giggs, only the forty-ninth and his relative freshness was used to devastating effect. He started to run. With a faint sidestep he evaded Vieira's gesture of a challenge. He also went outside Lee Dixon before cutting back in, drawing Dixon and Martin Keown together and spurting between them into the penalty area, where Tony Adams hurtled across but was too late to block a rising drive whose sheer pace left David Seaman helpless as it zipped into the ceiling of the net.

Off came Giggs's shirt, which was whirled above his head, and Ferguson, grinning, applauded as he strode towards his new assistant, Steve MClaren, who remained thoughtful, impassive, scanning the pitch, as if seeking to identify factors that might endanger the likelihood of Giggs's being the conclusive goal, setting aside the irrelevance of its beauty. It was nevertheless one of the FA Cup's most memorable. And a significant moment in United's history. 'After it,' Schmeichel was to declare in his reflections on an extraordinary multiple climax, 'we felt invincible.' By the time Ferguson faced Gary Newbon for the post-match interview on ITV, his task was to dampen euphoria. 'Look, Gary,' he said. 'It could all blow up in our faces at the end of the day.' Fans and players alike would be talking about this event for many years. But all it had done was put something in the bank. 'We're in the final. Now let's go and win this League.' There were seven matches left and United won the first, 3-0 against Sheffield Wednesday at Old Trafford, before heading for Turin and the most fanciful element, surely, of the treble quest.

Juventus, after all, clearly knew how to get to finals; they had been in the last three. They had conceded only eight goals in nine matches. They oozed class; Didier Deschamps and the incomparable Zidane had won the World Cup with France less than a year before. And, if there was any doubt that they had a cutting edge too, Pippo Inzaghi removed it by scoring twice in the first ten minutes at the Stadio delle Alpi.

So was that it for another year? But for Roy Keane's finest hour, it probably would have been. It was in the twenty-fourth minute that Keane raged in to meet a Beckham corner and send a glancing header wide of Angelo Peruzzi. It was in the thirty-fourth that Yorke nodded Cole's lofted pass out of the goalkeeper's reach to put United ahead on away goals. And it was in the eighty-fourth, after both Yorke and Irwin had struck a post, that Yorke was brought down in the act of rounding Peruzzi but required no penalty kick because Cole was following up to score.

This time, Ferguson had Lippi beat. United were going back to Camp Nou for the final, and deservedly so. The only regrets were that both Keane and Scholes would be missing after collecting yellow cards in Turin.

A draw at Leeds on the Sunday left United behind Arsenal in the domestic rankings, but they had a match in hand and were to win it, at Middlesbrough through Yorke's last goal of the season. His penultimate had given United the lead a few days earlier at Liverpool, but this match became turbulent and bitterly controversial: the nadir of Ferguson's relationship with David Elleray, who left United with ten men after showing Denis Irwin a second yellow card for kicking away a ball that had run over the touchline.

Irwin had increased United's lead with a penalty, but Jamie Redknapp, also from the spot, pulled a goal back and Paul Ince equalised near the end. Afterwards a fuming Ferguson said of Elleray in a televison interview: 'We will not let this man deny us our title.' More surprising to Elleray was the quip of his chairman. 'Martin Edwards said that, if Arsenal won the title, they should give one of their medals to me,' said Elleray, 'and that led to the worst period of my career in

refereeing, with death threats, police protection and eventually withdrawal from what would have been my last match of
the season.'

He admitted having forgotten the first yellow shown to
Irwin, whom suspension was to rule out of the FA Cup final
– but added that he would still have issued a second. 'He'd
kicked the ball forty yards. But I'd also given three penalties
and when the match finished I was glad to see Bernie, the great
policeman who used to look after the match officials at Anfield.
He had this big old-fashioned truncheon, with all those nicks
on it which I imagined came from cracking skulls around
Toxteth, and he kept Ferguson away from me in the tunnel,
which is very narrow at Anfield.

'After that I had a really grim time. There was abuse in the
street, telephone calls, hate mail. I think it was more because
of what Martin said than Alex. But it was a combination.'

Elleray, who intertwined refereeing with his duties as a
housemaster at Harrow School, was often portrayed as United's
(and therefore Ferguson's) arch-enemy. Yet he spoke of pleasant
encounters. 'There's a great contradiction with him. Once I
did a match at Old Trafford and got there extremely early with
my guest for the day, Bill Davis, who was the head of the
Combined Cadet Force at Harrow. We ran into Alex three or
four hours before the kick-off and I told him Bill was an avid
United fan. 'Fine,' said Alex. 'Just leave him to me.' And he
took this guy away and personally gave him an insider's tour
of the stadium. They were away nearly an hour.

'Another time Alex was chief guest at the Independent
Schools FA six-a-side tournament in Manchester. He was
talking to all those schoolmasters about pressure on young
players, and talking a lot of sense. He could just have turned

up and spoken at the lunch but instead stayed for the whole tournament, right to the awards at the end, going round talking to the boys, having his photograph taken with them and generally being the diplomat *par excellence*.

'Every time I've encountered him away from a match, I've been impressed. The analogy I've always used is with people who become very different when they get behind the wheel of a car. When he gets close to a match, he becomes a different person. How much of that is studied I'm not sure.'

We were speaking early in 2010, at a time when Ferguson appeared to be criticising referees every time United failed to win. He had attacked Alan Wiley's fitness after Sunderland drew at Old Trafford, Chris Foy's timekeeping when Leeds United pulled off a shock win there in the FA Cup and Mark Clattenburg's perceived inconsistency in a drawn match at Birmingham; it was all bizarrely, even tediously, excessive. If Ferguson could behave so scornfully in public, how intimidating had he been in the privacy of a stadium's bowels?

'For me,' said Elleray, 'he was never as bad as the media made out. A lot of the ranting and raving after the match you could ignore. You get it from plenty of managers and you're used to it. But Ferguson was quite clever and I think he was at his most dangerous at half-time. With a comment as you were coming off the field or going back out – to get into your brain for the second half.'

Such as? 'A lot of the time he'd be complaining that you weren't protecting his team. There would be something like "You need to get a grip on them [the opposition] – otherwise there's going to be a problem." I remember he had a go at me at the interval of that semi-final against Crystal Palace, for not protecting Keane. He'd been tackled and his foot was cut and it was made clear to me that he was going back out in not a very good mood.' In the second half, Keane responded to another aggressive challenge with a stamp on Gareth Southgate that left Elleray with little room for discretion.

Elleray later heard a story about Ferguson: 'Manchester United were playing at Chelsea and Alex was unhappy with the referee chosen for the game. When asked who he would like instead, Ferguson said "David Elleray". On being told, "But you don't like David Elleray!" he replied, "Whether I like him or not is immaterial – he protects my players."'

Winning Plenty Without Kidd

Elleray was nevertheless in need of protection himself – and from threats of rather more than a cut foot in the fearful aftermath of Anfield – when United regained the leadership, so that victory over Tottenham at Old Trafford on the final day of the 1998/9 season would win them back the title. They won 2-1.

By now only the result mattered, but United's performances had betrayed a jaded air that was understandable. There had been a tense and scoreless draw, for instance, at Blackburn, who were thereby relegated. Their manager was Brian Kidd, who had resigned as Ferguson's assistant during the season.

Kidd's replacement was Steve McClaren, who had built quite a reputation in a short time under Jim Smith at Derby County. McClaren was the ice-cool figure next to Ferguson amid the celebrations of Giggs's winner at Villa Park. His first few months were certainly proving eventful.

Ferguson, in his autobiography, which was published towards the end of that year, at times referred gracelessly to Kidd. He acknowledged the high value of Kidd's work for him at United, where the former European champion had graduated from youth development to first-team training with distinction. He made no secret of how he had urged Martin Edwards to improve Kidd's contract the previous summer, when Kidd had told the chairman he was wanted by Everton as manager. But he was acid in his references to the personality of a man who, it was true, had little in common with Ferguson's straight-shooting soulmate Archie Knox. For example: 'When I put to him [Kidd] what Martin Edwards had said, he chuntered on for ages in a manner that had become familiar to me . . .'

Would Ferguson have liked to be the victim of such indiscretion? Almost certainly not. Nor would he have appreciated the interference Glenn Hoddle, as England manager, had to to put up with in the World Cup summer of 1998. Then, Ferguson broke with convention in criticising Hoddle for asking David Beckham to appear at a media conference after he had been dropped for a match against Tunisia. This seemed none of Ferguson's business, at least in public – if he had deemed it in Manchester United's interest to console the player, Beckham's number was in his phone – yet he chose to air his views in a newspaper column. Hoddle described it as unprofessional.

Ferguson's critique of Kidd was more wounding. He doubted that his long-time assistant was made of management material. However gratuitous, this was not an unreasonable opinion and almost as Ferguson's book hit the streets, Blackburn's owner, Jack Walker, came to a similar conclusion. Kidd was sacked.

Ferguson's own stock could have been no higher after the glory of Barcelona. Picking the team to face Bayern there had been complicated by the suspension of Keane and Scholes, although Keane would probably have missed the match anyway due to an injury sustained when Gary Speed tackled him aggressively in the opening minutes of the FA Cup final. The captain was replaced by Teddy Sheringham, who soon scored the opening goal of a drearily one-sided match against Newcastle; Paul Scholes made it 2-0 in the second half and United became the first club to complete a hat-trick of Doubles.

Even in such an important match, Ferguson managed his resources, starting with Ole Gunnar Solskjær up front instead of Dwight Yorke, who came on for Andy Cole. But Yorke and Cole were always going to take the field for the European climax. Sheringham and Solskjær sat on the bench. Peter Schmeichel, of course, kept goal and, because Ronny Johnsen was fit, the back four picked itself; the others were Gary Neville, Jaap Stam and Denis Irwin.

The problem was how to arrange the midfield without Keane and Scholes; clearly Nicky Butt would take one of the central positions and Ferguson, though he claimed always to have regarded David Beckham as a wide player, gave him the other. He later explained: 'I wanted him on the ball. I needed a passer in the central midfield and I wasn't worried about people rushing by Beckham because Jens Jeremies was doing a holding job with Lothar Matthaus and Stefan Effenberg was very much a playmaker, not the type to go bursting past anyone.'

The wide-right role went to Ryan Giggs, with Jesper Blomqvist on the left. 'The idea was to get some penetration through Giggs beating men, Beckham passing and Blomqvist using his left-foot ability.' Asked why, of the two left-footers, Giggs, the superior player, was asked to switch, he replied: 'I didn't think Blomqvist would have the confidence to play on the right.' Besides, Giggs could do some damage. 'Their slowest player was the left-back. Tall lad. Went to Manchester City.' Michael Tarnat was indeed troubled by Giggs's pace and trickery. But little else went to Ferguson's plan.

After only six minutes, Johnsen fouled Carsten Jancker and, after Markus Babbel had craftily manoeuvred Butt out of United's defensive wall, Mario Basler shot through the gap. And 1–0 was how it looked likely to end when the first substitute appeared in the sixty-seventh minute, Sheringham replacing Blomqvist.

Sheringham was told to play on the left and occupy Babbel as part of the aerial battle; the central defenders, Sammy Kuffour and Thomas Linke, were not especially tall, so there might be some potential there. Giggs changed sides to play behind Sheringham with Beckham on the right and Butt in the middle of a three-man midfield that was almost immediately swamped.

It seemed that Hitzfeld had utterly won the tactical contest because his first substitute, the elegant midfielder Mehmet Scholl, who had come on four minutes after Sheringham, linked with Effenberg to take control. Schmeichel saved from Effenberg but could do nothing when first Scholl cleverly chipped against a post and then Jancker, with an overhead kick, struck the crossbar.

United looked soundly beaten when the clock showed ninety minutes and up went the illuminated board. On it was '3'. In the first of those minutes, Schmeichel ran the length of the pitch to meet a corner – without Ferguson's permission – and caused confusion amid which the ball was miskicked to the edge of the penalty area, where Giggs scuffed what could only have been an attempt at a shot back into the goalmouth for Sheringham, with yet another miscue, to equalise.

An estimated 50,000 United supporters went berserk and somehow everyone suspected that, for the shell-shocked Bayern troops, the worst was not yet over. Injury time would, of course, be extended to allow for the age it had taken the Germans to drag themselves to the centre circle and three minutes and thirty-six seconds had passed when again Beckham whipped the ball in from the left and Sheringham headed on and Solskjær, with whom Ferguson had replaced Cole in the eighty-first minute, instinctively stabbed it high into the net. Cue delirium.

Both Ferguson and Gary Neville found the *mots justes* afterwards. 'Supernatural,' said Neville. 'Football,' said Ferguson, 'bloody hell!' It was indeed one of the most extraordinary manifestations of a game with a mind of its own and, as the celebrations spread through Barcelona, some of us spared a thought for the vanquished. Hitzfeld especially. Had he not been cruelly denied? Ferguson was to consider the point at a distance of some seven years and insist: 'The people who said we were lucky got it wrong. Bayern, because they hit a post and so on, looked more effective than us, but in those last twenty minutes we had five chances. Five great chances!'

Not all of them, however, were chronicled by the next issue of the extremely reliable magazine *World Soccer*. Mysteriously, its respected reporter Keir Radnedge mentions only saves by Oliver Kahn from Sheringham and Solskjaer while at the other end woodwork nervously shuddered. Even if you include the goals, you don't get a total of five chances.

As for Hitzfeld's apparently timely introduction of Scholl: 'We knew that beforehand. They did it every game in the last twenty minutes, taking Basler and [Alexander] Zickler off and putting on Scholl and [Hasan] Salihamidžić.' More convincing was Ferguson's assertion that Bayern suffered for Hitzfeld's withdrawal of Matthaus, the vastly experienced team leader, in favour of the centre-back Thorsten Fink in the eightieth minute. 'Matthaus organised their offside. Scholl replaced him on the post [at corners] and, when the first goal went in, Scholl was late coming out, playing Sheringham onside.'

That was the detail with the devil in it. The whole stadium suspected offside. We had all switched our attention to the relevant linesman. 'So had I,' said Ferguson. 'So had Sheringham. But Scholl had played him on.' Next to Ferguson, Steve McClaren kept his composure and advised a reversion to 4-4-2 for extra time. There was no extra time.

What a Knight

Ferguson had followed in the footsteps of Mr Jock Stein, Sir Matt Busby, Mr Bob Paisley, Mr Brian Clough (and Mr Tony Barton, who had won the European Cup with an Aston Villa team built by Ron Saunders) and, even though, unlike Busby, he had not broken new ground even for his club, his connections made the offer of a knighthood a formality. Indeed, Alastair Campbell had thought ahead and taken advice from the Cabinet Secretary, Sir Richard Wilson. Almost as soon as the final whistle blew, he remembered what to do, and vaulted from his seat into the VIP area at Camp Nou to ask Cathy Ferguson if she thought he would be 'up for it'.

Football was a natural relaxation for Campbell. It dovetailed with his job. He made sure of that, but the FA Cup final between United and Newcastle had been an easy fit because he travelled to Wembley with his sons Rory, who had switched allegiance from Burnley to United after getting to know Ferguson, and Calum in the escorted car of Tony Blair. On the way, the Prime Minister worked on Northern Ireland, having 'a couple of difficult calls' with David Trimble and Gerry Adams. At Wembley, after he had socialised with, among

others, David Beckham's wife Victoria, Newcastle's performance was a disappointment to him.

The crisis in Kosovo, the main issue at the Cabinet meetings of the time because of the deaths of civilians, provided
the background as Campbell, with Rory, flew to Barcelona
four days later. He put no spin on United's performance.
'Bayern should have buried them in the second half,' he said.
When he mentioned the knighthood to Cathy, she was against
it, adding: 'Don't you think he's won enough already?'

Campbell left for the airport and made a call to Ferguson
himself, who rang back to say that, for him, the question was
whether his parents would have approved or not and that,
although he would leave the decision until the morning, his
inclination was that they would have favoured acceptance.

Later that year, he wrote in his autobiography: 'When I
learned during the summer that I was to receive a knighthood, I had to smile at the thought of how far football had
brought me.' He mused on Govan and hand-me-down football boots – and swore gratitude to Manchester United. A
couple of years later, he was inviting offers of alternative
employment and refusing to rule out rival English clubs.

Managing to Hurt

Brian Kidd was not the only victim of Ferguson's auto-biography, but due to events in the time between its composition and publication, he did receive his kicking when he was down. While Steve McClaren had revelled in a pinch-yourself introduction to his old job alongside Ferguson, Blackburn under Kidd had hardly won a match in being relegated and unemployment beckoned.

At least Gordon Strachan was still in the Premier League. Indeed he was celebrating three years in charge of Coventry City with a sequence of four home wins that left them just below mid-table when he read an account of his negotiations with Cologne when at Aberdeen, coupled with an accusation that he had later been less than candid about a conversation with Martin Edwards at United, and Ferguson's conclusion: 'I decided that this man could not be trusted an inch.'

Strachan had been prepared for something critical – when he had visited Old Trafford with Coventry the previous season, not even a handshake had been on offer – but this shook him. When I met him at Coventry's training ground a few weeks later, he said he had tried to avoid the subject with a standard reply ('It's sad that Alex cannot use his book solely to celebrate his achievements') but it rankled because the accusation simply did not stick. 'He, of all people, should know I can be trusted.'

He and Strachan, of course, went back longer than most. Strachan recalled the days when Ferguson had that tape of the awful Glaswegian singer played on the team bus and even confessed to being the player who hurled it off. 'So maybe I can't be trusted after all,' Strachan sneered. That may have been his anger surfacing, for he later admitted it was someone else. He also spoke of the agent Bernd Killat, who did work for them both. He referred to the friendship between his wife, Lesley, and Cathy Ferguson, who, by Ferguson's own account, had been left to bring up three boys virtually alone.

At times, inevitably, Cathy had been near the end of her tether, requiring sympathy and understanding, and, when her husband was not there, Lesley Strachan had not been slow to rally round. So Lesley was hurt, too.

But Strachan spoke less in anger than sorrow. 'It's a shame,' he said of his relationship with Ferguson. 'Ever since I left Old Trafford we've had arguments, niggles, bits and bobs, and I'd love it if we could just start again. With his confrontational style, I suppose this sort of thing is always liable to happen. But it's a real pity. To be able to greet each other and talk about the old times would be wonderful.'

Strachan had to wait several years for that. His fifth season at Coventry ended with the club's relegation after thirty-four years in the top division. He then revived Southampton, guiding them to eighth place and the FA Cup final, before quitting and taking a sabbatical, from which he emerged to take charge of Celtic in June 2005. Under him, they won three championships in a row and it was when United came to

Parkhead for a friendly that Strachan seized an opportunity for rapprochement. 'Can I have a word with you?' he asked, and before Ferguson had left his room there was an understanding.

'Now, when we meet, we can talk fitba,' said Strachan (this was in the summer of 2009, before he came out of another period of rest to join Middlesbrough). 'We don't hug – it's not his style – but we can have a laugh and a chat.' Strachan smiled. 'It's fine.'

Only then did I discover that, a few years after Ferguson had labelled him untrustworthy, Strachan had been approached by Michael Crick in connection with the book Crick was preparing about Ferguson. He declined the interview in case Crick was 'looking for dirt' (although Ferguson was to speak nothing but ill of *The Boss*, it turned out to be a fair and not unduly aggressive book). Never had Strachan been interested in opportunities to retaliate in kind.

And never, in nearly twenty years since the insult was delivered, had he forgotten that old feeling of being ready to run through a brick wall for Ferguson. 'To this day,' Strachan added, 'if anyone says something about him, I'm the first to stand up for him.' Closely followed by his old friend Mark McGhee, whom Ferguson so suddenly and mysteriously ostracised.

Football – bloody hell!

UNITED:
THE ENCORE

Goals Galore

After the treble came the encore: a magnificent Premier League season featuring ninety-seven goals, a record (and, to put it in startling perspective, twenty-four more than Arsenal scored four years later when their 'Invincibles' went through a League season unbeaten). The competition in 1999/2000 included Wenger's Arsenal, of course, a vibrant young Leeds United and a Liverpool showing signs of resurgence under Gérard Houllier. But United left them all trailing.

Yorke, Cole and the supersub Solskjær, who had set a record of his own by springing from the bench to score four times at Nottingham Forest the previous season, were finding the net so regularly that defensive problems could be absorbed. Stam was still sound, but alongside him Mikael Silvestre, the Frenchman whom Ferguson had bought from Internazionale for £3.5 million because of Johnsen's injuries, inspired less confidence. Although usefully able to play left-back as well, Silvestre was never to make much more than a squad player.

Not that you could call his acquisition a Ferguson blunder; to identify one of those from his post-treble summer, you would cite Massimo Taibi. He also came from Italy – from Venezia, after being discarded by Milan – and cost £4.5 million and was not around very long. The problem was that Peter Schmeichel, now thirty-six, had left for a lighter workload at Sporting Lisbon. Ferguson's first solution was to bring in Mark Bosnich from Aston Villa, where the Australian had become recognised as one of the Premier League's top goalkeepers, but it soon became apparent that he lacked the work ethic demanded by the manager.

Taibi had four matches. In one against Southampton he conceded a goal so comically, letting it run between his legs, that someone dubbed him 'the blind Venetian'. In the last of his four outings, United lost 5-0 at Chelsea. It was an extraordinary result for champions to sustain and, although the Italian was not wholly to blame, he was not picked again.

At the end of the season Bosnich was replaced by Fabien Barthez and this time Ferguson had got it right, though Barthez was hardly a discovery out of nowhere, given that he had won the Champions League with Olympique Marseille and both the World Cup and European Championship with France.

Bosnich went to Chelsea, where, in September 2002, he failed a drug test, incurring a nine-month ban from football. He later ascribed a cocaine habit to his relationship with the model Sophie Anderton. Eventually he rebuilt his career in Australia.

There was little else to report on the domestic front because Ferguson sent a limp gesture of a team to Aston Villa in the League Cup – Bosnich and Solskjær were the only semblances of first-teamers in a side beaten 3-0 – and United did not take part in the FA Cup at all, even though they were the holders. They were criticised for it, but the decision to go to Brazil for Fifa's inaugural Club World Championship instead had been taken after a request from the FA themselves, who were bidding to bring the World Cup to England in 2006 and had Sir Bobby

Charlton as the figurehead of their campaign. In the event Germany and Franz Beckenbauer were to win the Fifa vote, but United's dilemma was genuine.

However, the benefits to United of a mid-winter break in sunny Rio de Janeiro (they did not seem to take the tournament over-seriously, even though David Beckham was sent off in a match against the Mexican club Necaxa) must have been taken into account. They would certainly have been discernible to Ferguson, who wanted his players as fresh as possible for the closing stages of both the domestic championship and the Champions League.

It was a bigger than ever Champions League. Indeed, it seemed to go on for ever as Uefa's clubs all but killed the goose that laid the golden egg. There were two rounds of the group stage, which meant that successful teams would have played eight matches before Christmas – and even then been only a third of the way through the second group stage, with quarter-finals, semis and the final perhaps to come.

United, back from Brazil, topped their group but, after drawing scorelessly with Real Madrid in the Bernabéu, were knocked out at Old Trafford by the eventual winners.

After Roy Keane had sliced a cross past his own goalkeeper, Raimond van der Gouw, Raul scored twice, assisted by a piece of sorcery from Fernando Redondo that even United fans were moved to applaud. It was over. Beckham scored a dazzling solo goal and Paul Scholes put away a late penalty. The two further goals that were required in as many minutes proved beyond the powers of even Sheringham and Solskjær, whom Ferguson had sent on with the score 0-3. The holders were out. And it would take Ferguson another eight seasons to return to Europe's summit.

Threatening to Quit

The next season, 2000/2001, saw United again win the domestic League and fall in the Champions League quarter-finals. Again they had to plough through twelve group matches before the competition acquired an edge, but immediately Hitzfeld and Bayern Munich wreaked a measure of revenge for 1999, beating United home and away. Leeds United went one better, losing in the semi-finals to Valencia.

Barthez contributed a mixture of excellence and eccentricity in goal, Wes Brown continued to impress at the back and up front Sheringham and Solskjær outscored Yorke and Cole. The FA Cup, from which United were removed by a Paolo di Canio goal for West Ham at Old Trafford, and the League Cup both went to Liverpool, who completed a hat-trick by beating the Spanish club Alaves in the Uefa Cup final.

Ferguson had much – in the form of Cantona – for which to thank Liverpool's French manager and his relationship with Houllier remained excellent. If there were any mind games involved in their team's collisions, Houllier never noticed them. 'I think he had liked it when I defended David Beckham – I couldn't understand why English fans were booing him

[Beckham's popularity had been affected by his red card against Argentina in the 1998 World Cup] – and another time when I praised the passion for United shown by Gary Neville. Phil Thompson, who was my assistant at Liverpool, wondered if I'd gone a bit too far there!

'So Alex and I always got on well. He even told me he was gutted that I didn't get Manager of the Year in that season when we won the trophies [the award went to George Burley, whose Ipswich Town finished fifth in the League].'

That season Houllier's team beat Ferguson's home and away in the League. Wenger's Arsenal were the only other team to beat United until the closing stages of the season, when the title was won and Ferguson made a surprising declaration that his future might lie with another club.

He had been busy in the build-up to the concluding match, against Tottenham at White Hart Lane. On the Thursday he had attended a Labour election rally in Manchester alongside his friend Mick Hucknall, of Simply Red, and the veteran actor Sir John Mills. On the Friday he had raised football's eyebrows by announcing that he would sever his connections with United on the expiry of his contract in the summer of 2002, a year hence. The intention had been to hand over the manager-ship then and take an 'ambassadorial' role, but discussions between the club and his son Jason, who was now acting as his agent, had broken down.

This led some newspapers to bill the Saturday match as his last in charge of United. For a solid thirty minutes of the first half, which he spent in the directors' box, the travelling fans chanted his praises. As a follower of politics, he might have noted with satisfaction that even Michael Heseltine had never received that long an ovation from the Tory blue-rinses. In the second half, which Ferguson spent in the dugout, Spurs scored twice and United lost 3–1. But they did keep their manager.

It would, Ferguson said afterwards, be for one year only. He was open to suggestions about what to do thereafter. If another club wanted him as their manager, let them say so.

In the meantime, he would approach the next season at United with relish: 'I want to go out with my head held high, knowing I've enjoyed the sixteen years I'll have completed with the club. That's something worth remembering.'

As he spoke, Ferguson-watchers had to suppress pull-the-other-one smiles.

We remembered the leaks from him at around the same stage of the title-retrieval season of 1995/6, when he had been demanding a six-year contract to take him to the age of sixty. We suspected we were watching just another, albeit particularly dramatic, piece of negotiation – and so it proved – but my report for the *Sunday Telegraph* did add: 'He has always been determined to avoid the fate of the other great long-serving managers, notably the Scots with whom he most closely identifies: Jock Stein, who left Celtic after being offered the ridiculously inappropriate post of lottery manager; Bill Shankly, who said he wanted a clean break with Liverpool and became embittered after it happened; and of course Sir Matt Busby, whose continuing presence at Old Trafford was blamed for the failure of two successors, even if Ferguson, who came to the club much later, often expressed gratitude for the old man's advice.'

The further example of Scot Symon, whom Rangers so callously dismissed soon after he had signed Ferguson, I overlooked amid the urgency of the moment, but this had undoubtedly left a deep and lasting impression on him. Ferguson had developed a theory that management had become an increasingly complicated task, not least because of the proliferation of the media and the activity of agents, and that he could alleviate the burden of his successor as team manager by remaining at the club.

Sensing this during an interview before Christmas 2000, I had asked if Steve McClaren might be moved into the job with Ferguson as general manager, on the Italian model. 'That will be the club's decision,' he replied. 'But I don't think it would be easy for any one person to come in and do the job the way I'm doing it.' This was when he referred to the strength he had drawn from Busby: 'I was desperate to talk to Matt. One of the things people don't understand about managers is that sometimes you're alone and you don't want to be alone. People assume you're too busy.'

It was an argument that failed to persuade the board, despite the promotion from deputy chief executive of Peter Kenyon to replace Martin Edwards that year. Various ideas were explored – Ferguson might become a global envoy for the club, like Sir Bobby Charlton, or supervise youth development, or both, taking the title of president once held by Sir Matt – but negotiations kept stalling and a factor might have been the approach to them of Ferguson's representative. Jason Ferguson shared his father's fiery temper – he had it to a far greater degree than Darren, while Mark was relatively tranquil – and would sometimes show it during the discussions. Not every party to the talks thought this was such a helpful tactic.

Eventually his father had to go to the brink. Hence the end-of-season announcement that negotiations had failed and the threat that he might join a rival after his final year with United. It worked. To Kenyon's satisfaction, the board awarded Ferguson £3 million for the next year and thereafter a five-year contract worth a total of £7.5 million.

The Business with Jason

Sometimes Jason got in the way. As a child, he had from time to time annoyed staff and directors at Aberdeen Football Club with his scamperings. On one occasion, as a teenager, he had danced on the Wembley pitch after United's FA Cup final replay victory, briefly occupying the attention of police and stewards until his father intervened.

Upon settling down to the world of work, Jason had done well as a researcher with Granada television after being eased in by Paul Doherty, the head of sport and a friend of his father's. Andy Melvin, a former football reporter from Aberdeen who also knew his father, then got Jason into Sky when Rupert Murdoch's satellite broadcaster won the Premier League rights and here Jason truly impressed, rising to senior football director at the age of twenty-seven.

If only he had stayed in television.

Encouraged by his father, who thought him underpaid at Sky, he became an agent, a director of a little firm called L'Attitude in which his wife already had shares. In this venture Jason joined Kieran Toal, a former United youth player, and the man with the funds, Andy Dodd, who was a member of the Alex Ferguson network to the extent that he managed Mick Hucknall.

Jason continued to act for his father, helping to organise a testimonial year that was reported to have raised £1.4 million, some of which was donated to a cancer charity. In his autobiography, Ferguson had given a moving account of his dismay at conditions on the ward in which his late mother had been treated, and raged at 'the Tory government' for 'vandalising the National Health Service'; the charity bore his mother's name.

In the autumn of 2000, while the parties due to negotiate Ferguson's future were tuning up, United received an invoice for £25,000 from L'Attitude in connection with the transfer of Massimo Taibi to the Italian club Reggina for £2.5 million (£2 million less than United had paid). The money was reluctantly paid. But that proved the biggest earner of L'Attitude's short life and, after several vain attempts to make money on the rejects from United's youth system, the firm went out of business.

Its sales pitch had been straightforward and unsubtle according to two of the youngsters approached towards the end of the 1999/2000 season, Dominic Studley and Josh Howard, who were interviewed separately for Michael Crick's book two years later and between them told the most haunting tale of life behind United's glamorous facade.

Howard was a midfield player who had trained with United since adolescence, alongside Wes Brown among others, and become the captain of a youth team sometimes featuring Luke Chadwick, in whom Ferguson had such high hopes. The manager decided that Howard would fall short of the first team but told him he would 'make a living out of the game' and said other clubs had already been in touch. 'He asked who I had representing me and said I would need some help . . . then out of the blue I got a phone call off that Jason Ferguson . . . I thought it was a bit strange how he got my number.'

Howard went to meet Jason and Kieran Toal at L'Attitude's office in Manchester, where Jason said he had 'a lot of contacts' and promised to 'get some clubs interested'. Among those who subsequently got in touch, said Howard, were Aston Villa, Birmingham City and Preston North End. He and Studley, however, then encountered another agent, Mel Stein (well known to Alex Ferguson as the adviser to Paul Gascoigne, who had joined Tottenham instead of United because much more money was on offer), and the fee Stein was seeking – 3 per cent of any deal – seemed markedly more modest than L'Attitude's proposal.

The lads signed with Stein and, when Alex Ferguson found out, said Howard: 'He called us in the office and said "What the fuck are you doing signing with him?" Then he just said to us, "You can fuck off out of here and I hope he gets you a club because I won't."'

That night, said Studley, he and Howard rang Stein, who wrote Ferguson a letter of complaint about the lads' treatment and threatened legal action. They were called back to Ferguson's office. 'He was a bit slimy this time,' said Studley. 'He had Mike Phelan in the office with him . . . and me and Josh felt a bit intimidated by this because we were only young, only nineteen . . . and he read out the complaint that Mel Stein had written in to him and said to us, "Why have you said to Mel Stein that I said this? I didn't say this." And me and Josh just agreed with him and said "Yeah" because we felt intimidated . . . We just said to him, "We didn't say those things to him, he must be making it up."' Both Studley and Howard remembered Ferguson nodding to Phelan, as if confirming that his underling was witness to the retraction.

For the second time, Studley left Ferguson's office in tears, convinced that his career as a professional footballer was over, which was to prove more or less true. He drifted into parks football before making a semi-professional return in 2004 at Mossley, of the Unibond League Division One, but worked mainly as a personal trainer in Manchester.

Josh Howard got to Preston but could not adjust to living in 'grotty' lodgings and moved to Stockport County. There were further brief spells with Bristol Rovers, Barnet and three semi-professional clubs near his home north-east of Manchester — Stalybridge United, Hyde United and Mossley (with Studley) — before he settled with FC United of Manchester, a club formed by disillusioned Manchester United fans, in the North West Counties League Division One. He retired in his late twenties to pursue 'successful businesses'.

So neither Studley nor Howard ended up with glittering careers at Real Madrid or Barcelona and it would be ludicrous to claim that Ferguson ruined their prospects of such glory. Howard, reviewing the episode in 2010, a decade on, was realistic about it, volunteering the opinion that the likes of Chadwick had more talent and freely agreeing that Preston, whom he joined immediately after United, were one of those clubs whose calls followed the meeting with Jason Ferguson and Toal.

It is possible that Ferguson's anger was caused by a genuine belief that Jason and Kieran Toal represented the lads' best hope of continued employment in the game, and it may also be that Ferguson's recollections of these events differ from those of Studley and Howard.

Power and Control:
Alastair Campbell
(*top right*) and
Ferguson became
close as New Labour
rose to power.

Jason Ferguson's (*middle left*) involvement
as an agent in United transfers attracted
difficult questions, not least from John
Magnier (*middle right*) and J.P. McManus
who went to war with the manager
over stud rights to their shared horse,
Rock of Gibraltar (*right*).

Knocking them off their perch: Liverpool, managed by Kenny Dalglish (*above left*), and Arsenal, managed by George Graham (*above right*) were top dogs before Ferguson arrived at United.

Loving it: Ferguson also got the better of Kevin Keegan, after one of his infamous 'mind games' appeared to derail the Newcastle United manager.

Red, red whine: Jose Mourinho (*above*) regularly bettered Ferguson, who nevertheless shares a close rapport (and often a bottle of red) with his Portuguese nemesis. His relationship with Arsenal's Arsène Wenger (*below left*) (pictured with Carlos Queiroz, one of Ferguson's most capable assistants) and Rafa Benítez (*below right*) is much frostier.

Out with the old: Ferguson did not shy away from moving on big-names who crossed him like Jaap Stam and Ruud van Nistelrooy, (*above*) or those who ran out of steam like Roy Keane, (*below*).

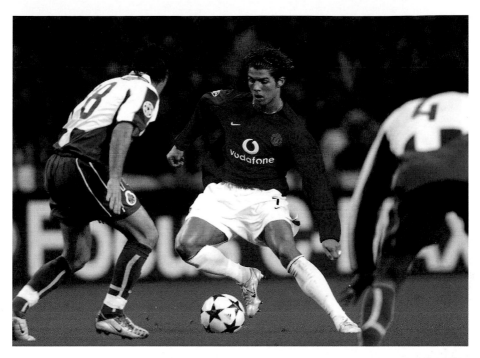

In with the new: Cristiano Ronaldo (*above*) bewitches defenders after arriving from Sporting Lisbon while Wayne Rooney, England's bright young star (*right*), was also a teenager when Ferguson secured him from Everton for £27 million.

Up for the cup: Cristiano Ronaldo's header gives Manchester United the lead in the 2008 Champion's League final against Chelsea.

Down and out: John Terry is inconsolable (*left*) after his missed spot-kick (*above*) costs Chelsea dearly in the subsequent penalty shoot-out.

Ronaldo celebrates winning the European Cup. A year later United's prize asset joined Real Madrid for a world-record fee.

Ferguson shows off the second European Cup that ensures his status as one of the all-time great managers.

Credit crunch: Malcolm Glazer's (*left*) takeover helped rescue Ferguson from Magnier and McManus, but the debt the Glazers burdened on the club has angered the Old Trafford faithful.

'Typical Germans': The current Manchester United team line-up prior to being knocked out of the 2010 Champions League by a Bayern Munich side that Ferguson claimed had influenced the referee.

Yet it still rankled with Howard that a 'headmaster' – that was how Ferguson had appeared to the errant pupils in his study in 2000 – could have behaved as he did. Or, as Studley put it: 'It just takes the piss a bit the way he did say it and then got us in the office again and had the cheek to say he actually didn't say it. He probably thought, "Oh no, I might get myself into trouble here . . ."'

If Studley and Howard were right, Ferguson was exhibiting a strange concept of loyalty, a refusal to be countermanded by someone weaker that takes the mind back to June Sullivan, the secretary at St Mirren all those years earlier whom he treated harshly – and was himself judged adversely for it.

The demise of L'Attitude followed in a matter of months. Not that this was to finish Jason's career as a transfer dealer. We were to hear a lot of it after his father fell out with two of United's major shareholders, John Magnier and J. P. McManus, over the racehorse Rock of Gibraltar, and it also contributed to the long-running feud with the BBC.

At the end of the summer of 2001, by which time Jason had joined a new agency, Elite Sports Group, came the sudden announcement that Jaap Stam was going to Lazio. Those who knew Ferguson's control-freak tendencies assumed it was to do with the embarrassment caused by Stam's book, but Ferguson insisted the deal was just good business. He had bought Stam for £10.6 million and here was the Italian club offering a profit of nearly £6 million on a twenty-nine-year-old who, Ferguson felt, had 'lost a bit' after an Achilles tendon injury. He later admitted being mistaken about that.

At any rate, it became known that Jason's Elite Sports Group had been key to the deal. This time the invoice was for a great deal more than £25,000 – and it went to Lazio. Yet Lazio also dealt with Mike Morris, an English agent based in Monaco, and at least one other agent was involved. Transfers can be murky affairs but what bothered United, and in particular the plc chairman Sir Roland Smith, was the involvement of the manager's son.

By now Ferguson senior earned £3 million a year plus endorsements and other income of which Jason, having turned his back on a career in television, was taking a slice; was it really necessary, the board asked, for him to risk the club's reputation by taking part in transfers? The question was to be put again, and in public. The answer seemed obvious enough. Of course it was not necessary. But it paid well.

No Wenger, No Eriksson –
Ferguson Stays

Jaap Stam was replaced by Laurent Blanc, who was slower than the supposedly creaking Dutchman – not surprisingly, at thirty-six and having apparently passed his best at Internazionale – and United conceded forty-five goals in the League.

They scored plenty with Ruud van Nistelrooy notching twenty-three in the thirty-two appearances of his first Premier League season. His capture had been classic Ferguson activity in the transfer market. It had started more than a year in advance. Every student of European football knew that the PSV Eindhoven striker was equipped for the very top. His value had swiftly risen from the £4.2 million PSV had paid Heerenveen to the £19 million United agreed. And then he collapsed in training; a cruciate ligament had gone and he would be out of football for a year.

In that time we saw two sides of Ferguson; by visiting Van Nistelrooy, constantly reassuring him, he showed enlightened humanity, but it irked PSV, who felt that he was disturbing the player's rehabilitation, for which the Dutch club, having already footed the bill for his operation, were paying. Whatever the rights and wrongs of Ferguson's visits, Van Nistelrooy recovered splendidly and proved an instant hit at old Trafford.

United could still finish only third, behind Arsenal and Liverpool. They made no impression on the domestic Cups and once again concentrated on the Champions League, looking especially strong in the second group stage and then in the quarter-finals as Deportivo La Coruña, who had beaten them at Old Trafford in the first group stage, were swept aside.

The final was to take place at Hampden Park, Glasgow, where a teenage Ferguson had gaped at the majesty of Real Madrid's triumph over Eintracht Frankfurt in 1960, and Ferguson, who seldom missed an opportunity to strengthen his team psychologically, encouraged the belief that some force might be drawing them to his home city in the evening of his career. The prospect that Real might be their opponents only enhanced this line of thought. In 2008 he was to use the fifth anniversary of the Munich air disaster to motivate his players, and with more emphasis, and, it might be claimed, successfully, for United were to beat Chelsea on penalties. But in 2002 they did not even reach the final.

They were ousted, like Rangers in 1960, by the German team destined to lose to Real in the final. Bayer Leverkusen came to Old Trafford with a young Bulgarian centre-forward of whom the stadium was to see more. But Dimitar Berbatov had left the field when the crucial goal was scored. Oliver Neuville, who had replaced him, made it 2-2.

Neuville also equalised at the BayArena, but it was his away goal that took Leverkusen — an excellent side, with Michael Ballack, Bernt Schneider and the wonderfully adventurous Brazilian centre-back Lúcio — to Glasgow, where they were undone by Zinedine Zidane's magnificent left-foot volley (a finer goal than any of the ten scored at Hampden in 1960).

And again Ferguson stayed on. It had been a strange season whose inconsistencies – encapsulated in a match at Tottenham that saw them deservedly 3-0 down at half-time yet emerge magnificent 5-3 winners – brought criticism from Roy Keane, by now seen as very much the manager's voice on the pitch. Keane had already poured scorn on the club's executive fans, with their 'drinks and probably their prawn sandwiches' and their ignorance of football, when he turned his attention to unnamed team-mates who were, he thought, shirking (Ferguson later ascribed a loss of dressing-room concentration to his own announcement that he was to quit).

In *The Times*, after one of two more defeats at the hands of Houllier's Liverpool, it was said to be 'a season too far, a fight too many for the ageing heavyweight' Ferguson. He added to an air of indecision with conflicting messages to pals in the press, telling Bob Cass of the *Mail on Sunday* that he might change his mind about leaving and, when other papers rightly made a fuss of this, saying to Glenn Gibbons of the *Scotsman*: 'I'm going all right. That's been settled for some time now.'

While *Scotsman* readers were digesting that, Ferguson and his family went out for lunch. They had converged on his Cheshire home to celebrate the New Year and, after returning from the meal, continued to talk while Ferguson went to sleep in an armchair. This was the account he gave me years later. I had reminded him of the apparent relish with which he had spoken of retirement; he had even named an event, the Melbourne Cup horse race, which he planned to attend in Australia in the autumn. Not only that; he had stressed Cathy's entitlement to more of his time. 'Then I changed my mind,' he said. 'Or Cathy changed it for me.

'I was regretting what I'd done anyway. I realised I'd been a bit hasty. So there we were as a family, all together, and I was snoozing when Cathy came and kicked my foot. I opened my eyes and the three of them [Mark, Darren and Jason] were standing behind her. And she said, "We've decided you're no' retiring." I think Manchester United had interviewed someone for the job.'

This was an understatement. They had lined up Sven-Göran Eriksson after failing in an audacious attempt to wrest Wenger from Arsenal about which Ferguson, his great rival, may not have known. Around that time I asked Ferguson if Wenger might not be a good choice. He shrugged and ventured the thought that the Old Trafford crowd might not accept him. It was a chance the board appeared more than willing to take. But Wenger decided to stay at Arsenal and so they went for Eriksson. It was some time after they and Eriksson had shaken hands that the board realised they would not be needing him. For Ferguson had kept the outcome of the family conference to himself for several weeks.

Fifteen months earlier, he had become involved in the FA's search for a replacement for Kevin Keegan as England manager. Adam Crozier, a fellow Scot who was FA chief executive at the time, came to him principally to ask if Steve McClaren could join a team of English coaches to work with the new man; he agreed to this. Then Crozier took the opportunity to ask Ferguson's opinion of Eriksson, who was then with Lazio in Italy; again he spoke positively. But his regard for Eriksson seemed not to have survived the Swede's apparently impressive first year with the England team – it had featured a 5–1 victory over Germany in Munich – and this may have owed something to United's notion that Eriksson could succeed Ferguson.

Ferguson waited a year and then gave an interview to *The Times* in which he sneered: 'I think Eriksson would have been a nice easy choice for them. He doesn't change anything. He sails along and nobody falls out with him . . . I think he'd have been all right for United – the acceptable face.' Carlos Quieroz, who had replaced McClaren as his assistant when the Englishman went to manage Middlesbrough in the summer of 2001, knew Eriksson from Portugal, where Eriksson had been in charge of Benfica. 'Carlos says what he did well was that he never fell out with anyone. He was best pals with the president and the press liked him. I think he does that. The press makes a suggestion and he seems to follow it.'

Eriksson never responded to that. Not even when, as manager of Manchester City in 2007/8, he supervised home and away victories over Manchester United. 'I do feel things strongly,' he once said during his time as England manager. 'It's just that I'm not very good at expressing emotion.' We may never, then, know how he felt upon hearing that United no longer wanted him. Possibly a bit like Blackburn Rovers felt when, in 1997, he changed his mind about joining them and went to Lazio instead.

Terms had been agreed between United and Eriksson, but he was not to have started at Old Trafford until he had seen England through the World Cup in the Far East that summer. A United deputation had arranged a meeting in London with the FA – the subject had not been specified, but it was to be the official proper-channels approach for Eriksson – and the very day before the relevant directors were due to travel south Ferguson rang one of them, Maurice Watkins, and announced his change of heart.

At the subsequent board meeting, joy was not unconfined; there would be more arguments over money, more ear-bashings, more furies – despite Bobby Charlton's bizarre assertion in his autobiography that he had never seen Ferguson lose his temper, another director testified to a tray of glasses having been dashed to the boardroom floor – and more years of hiatus in which the post-Ferguson era had merely been deferred. And no guarantee that the Keystone Kops defending of the first half of the season was not a sign of things to come. And maybe more signings as ill-starred as that of Juan Sebastián Verón, who cost nearly £29 million and whose first season in the midfield had done little but disrupt it. Ferguson was lucky to have the almost fanatical support of Peter Kenyon, who, upon taking over from Edwards as chief executive, had publicly declared that his first priority was to get the manager to think again about retiring.

Three more years were agreed. Ferguson asked for £4 million a year and got £3.6 million. Then, in the summer of 2005, he said, there would be a clean break.

Most observers were pleased he would be around a little longer. United, while incapable of living with an Arsenal who won the Double in a style epitomised by Thierry Henry, had played attractively in the second half of the season. Particularly once David Beckham, by now frequently falling out with Ferguson over the celebrity lifestyle he was developing since his marriage to Victoria, aka Posh Spice, had returned after a few matches' 'rest'.

And, as for Ferguson himself, most people had understood that his appetite for the game remained. We had been reminded of St Augustine's attitude to chastity. Ferguson wanted the joys of leisure, diversity and travels with his wife . . . but not yet.

To a Long Life

Ferguson ascribed his longevity as a manager to four factors. One concerned mental equipment and fell under the sub-heading of enthusiasm and determination. Another was health. He also claimed to have reaped the benefits of delegation and, finally, learned to switch his mind from football to the joys, which included fresh air and banter, of horse-racing.

The story of Ferguson's relationship with horse-racing while manager of Manchester United is a fascinating one. It began with him in debt and ended with United owing infinitely more. The main beneficiaries were bookies and banks.

But first let us deal with delegation. Ferguson had been at Old Trafford only a few months before its attractions became evident to him and a staff of eight began to grow to nearly forty. He managed to resist the inevitable letters from sports psychologists with their talk of positive thinking and visualisation. Then Trevor Lea materialised: 'A sports nutritionist. He was the start of it, of introducing things.'

To hear Ferguson talk of Lea's revelations – this was in 2006 and even the infamous reliance on lifestyle coaches of his friends the Blairs seemed more than a little passé – cast him in a charmingly naive light: 'Trevor was working at the University of Manchester and, when somebody told me about him, I called him in. And he started telling me about what my body was. It was fantastic. He explained to me that it was historic. Your body thinks a famine is coming and that's why you gorge yourself – because you don't think there's another meal coming. I'd never heard that before. And then he started to explain what he does, and I took him on.

'Then we had a doctor come in to do a weight-training programme, and he said we really should get a full-time weight trainer. So we did. For speed and strength. Then we got a full-time doctor. I always remember that, at Aberdeen, my biggest challenge was to get a second physio. And they let me have one three months before I left! Here I've got five physios.'

He was like a kid in a sweetshop: 'We got an optometrist – and a podiatrician who comes in three days a week to look after the players' feet. Bit by bit, we've added things because we know they are important. And you have to let them get on with it. You have to delegate.' In this context, the academy system had helped him because he was obliged to delegate to Eric Harrison and later Brian McClair, whom he appointed academy director.

Long gone were the days when Ferguson constituted his own youth-development staff. Now McClair and Ferguson's longest serving assistant, the former Luton Town manager and United winger Jimmy Ryan, would identify the young talent, whether in England, Europe, Africa or South America, and all Ferguson had to do was charm the parents. 'I come in at that stage. I let the experts do their jobs and it's been easy for me because age makes you delegate. If I was still in control of the youth side, I think I'd be worn out by now.'

And it was partly an instinct for self-preservation that drew him to the horses. He had always bet on them, of course, but then he experienced an urge to get closer. It was to do with the job; he was still trying to do too much. 'I was going home at night and getting straight on the phone to the scouts. It was becoming an obsession. Football was taking me over and eating into me. In the sense that I'd nothing else. *Nothing.*' And then one day he was invited to the Cheltenham Festival as part of a group hosted by Mike Dillon, public relations manager for Ladbrokes and a United fan.

He took Cathy – 'it was our anniversary,' he explained – and enjoyed it immensely. 'So I says to Cathy, "Do you want to buy a horse?" She says, "What do you want to buy a horse for?" I said I thought I needed a release. She said I was right there – but why a horse? I said, "I don't know – I've just got a wee bit of excitement about it." So she says okay. And I did find it a great release.

'You'd go down to Newmarket after a European tie on the Wednesday night, say, getting the 6.40 flight to Stansted on the Thursday morning. You could be at Newmarket in twenty minutes. You're out there on the gallops – and nobody can get you! You're watching the horses train and taking in the fresh air. And I'd come back into training on the Friday and be fucking buzzing!'

According to Ferguson, this was a significant factor in his career's extension far beyond the 2005 deadline set when Eriksson was lined up and stood down (the Swede went on to guide England to the quarter-finals of two World Cups and a European Championship before being replaced by McClaren). Ferguson stopped visiting Newmarket after a few years, but still could not resist the horses. In 2006 he confessed:

'I bought a new one in the October sales for a lot of money. I didn't tell Cathy about it. But she found out. She read it in a newspaper. She came to me pointing at it and said, "What is this – are you trying to bankrupt us?" So I put the horse in her name to keep her happy – and let her name it.'

Racing, though, had proved a mixed blessing – and far from the blissful release from football-related worries that Ferguson had envisaged.

It was his own fault. His tendency to get over-involved soon surfaced as Dillon introduced him around and he became a member of an owners' club (later he helped to start one for Manchester United supporters that flopped dismally). As a sporting celebrity, he was warmly welcomed at meetings. Except, he felt, by the snobbier members of the sport's establishment. So he was always going to get on with John Magnier. They were both what the middle classes would call 'chippy'.

Magnier was self-made. He had bought Coolmore Stud in County Tipperary in Ireland and become one of the world's top breeders. He was therefore extremely rich. He and his friend J. P. McManus, a big-time gambler and fellow Irishman, gladly took Ferguson into their circle and soon – in the summer of 1999, while Ferguson was basking in the afterglow of Champions League triumph and trying to fit book-signing sessions into his schedule – came the first reports of Magnier and McManus taking an interest in Manchester United.

There was little alarm among the sort of fans who monitor such matters; they liked the idea of an alliance between Ferguson and rich men who were presumed (quite wrongly) to have only football at heart.

A few months later, it emerged that the Irishmen had set up a company, Cubic Expressions, which had bought a small package of United shares. Within six months they were United's second biggest shareholders, owning nearly 7 per cent. And still fans fantasised that they would constitute Ferguson's power base and keep him at the club, stronger than at any stage under the chairmanship of the lucratively fading Edwards, who had already made nearly £80 million from selling shares.

A year on, Magnier offered Ferguson a share in the two-year-old stallion Rock of Gibraltar, which promptly won seven Group One races in succession. Ferguson was at Longchamps in September 2002 as it passed the six-race mark set by Mill Reef thirty years earlier. So this was no ordinary beast and, when it was retired that November, its stud value was estimated at £50 million.

Amid speculation that Ferguson might be about to earn more than £4 million a year from his gift's sexual activities, he wrote to Magnier shortly before Christmas asking about his 'rights' and the slow-burning fuse was lit on a very large bomb.

There was plenty to keep him occupied with his core activity at Old Trafford. Not only those European nights after which he would clear his head at Newmarket; perhaps influenced by the trophy drought of the previous season, he sent a strong side into the League Cup fifth-round meeting with Chelsea at Old Trafford and was rewarded with a winner from the Uruguayan striker Diego Forlán, for whom he had paid the Argentine club Independiente nearly £7 million on the recommendation of his brother Martin. Another summer signing, the expensive Verón, also played and, unlike Forlán, stayed in the side until the final, which United lost to Liverpool at the Millennium Stadium, Cardiff.

They were knocked out of the FA Cup by Arsenal in the

fifth round, at Old Trafford, in a match that left little doubting the rancour between the teams and their managers and so irked Ferguson that he accidentally injured Beckham by kicking a boot during a post-match tantrum (an outraged and bleeding Beckham had to be dragged away from him, like Mark McGhee at Aberdeen all those years before). But by then United had the higher priority of a charge towards the League title.

The Iraq Diaries

United had begun the 2002/3 season poorly and it was the day before a Kevin Nolan goal gave Bolton Wanderers victory at Old Trafford when Ferguson rang Alastair Campbell to say he was 'really worried' – about Iraq.

To be more precise, he was worried about the Government's involvement with the United States in the impending invasion of that country. Despite all the footballing issues on his mind, Ferguson's political antennae were at work and he cared enough to pass on their message. According to Campbell's diaries: 'He said he thought it [Iraq] was a very dangerous situation for TB [Tony Blair]. I said TB had a real sense of certainty on this one.'

Apparently Ferguson was also 'on the rampage' about the press and 'said we had to do something, they were out of control'. It is unlikely that, when Ferguson and Campbell spoke, the words 'press' and 'control' were ever very far apart.

In more than politics they seemed to dovetail: they shared a distrust of the media. In *A History of Modern Britain* Andrew Marr notes that Campbell had worked in 'the dirtiest, most cynical end of the newspaper market' and come away thinking most journalists were idle liars, as well as biased against Labour. 'He was tribal and assumed the rest of the world was too.' On his watch New Labour became the most media-obsessed party in British political history (perhaps understandable given his experience of the Kinnock years) but, wrote Marr, damage was done to politics generally.

Meanwhile, Ferguson, at least on the occasions of his touchline rants, criticism of referees and ill-concealed antipathy towards what would otherwise have been a relatively friendly section of the media, could be said to have done little for the dignity of football, even if the attractive manner in which he got his teams to perform unquestionably brightened our lives.

The Premier League that 2002/3 season was won — United's eighth under Ferguson — and the manager was heading for America on holiday when, early one morning on the *Today* programme on BBC Radio Four, John Humphrys interviewed the defence correspondent Andrew Gilligan, who alleged that Downing Street had 'sexed up' a dossier about Iraq's having weapons of mass destruction.

At length it became known that Gilligan had spoken to David Kelly, a respected scientist who worked for the Government. A committee of MPs summoned Kelly and asked if he was the informant. He denied it, but unconvincingly, and then took a knife and some analgesics and went for a walk in the woods from which he did not return.

Two weeks later, Campbell received a call from Ferguson in the United States and told him, who knew he had been restless for some time, that he was to resign. Ferguson was sympathetic to both Campbell and his partner, Fiona, to whom he offered 'my congratulations'. He told Campbell he had 'done a great job' and should now do what he felt was right for himself and his family, adding: 'You've given enough.'

Campbell departed at the end of the first inquiry, chaired by Lord Hutton, into events leading to Dr Kelly's death. Its report found largely in the Government's favour and against the BBC. The impression it left was that Kelly had spoken loosely and without as much knowledge as Gilligan had suggested. But a second inquiry, in March 2010, under Sir John Chilcot, saw Campbell and Blair called to a court of increasingly hostile public opinion about the war as a whole.

Ferguson's words of warning back in 2002 had been vindicated and Campbell and Blair, though the latter's 'real sense of certainty' appeared still to be in place, may have had more than one occasion on which to reflect on the educated political instinct of their friend from Old Trafford.

Then came the collapse of the global economic system and, although the scandal over MPs' expenses affected all parties, the Government headed by Gordon Brown bore the brunt of public disaffection. In the election of May 2010, the Labour Party lost the keys to Nos 10 and 11 Downing Street. Ferguson had remained loyal to the cause, appearing in a television programme to extol the virtues of Brown and the party. Perhaps the supportive profile was a little lower than before. Or maybe it was just that Ferguson's energies were focused on the other cause, lost three days after the election when Chelsea's title was confirmed. At any rate, as one observer put it, 'the curtains were drawn on New Labour'. Thirteen years, it was, since Ferguson had rung Campbell to suggest he draw Tony Blair's curtains on the new dawn.

The Rock and a Hard Place

That 2002/3 season had been one in which Ferguson, when he managed to turn away from work, became increasingly concerned about not just Iraq but his understanding with Magnier and McManus over the horse; he wanted to know just how rich he was going to become.

On the field, though, things went as he liked them to go, at least in the League, with a gathering momentum that might have reminded him of the Rock's pounding hooves.

In late November, missing their injured captain, United had lain as low as fifth, but Roy Keane returned and, with Van Nistelrooy in riotous form, led them to the top. Their last League defeat was on Boxing Day. Once more Arsenal had been eclipsed (though Wenger's men lifted the FA Cup) and towards the end of the season record Premier League crowds of nearly 68,000 at Old Trafford underlined United's growth, although already Ferguson was pushing the directors to expand the ground further.

In the Champions League, United had been obliged to pre-qualify, but then it was the usual procession through the two group stages, lent additional excitement by the quality of home and away victories over Juventus and the mouth-watering fact that the final was to be at Old Trafford. Beat Juventus and you win the trophy: it was not a bad rule at the time and it proved reliable. Milan beat Juventus in the final, Andrei Shevchenko converting the decisive penalty on the turf that Beckham, Keane and Van Nistelrooy called home.

United had gone out in the quarter-finals to Real Madrid, who were 3-0 up at the Bernabéu when Van Nistelrooy pulled one back. The return match was wonderfully dramatic, even though Ronaldo, the Brazilian who had been leading scorer at the previous year's World Cup, seemed to have killed it as a contest with his first goal in the twelfth minute. He scored again after Van Nistelrooy had struck, and yet again after an Ivan Helguera own goal and departed to a standing ovation from United and Real fans alike. Beckham then scored twice, following up a free-kick with a less characteristic dribble and drive, to give United victory on the night.

Almost overlooked in the excitement was Ferguson's apparently bizarre decision to start the match with Beckham on the bench; their relationship had become increasingly tense amid rumours that Real were taking an interest. As soon as Beckham had taken over from Verón, the threat of a thrashing was lifted and United obtained the consolation of victory on a glowing night. Roman Abramovich was a guest at that most memorable match – his ticket had been ordered by the agent Pini Zahavi – and legend has it that he decided there and then to buy a Champions League club. Price, availability and location, apparently, all gave Chelsea the edge over United.

United shares, meanwhile, had been steadily accumulated by Magnier and McManus, but any popular notion that Ferguson would benefit had been dispelled. Quite the opposite;

early in 2003, just as United were finding the form that was to carry them to the title, Ferguson began to pursue the matter of the stud fees for Rock of Gibraltar. He followed up his letter to Coolmore with a telephone call and then contacted the stud registrars and, with the feeling a man gets in the pit of his stomach when a multi-million-pound invoice is disputed, learned that his name was not specifically entered next to the Rock's.

Ferguson and Magnier started to talk (McManus stood aside, while supporting Magnier's version of events). Magnier made various offers over a period of months, culminating in one of £300,000 a year for the entirety of the Rock's stud career – expected to be about twenty years – or a flat payment of £7 million. Ferguson rejected this but now reduced his demand for 50 per cent of the horse's earnings to 20 per cent.

Talking to both parties all the while was Dermot Desmond, the leading shareholder in Celtic. He was friendly with Ferguson, who had helped him to persuade Martin O'Neill to manage the Glasgow club, and very close to Magnier and McManus, not just at Coolmore but in other ventures, including a Barbados hotel.

Desmond had also bought some shares in United; his stake was about 1.5 per cent. The Glazer family, owners of an American football franchise and, at that stage, thought to be merely exploring the potential of European 'soccer', held a little more. Harry Dobson, a Scottish mining entrepreneur, had bought 6.5 per cent and John de Mol, the Dutchman responsible for *Big Brother*, 4.1 per cent. Cubic by now had 10.4 per cent, taking it above the 9.9 per cent of Sky, making the Irishmen the club's leading shareholders. And still the public perception was of Ferguson's horse-racing cronies steadily buying in. It even survived a report that Paddy Harverson, United's head of communications, had spoken disparagingly of the Irish to a journalist. Naturally this angered Magnier. If Ferguson, whom he regarded as part of the United establishment, wanted a fight, he could have one. Heels were dug in. Ferguson engaged Dublin lawyers for a court case over the stud fees that would have to be heard in Ireland.

Magnier's Gloves Come Off

The dispute hit the streets around the time that United were completing the £12.4 million signing of Cristiano Ronaldo.

At first – strange as it may be to recall – the Portuguese teenager was widely regarded as flashy, a show pony, an inadequate replacement for Beckham, who had been sold to Real Madrid a couple of months after their spectacular visit to Old Trafford. Signings also included Eric Djemba Djemba, Kléberson and David Bellion. The assumption that Ferguson had a just case against Magnier protected him from criticism; the newspapers took his side.

Ferguson and controversy were, however, recurrent companions. The previous season, at around the time he was absorbing the realisation that Magnier would fight him for the stud money, there had been the incident of the flying boot in the dressing room that cut Beckham's eyebrow and had the player advancing on Ferguson until Ryan Giggs restrained him. Now Ferguson, after haranguing match officials at Newcastle, was banished to the stands.

Then he took on the FA when Rio Ferdinand missed a drug test, making irate phone calls to the organisation's head of communication, Paul Barber. 'This is a fucking disgrace,' he stormed, once again rallying behind a member of the United family in his perceived hour of need. 'You're killing the boy's reputation.'

The truth was that any damage to Ferdinand's reputation was self-inflicted in that he had forgotten to take the routine test at Carrington – he had driven off to go shopping while the three other chosen players gave their samples – and left the FA with no alternative but to omit him from the England squad to travel to Istanbul for a European Championship qualifying match. Had he been included and played, Uefa would have been entitled to throw England out of the tournament. Ferguson should have known this. Instead, he furiously accused the FA of 'hanging the boy out to dry' – a phrase repeated by Gary Neville as the players rallied round their grounded colleague, even debating a boycott of the trip that would have benefited only the Turkish hosts.

It was an example of how Ferguson's United circled their wagons. Even David Gill, who had recently taken over from Peter Kenyon as chief executive, stood defiant alongside Ferguson and his errant defender.

And then Ferguson asked for a new contract to take him to 2007 and the age of sixty-five.

This only confirmed Magnier's assumptions about the politics of Old Trafford. Ferguson had the board and the new chief executive – Gill had been promoted when Abramovich's riches lured Kenyon to Chelsea – firmly with him. The battle lines were being drawn and the power of Magnier's artillery soon became evident as it emerged that Cubic had bought out Sky, increasing its stake to 23.15 per cent. The Glazers had 9.6 per cent and by now were seen as the good guys.

In November, with United trailing not only a rampant Arsenal but Chelsea under Claudio Ranieri, Ferguson's writ arrived in Dublin. He was now arguing that the Rock's value had been enhanced by association with his name and Magnier's lawyers, dismissing his case as 'without merit', promised a vigorous retort.

A token of Magnier's determination was detected at the United AGM, during which noticeably well-informed share-holder representatives, whom Michael Crick found to be actors, asked questions about the conduct of transfers. Around the same time stories about various deals appeared in the *Sunday Times*. Anyone seeking to probe Ferguson's vulnerabilities – and Magnier had hired corporate investigators – would have concentrated on this area. In particular there had been the embarrassment over the activities of Jason Ferguson in trans-fers and Sir Roland Smith's unhappiness, before his death and replacement as plc chairman by Sir Roy Gardner, about Elite's having received up to £1.5 million in connection with Jaap Stam's move to Lazio.

The fact that Lazio had paid it might well have heightened Sir Roland's concern. He could have been forgiven for asking himself: why had the Romans been so grateful – might United have got a better deal?

Jason and his father also featured in Tom Bower's acclaimed book *Broken Dreams: Vanity, Greed and the Souring of British Football*: 'Agents discovered that Sir Alex encouraged players seeking transfers in and out of the club to abandon their estab-lished agents and engage Jason Ferguson . . .' He may, of course, have done so because of his absolute trust in Jason and distaste for agents in general (with exceptions, such as the disgraced Hauge). But he must have known that others might take a different view of Jason's involvement in Stam's departure, the engagement of Laurent Blanc and the arrival from Wigan Athletic of Roy Carroll, a goalkeeper with a weakness for gambling.

A failure to take account of this proved self-damaging. When Magnier heard that Ferguson was not only seeking a long-term contract extension but expressing confidence that Gill would arrange it, the gloves came off.

Even the discovery that Ferguson, after encountering a heart murmur, was to have a pacemaker fitted became relevant: was it responsible in these circumstances for the club to commit itself for four more years? Ferguson laughed off his difficulty, saying the players had been shocked to discover he had a heart. But Magnier was no laughing matter – and not for turning back.

In January 2004 he sent the board a letter containing the famous '99 questions'. They found their way into the *Daily Mail* (by coincidence a paper against which Ferguson had held a long-standing grudge) and the issues raised included 'conduct of player transfers', 'commissions paid in relation to large transactions', 'accuracy of presentation of financial data in annual accounts' and 'conflicts of interest'. This seemed to be the crux of it: 'There are some individual transfers where the fees and payments made to players and agents are particularly large . . . what we cannot understand is the necessity for the relative secrecy in which the agents conduct their role and also the astonishing fees which have been charged to the company on the completion of transfers.'

Manchester United was not the only club where such questions could be asked. Football was – and is – a very dubiously run industry and few were greatly shocked when, towards the end of 2009, it was disclosed that Premier League clubs alone had paid a total of £71 million in one year to intermediaries in transfers.

Why anything needs to be paid to these people, who used to be confined to the perfectly legitimate and desirable sphere of player representation, is the big question. Clubs are perfectly capable of arranging their own transfers and many observers of the game have long believed that the practice of agents acting for clubs (as distinct from players) is institutionally corrupt, however legal, accepted and commonplace.

So naturally, as Ferguson paid a call on his old foes the FA to assure them he had nothing to fear from the investigation, there was some relish for the notion of Magnier shining a light into the corners of United's business. But I warned the readers of the *Sunday Telegraph*: 'Just lose no sleep in your excitement at the prospect of a court battle bristling with allegations – because there won't be one. While Magnier and Ferguson share a gift for the taking of tough postures – one is strong and silent, the other amusingly ebullient – nothing scares such men like disclosure. The case will be settled.'

Sadder and Wiser

Ferguson must have wished it could go to a jury of United supporters. At the next home match – a 3-2 victory over Southampton in which Louis Saha, signed from Fulham, scored on his debut – a chant of 'Stand up if you love Fergie' was ignored only by the visitors' section (and the press and directors' boxes, where etiquette forbids such display). There were less supportive chants about Magnier and where he could stick his ninety-nine questions. But the red hordes and their circled wagons could not protect Ferguson now. There was only one way out and, upon telephoning Magnier in Barbados, he discovered that it amounted to surrender.

Yes, said Magnier, there could be an out-of-court settlement, but it would be on his terms. There would be no half-share of the £100 million some had guessed the Rock might eventually earn, or anything like it. There would not even be the £7 million Ferguson had so rashly turned down, or even half of it. He got £2.5 million. Having lost the Rock, he was scarcely in the hardest of places. But the relaxing properties of the racecourse? Ferguson and Cathy were a sadder and wiser couple.

As Ferguson had often said of his football teams, however, the mark is made not by defeat but the response to it. On the night of 9 March, as he came to terms with Magnier's victory, United went out of the Champions League at Old Trafford. They led Porto on away goals until the ninetieth minute, when Tim Howard could only claw down a free-kick from Benni McCarthy and Costinha stabbed the loose ball into the net. Porto's manager celebrated wildly, running along the touchline in a coat that was to become familiar; the following spring José Mourinho was to return to Old Trafford in charge of Chelsea, its newly hailed champions.

In that 2003/4 season, he guided Porto to further victories over Lyon, Deportivo La Coruña and, in the final, Chelsea's conquerors, Monaco, adding the Champions League to the Uefa Cup that Porto had won the previous season. At Old Trafford, they had been lucky in that Paul Scholes was denied a second goal before half-time by a flag erroneously raised for offside. But Ferguson took defeat with a sportsmanship that did him credit, especially given that United had failed even to reach the quarter-finals (the Champions League had finally abandoned the second group stage, instead having a round of sixteen) for the first time in eight years. As Glenn Moore noted in the *Independent*: 'In times past, Ferguson would have headed, this morning, for the gallops. Now even that release is denied him.'

A few of us briefly entertained the notion that Ferguson might be entering his darkest spell since the winter of 1989/90. Only briefly. On the Friday after the European exit he looked forward to a derby at the City of Manchester Stadium (rivals City having moved from Maine Road in 2005) despite a rash of injuries: 'I'm not telling you how many are out – you wouldn't bloody believe it!' United lost 4-1, but by now they had only one realistic target and eventually they hit it by beating Millwall, from the division below, at Cardiff in the FA Cup final. Along the way they had overcome Manchester City, Aston Villa, Fulham and in the semi-finals – with the unceremonious approach to tackling that often marked confrontations with their keenest rivals – Arsenal. In the final one goal came from Ronaldo and another two from Van Nistelrooy, who finished with thirty in all competitions. Only Arsenal's Thierry Henry, who took the second of three Footballer of the Year awards, was more feared.

And Ferguson could look forward to the summer, in which he would watch Ronaldo's Portugal put an England without Ferdinand out of the European Championship as Beckham failed from the penalty spot, knowing that the argument about who should profit from the sex-slave horse was behind him. As I wrote at the time: 'Although we are told Magnier and McManus still want answers to the 99 questions they have put to the United board, anyone working on the assumption that the Irishmen are ethical zealots is probably also in the habit of saving extracted teeth for the fairies and going to sleep on the night of December 24 only after making sure the sherry and mince-pies are ready for Father Christmas.'

Ferguson had known that much about his adversaries. He had lost his high-stakes gamble and, in the process, his campaign for a long-term contract; he was handed a one-year rolling agreement. The board decided to publish payments to agents in future and not to use Jason or Elite. But the immediate threat to the manager's position had been lifted and early the next season he would have Ferdinand back. The defender had incurred an eight-month ban for missing the drug test.

He had appealed and, before the hearing, Ferguson was asked if he would obtain a reduction. 'If he doesn't,' said Ferguson, 'I'll be going to the United Nations.' Kofi Annan was spared that experience. But Ferdinand had to serve his time.

UNITED:
RONALDO AND ROONEY

Wine with Mourinho

The 2003/4 season had been dramatic enough, but in a chilling way: one in which the wind of change had come all the way from Siberia.

It was Roman Abramovich's first season as owner of Chelsea and, although the team had finished a creditable second to the 'Invincibles' of Arsenal, he ended it by sacking the Italian manager, the affable Claudio Ranieri, whose desk had hardly been cleared when José Mourinho introduced himself.

For the Special One it was to be a far from ordinary inauguration to England's Premier League – the 2004/5 season began with a visit to Stamford Bridge of Ferguson's United – and Mourinho remembered it clearly, in detail.

Not least because of the culture shock: 'It was the first time in my life I went to an important game without being with my team in a hotel. The game was at three o'clock and we met at Stamford Bridge at 12.30. For me this was a completely new experience. In Portugal, in Spain and in Italy people concentrate for one, two or even three days before – everyone else is outside the walls.

'This was England, so I tried it the English way. I walked

through the streets because my house was near the ground and, as I'm crossing the King's Road with my assistants, I'm thinking – in a couple of hours we're playing Manchester United! Stamford Bridge was empty. Everything was so quiet. Incredible!

'I remember the game clearly too – a typical first game of the season. Not good quality. Not big emotion. A game for the first team to score.' Eidur Gudjohnsen scored for Chelsea. 'After that, we defended. We closed the door. They had a couple of chances, but we won.'

And afterwards Mourinho came to understand one of the traditions Ferguson enjoyed: that of sharing a good bottle of red wine.

They had got on well the previous season, despite Porto's late victory and the linesman's blunder that had permitted it. But those two matches in the Champions League did not signify the first acquaintance, even if Mourinho doubted that Ferguson would recall meeting him with Sir Bobby Robson back in 1996, when Robson was manager of Barcelona and Mourinho officially his translator (though Robson had seen enough of the younger man at Sporting Lisbon and Porto to have encouraged his involvement in training and match preparation).

Day after day, Robson would talk to Mourinho about the English game, its characteristics and its personalities. 'Sir Alex was one of the legends,' said Mourinho, 'and even Bobby, who was a legend of English football in his own right, spoke of him with great respect. And of course Manchester United had a great meaning for me as well.'

One day Ferguson flew over with Martin Edwards and Maurice Watkins to arrange the transfer to United of Jordi Cruyff. The host delegation chose a restaurant. On one side were the Barcelona president, Josep Lluís Núñez, and vice-president, Joan Gaspart, with Robson and Mourinho. On the other were Edwards, Watkins and Ferguson. 'And here I was,' Mourinho recalled, 'in the midst of a business deal between these two big clubs.

'This was typical of how I learned about managerial stuff with Bobby. In Portugal or Spain, it would not have been normal for the coach to be involved. I realised then that England was different. It was a perfect example of what Bobby had been telling me.'

Even after a decade at United, Ferguson appears to have been just as hands-on as at Aberdeen when it came to transfers. He was very much involved in the Cruyff deal. 'His ideas were very clear,' said Mourinho. 'He was fighting hard for his club. And an understanding of that dimension of management made me take an even greater interest in the English game, to fall in love with it even before I came.

'I had always thought that the coach should not just do a training session a day, then go home and watch a couple of videos of the opposition and come in and do the same thing the next day. And here I saw the English style of management – and it was Sir Alex.'

At that time it was plain Alex. Nearly eight years later, Sir Alex's United drew Porto in the first knockout round of Champions League. First they played at the Dragão and there was no opportunity for post-match memories of Barcelona. Towards the end United, who had led through Quinton Fortune, lost to Benni McCarthy's second goal and had Roy Keane sent off for what seemed a light tread on the back of the home goalkeeper, Vitor Baía. 'Most people thought Sir Alex was going mad about it after the game,' said Mourinho. 'But for me — especially now that I have got to know him — he was not mad. He was starting to play the second game.'

It began in the tunnel. 'He and I were walking to the dressing rooms at the same time and he was shaking hands with me but not looking at me because the referee was coming behind us and Alex was complaining in his Scottish accent about the referee's decisions. I didn't interfere. I just let him get on with it.

'At that moment, I think, he felt he was in trouble. I think Manchester United had gone into the game with respect, of course, but expecting to beat Porto. And now he knew Porto was a team of some resources too. And so he started, as I have done all my career — and he's the master at it — to play the next game before it starts. In this case he was trying to create an atmosphere in which his own team would want revenge.

'He went into the press conference, mentioned that Porto had won a few titles and said maybe we had got used to buying them at the supermarket! He was trying to put the knife into his own players while making mine — young boys, mainly, unaccustomed to the Champions League — feel a little low, as if they had not deserved to win.'

After Porto had prevailed at Old Trafford, there was pandemonium in their dressing room. 'You would have thought we had won the World Cup,' said Mourinho. 'And then there was a knock on the door. It was Alex, with Gary Neville. As they came in, everybody fell silent, respectful. The party stopped. The party was over. And, as Gary Neville went round shaking hands with my players, Alex shook hands with me and said that, after the press conference, I was invited to come to his office for a drink.

'What a special person it was, I thought, who would do

anything to win but, if he lost, still do that. At that moment I made a decision. It was that, if I ever came to England, I would follow this example.

'I remembered something Bobby once said to me when we were at Barcelona. We had lost a game we should have won – it was against Hercules of Alicante – and I was devastated. "Don't be like that," he said. "Just think of the happiness in the Hercules dressing room. If you think of that, you won't be too sad. You'll share a little bit of the happiness of the others." And I wanted to come to that culture.'

When he did, however, he proved an often poor loser. Certainly not as sporting as Ferguson at his best. And sometimes as graceless as Ferguson at his worst.

At least in public. With fellow managers he was popular and observed the customs. Especially with Ferguson. 'Beforehand,' said Mourinho, 'we would play our game with words. Then there would be the game on the field. And afterwards – win, lose, draw – our tradition was to have a bottle of wine.

'He started it. He always had one in his office. So I decided it could not always be him and brought a bottle myself, a good one, Portuguese. And that started a competition. Who would bring the best bottle? Who would bring the most expensive? He came with a fine Bordeaux, I would retaliate – always with a Portuguese wine – and so it went on.'

Pizza with Wenger

No Gewürztraminer from Alsace would have crossed Ferguson's lips. Not at that stage anyway. His relationship with Arsène Wenger, his most consistently difficult opponent since the Alsatian's arrival at Arsenal in the autumn of 1996, had been far from cordial, at least when the media were around. Privately it was much warmer than the public perceived, according to Wenger, who had said in 2001: 'When we meet – at airports or in Uefa meetings, things like that – we don't hit each other. In fact sometimes it's quite fun.'

They had a great deal in common: they were football men to the core, workaholics with a passion for passing football, youth development and winning, although not necessarily in that order, as their falls from dignity in defeat testified. One difference was almost a nuance: while Wenger was often the most sour of losers, he was never an ugly winner.

The best known illustration of this took place in October 2004 and became known as 'Pizzagate' because the player who hurled a slice of pizza at Ferguson after a stormy match at Old Trafford became the subject of a cover-up on both sides. But the main drama, to which neither Ferguson nor

Wenger has referred in public, might have got genuinely violent.

It was a head-to-head between the managers in which fists might have been raised but for Ferguson's wise restraint. More than once, he has said that his Govan upbringing taught him never to shrink from confrontation in the dressing room; hence the 'hairdryer'. This, however, was just outside the dressing room and a different instinct, fortunately for all concerned, prevailed.

A lot had seemed to be conspiring against Ferguson at the time. Not least the feeling that he had met more than his match in Wenger, whose gift for language – indeed languages, for he spoke several and was usually described as 'urbane' or 'professorial' – Ferguson had been foolish enough to prompt. He had claimed that United, although they had finished fifteen points behind an unbeaten Arsenal the previous season, had played the more attractive football. When this was put to Wenger, he smiled and replied: 'Everyone thinks they have the prettiest wife at home.'

In addition there was the obvious threat of Mourinho for Ferguson to worry about as he pondered his team's poor start to the 2004/5 season; in nine matches they had won only twice.

And so Arsenal came to Old Trafford. Still they led the League, still they were unbeaten; indeed, they needed only to draw at Old Trafford to complete half a century of League matches without defeat. Ferguson's United responded ruthlessly, the Neville brothers appearing to target José Antonio Reyes, a Spanish attacker reckoned to be susceptible to roughing-up.

Arsenal might have been able to survive this but for two decisions by the referee, Mike Riley, that went against them.

In the first half, Freddie Ljungberg was bowled over by Rio Ferdinand when going for goal, but no red card was shown. In the second, Wayne Rooney was awarded a penalty despite a suspicion that he had dived over a challenge by Sol Campbell. United won 2–0 and afterwards the tunnel resounded to cries of 'fucking cheats' as players faced up to each other.

Who appropriated the slice of pizza from the Arsenal dressing room has always been a matter of conjecture, although Cesc Fàbregas has attracted fingers of suspicion since Ashley Cole's assurance in his autobiography, *My Defence*, that the culprit was neither English nor French (even though players from Germany and Sweden also played that day). At any rate, United's observance of the custom that food should be provided for opponents rebounded messily on Ferguson, as Cole chronicled: 'This slice of pizza came flying over my head and hit Fergie straight in the mush. The slap echoed down the tunnel and everything stopped – the fighting, the yelling, everything. All eyes turned . . . to see this pizza slip off that famous puce face and roll down his nice black suit.'

Again, Ferguson showed restraint. Thierry Henry, having just left the pitch, would have seen the first example of it when Wenger offered to 'sort out' their differences 'here and now' (the choice between verbal and physical weapons seemed to be Ferguson's) but not the second. Henry had requested a rerun of the penalty incident and accepted an invitation from Geoff Shreeves, Sky's man on the touchline, to see it in a room near the tunnel. 'After that,' said Henry, 'I could hear some people making a noise.

'I came back and remember being unable to get back into our dressing room at first because of the security guards. I know what had happened but it's difficult for me to talk about

it because – and I know this is an Arsène type of thing to say!
– I didn't see it.'

Henry was talking at a distance, in Barcelona, where he was
able to reflect warmly on battles that had appeared as bitter
as any in the English game. 'It was a good rivalry,' he said. 'I
always compare it to a boxing fight. You have two guys trading
insults and, at the end, they embrace and say how much they
respect each other. It's the same when two teams are at the
top. The respect was mutual, even though people thought we
hated each other and were surprised we could shake hands or
exchange shirts.'

He agreed that Ferguson and Wenger were, in many ways,
from the same mould. Indeed, later that evening he told a
story that illustrated it. Wenger, in training at London Colney,
had introduced to the Arsenal first-team squad a young
defender from the Ivory Coast called Kolo Touré who was on
trial with a view to signing. The idea was that he would start
by playing in a small-sided practice match, with Wenger
watching. Henry took the ball up to Touré and, not expecting
the visitor to know his tricks, tried one. Touré was taking no
chances. His tackle hit Henry like a blast from a scattergun.
'He took ball, man, everything. The ball soared into the air
and was falling just out of play when Arsène trotted after it
and snaked out a leg to control it. But Kolo was still running
furiously and, as the boss trapped the ball, hit him as hard as
he'd hit me. Arsène went head over heels. We all stopped and
gaped. Then Arsène got up. He had this great big grin on his
face.

'"Yes," he said. "I think we can go to war with this one." And
Kolo joined us.' It could just as well have been a former United
player talking about Ferguson.

Wenger and Ferguson had even become friendly in the latter years of their relationship. 'It reminds me of my relationship with my brother,' said Henry. 'When we were young, we always used to argue. I used to think my brother didn't like me and always wanted to show him that I could do better than him. And then suddenly we became the best friends in the world. But even now, when we play a game – when there is a competitive element – I will argue.'

The sibling rivalry between Ferguson and Wenger became less intense when Arsenal stopped winning trophies. Maybe that was coincidence. Ferguson, after all, never fell out with Mourinho when the Portuguese was top dog.

Fighting Back

Back in that first season of Mourinho's, their friendship did not constrain the Chelsea manager from accusing Ferguson of influencing the referee during the goalless first leg of a League Cup semi-final in the January. But Chelsea won the second leg 2–1 at Old Trafford and proceeded to collect Mourinho's first trophy in England by overcoming Liverpool at the Millennium Stadium.

Their fourth and final meeting of the season came almost at its end. Chelsea had won the title with three matches to spare, and the second of those was at Old Trafford. Ferguson arranged that his men should applaud them on the field and some, notably Roy Keane, did so with more grace than others; Gary Neville clapped sarcastically.

Chelsea, such a consistent side that the only League match they lost had been at Manchester City in October, gave one of their more flamboyant performances, with Eidur Gudjohnsen outstanding in a 3–1 victory.

Long before the final whistle – and even though it was United's last home match and an opportunity to send them to Cardiff for the FA Cup final with a bit of encouragement – the crowd had begun to drift away. More than half of the initial 68,000 had gone when the players did their trudge of honour, joined by Ferguson, who was limping. It would have been a cruel picture that showed him next to the relatively young and extremely handsome Mourinho and naturally we wondered if the new man, with all the wealth of Abramovich behind him, would be the death of Ferguson's career.

Ferguson was fortunate in one way. He was able to rue a series of embarrassing errors in the transfer market – Kléberson, Eric Djemba Djemba, Liam Miller, the young French flier David Bellion – while bedding in the classy pair who were going to feature in his, and United's, renaissance.

Cristiano Ronaldo had already spent a season with him when England went out of the European Championship in Lisbon in 2004, beaten on penalties after leading when the eighteen-year-old Wayne Rooney broke a bone in his foot. And Ferguson had booked Rooney for the next season. He would just have to wait for the foot to heal.

In just twenty-nine League appearances, five as substitute, Rooney was to get eleven goals, which made him United's leading scorer in a lean season by their standards (they finished third). With a further three in the FA Cup, he helped them to the scoreless final, in which they performed well but lost to an undeserving Arsenal because, although Rooney and others put their penalties away, Paul Scholes had his saved by the outstanding Jens Lehmann.

Again United had fallen in the first knockout round of the Champions League: to Milan, whom Liverpool, now under Rafa Benítez, were to beat on penalties in the Istanbul final after extraordinarily clawing back a three-goal deficit.

Meet the Glazers

So there was no trophy to celebrate at Old Trafford – but the fans still gathered there. Not so many as usual, and in a radically different frame of mind, for there was anger when, in May 2005, news broke that John Magnier and J. P. McManus had sold their 29 per cent stake in United to the Glazers.

As the Americans had built up their shareholding, the head of the family had replaced Magnier as Public Enemy No. 1. In Florida, Malcolm Glazer might have been known to Tampa Bay Buccaneers fans as 'The Leprechaun' because he was short with a ginger beard, but perceptions of him had come to play so badly across the Atlantic that, when shares sold by the United director Maurice Watkins were later bought by the Glazers, his car was daubed by militant supporters. When the purchase of the Irish shares gave them control, an effigy of the old man was burned at Old Trafford.

The stadium was no longer guarded, incidentally, by Ned Kelly, the former head of security, and his lieutenants. In 2002 he had been the victim of a sting by a newspaper which accused him of 'touting' tickets. He had been heartened by a telephone call from Ferguson, who said he had spoken to David Gill and been assured that a rap on the knuckles would suffice: 'Keep your nose clean, Ned. You'll be okay. Trust me.' Four days later, Gill sacked him and, Kelly recalled, he rang Ferguson, from whom there was an embarrassed silence, broken by a nervously mumbled 'Keep in touch, Ned' and the click of a receiver being replaced.

Security became more of an issue than ever once the Glazers' takeover had been completed in June 2005 — eight years after Ferguson had been introduced to Magnier and McManus, beginning the final stage of the process through which United turned from a footballing institution into a commodity. Malcolm Glazer's sons Joel, Avi and Bryan joined the board and the company went private again.

Magnier and McManus had taken £240 million for their 29 per cent, which gave them a profit estimated at £130 million.

United, once a model of prudence, had a debt of £650 million and this was what concerned well-wishers. While Magnier and McManus laughed all the way to Barbados and the Glazers worked out how best to manage their investment, the club had to pay interest to its new owners' banks and other lenders, including hedge funds.

The Winter of Keane

The 2005/6 season, with Van Nistelrooy and Rooney finding the net regularly and Ronaldo chipping in ominously, brought a trophy – Wigan were beaten 4-0 in the League Cup final – and a rise to second place in the League, which Chelsea won again. But that Portugal had become an unhappy hunting ground for results (if not players) was emphasised when United lost to Benfica in Lisbon, meekly departing the Champions League at the group stage.

They were coming to terms with the end of an era. It would be wrong to say that United were missing Roy Keane, for the leader had become one long winter of discontent; you could hardly hear his bones creaking for the grumbles: about fellow players, most notably Rio Ferdinand, that caused Ferguson to sanction the scrapping of an interview for MUTV; about the training facilities on a trip to Portugal – he fell out with Ferguson on that one; and, of course, about the kind of fans he imagined munching prawn sandwiches.

When Ferguson spoke of his fondness for strong-willed players – 'I'm happy seeing myself' – the man you envisaged was Keane. He was the Ferguson trade-off writ large. The unnecessary and unprofessional acts, the suspensions from big matches and the near-inhumanity of his utterings about Alfie Haaland after he went over the top at Maine Road were outweighed, to Ferguson's mind and those of the overwhelming majority of United fans, by inspirational performances. Even many Ireland fans forgave his rant at Mick McCarthy which caused him to be sent home from the 2002 World Cup before it had started.

And, to give Keane his due, a recognition that he was his own only true enemy seemed to lead to his finest form in his late twenties and early thirties. While remaining tough – a tunnel warning to his arch-foe, Arsenal's Patrick Vieira, not to pick on Gary Neville made unforgettable television – he played with more than enough discipline and intelligence to cement a place among the great United players of all time.

At thirty-four, however, he had lost his edge and in November 2005 Ferguson let him join Celtic, the club he had supported as a boy. He lasted six months before retiring and became a manager, initially with great success, at Sunderland.

Among those with the unenviable task of covering the ground Keane had vacated was Darren Fletcher, not an instant crowd favourite yet a midfield player who was to prove one of the most impressive graduates from United's youth ranks since the Beckham era. If ever Ferguson's faith in a footballer was vindicated, Fletcher was the example; a few years on, in 2009, when he was suspended from the Champions League final in Barcelona after being shown a late yellow card at Arsenal, almost as much dismay was expressed as when Keane and Scholes had missed out in 1999.

In 2005, just before the Champions League exit in Lisbon, the young Scot helped to set the tone for an improved League campaign with a home winner against Chelsea. But Mourinho's team more than avenged this with a sumptuous display in clinching the title with a 3-0 victory over United at Stamford Bridge and Mourinho believed that, but for the gradual breakdown in relations between himself and Abramovich and henchmen in his third season, Ferguson might not have got it back in 2006/7. Who knows? Mourinho's fourth season started badly and his job went to Avram Grant.

José and the Boss

José Mourinho was always going to have a choice of destinations. He chose Italy and it was there late in 2009, when he was striving to win a second successive Serie A title with Internazionale, that he reflected on his contests with Ferguson: 'Professionally, the easiest for me was in the Champions League with Porto. It was different when Chelsea and Manchester were the two big powers. People often say it is harder to coach a smaller club. But it is easier. With a big club you have to win every trophy, every game. That is why to have been at the top for more than thirty years is proof of how strong Alex is. Life at the top can make people very tired. The old man who wants to win every game can only be admired. He deserves a statue at Old Trafford.'

Their most recent meeting had been earlier that year, when United knocked Inter out of the Champions League (Ronaldo scored the second of the goals that settled the tie after a scoreless draw at San Siro) and Mourinho said: 'He was saying to me "Why should I stop? I feel strong, I feel happy, I have nothing to do at home, I love it – and I win!" I think the only thing that could push him out would be if he stopped winning. He's a winner. He could not live without victories.

'The period he was in trouble was the one when his pride was wounded – the period when Chelsea started winning. For two years, United won nothing [one League Cup, in fact]. Instead of giving up, he started to prepare a new Manchester United, which would again be champions of England and Europe.'

Was Ferguson a control freak? 'I don't know.' But the word 'control' meant as much to Mourinho as Ferguson. 'I think we both believe in control of the dressing room.' Ferguson had that. 'When people, for example, talk of the boot that flew at Beckham, or the "hairdryer", I never heard one player criticise that moment of aggressiveness. Why? Because they respect that person so much. They recognise in him such power, such leadership, that he can do anything he wants.

'There is only one thing I will not do and that is insult a player's mother. I will never do that. Anything else, yes. Why? Because the players know I am not doing it to insult, to smash. It is because I want something.

'The players trust Alex. They can be angry, of course, if he leaves them out of the team, but in the end they know he has the characteristics that bring success.' And that kept them under his control. 'It is a quality a coach must have.'

Ferguson also tried to obtain advantage by getting under the skins of referees, and of some of those opposing managers whose teams were perceived to threaten his. There had been his provocation of Kevin Keegan, and then the sometimes bitter rivalry with Arsène Wenger. Rafa Benítez was later moved to an outburst against him. But there had never been a dig at Benítez's predecessor, Gérard Houllier, and the mind games with Mourinho tended to be conducted in a friendly spirit.

Asked if he had ever beaten Ferguson psychologically, Mourinho replied: 'I never thought about it. We were different personalities, but neither was afraid of the other. No one could interfere with the stability of the other. Whatever I said, certainly, I did not think I could upset his self-confidence. He could block every word from outside.'

Mourinho, like Ferguson, was more aggressive with Benítez, whose team he once belittled even after Liverpool had knocked Chelsea out of the Champions League at Anfield – 'only Liverpool's crowd were better than us tonight' – and Wenger, with whose purist footballing philosophy he disagreed. So did he treat Ferguson differently? 'I think we both had a sense that we had to beat each other by football, not psychology. I always thought he was top at that level and his teams would be stable and prepared.' So he played by different rules against Ferguson? 'Yes.'

He had even been known to refer to Ferguson in private – and it was not Mourinho who told me this – as 'Boss'.

But he tended to give at least as good as he got, even in that last full season Mourinho had at Chelsea, 2006/7, when United regained the title; there were two draws in the League and Chelsea beat United in the FA Cup final, the first back at a rebuilt Wembley which seemed to have everything except a decent pitch, with a Didier Drogba goal.

Ferguson's good fortune had been that Mourinho, for all Chelsea's money, could not accommodate every top player in the world. With the help of Peter Kenyon and influential agents, the club had arranged in 2004 for the new manager from Portugal to have Petr Čech in goal and Arjen Robben, whom

Ferguson had long fancied, on the wing. Mourinho had asked for and got three Portuguese players: Ricardo Carvalho, Paulo Ferreira and Tiago. Claude Makelele, so good in the holding midfield role that they nicknamed it after him, was already there, with John Terry and Frank Lampard. No wonder they were to win the League twice. But Drogba was to be the centre-forward – and so they didn't go for Rooney.

In a market complicated only by the ambitious interest in Rooney exhibited by Newcastle United, then, Ferguson had got the best young English player for many years. The fee paid to Everton would reach £27 million and even then be a snip. And for less than half that amount United had already got the boy destined to be the best in the world.

Better than Quaresma

You looked at Cristiano Ronaldo in the spring of 2008, as he carried United towards the championships of England and Europe, and saw the Manchester United player writ large, scoring a goal a match, thrilling crowds at home and abroad and preparing to collect every honour in the game – already he had followed Thierry Henry as Footballer of the Year and this season's award would be a formality – and could hardly believe that Ferguson had thought long and hard about bidding for him.

Perhaps his greatest stroke of luck was described by Carlos Queiroz, whom Ferguson had appointed his assistant in 2002. In his year at United, before he left to become manager of Real Madrid, there had been several discussions about two young wingers at Sporting Lisbon, where Queiroz had been in charge. Ferguson was unsure whether to go for Ronaldo, then eighteen, or Ricardo Quaresma, who was eighteen months older.

'I had always followed Cristiano's career,' said Queiroz, 'and so delivered my opinion very strongly. We were not able to buy both of them – and I was sure about Cristiano. So when

I left for Madrid I made him my target. He was top of the list I gave Jorge Valdano, the sporting director. But unfortunately for me – and luckily for Alex – he ended up joining United instead. And it happened through me because Sporting asked me to ask United to inaugurate their stadium [the Alvalade had been refurbished for the European Championship] by playing a pre-season friendly. So I went to Alex and he was happy to do it. Sporting won 3-1, Cristiano had a fantastic game – and all the doubts disappeared! Alex had to make a quick decision now. Otherwise Jorge and I would have got Cristiano.'

He cost United £12.4 million.

Quaresma went to Barcelona for £4.5 million, fell out with Frank Rijkaard, returned to Portugal in the deal that brought Deco from Porto and, after failing to revive his career with Mourinho at Inter, joined the Turkish club Beşiktaş in 2010.

Queiroz was soon working with Ronaldo anyway. He lasted ten months at Real, whose president, Florentino Pérez, had discarded Makelele to make room for Beckham and instituted a policy of surrounding *galacticos* with products of the *cantera*, the youth development system. A trophy drought ensued and Queiroz was one of its first victims after Real had collapsed at the end of the season, letting Rafa Benítez's Valencia overtake them. Queiroz had kept in touch with Ferguson. 'Alex was a great friend during that time. He told me to make my own decisions and not to worry because there would always be a job for me in Manchester. That gave me strength. It kept my spine straight during a difficult time. So, even though I was offered some extremely well paid jobs, including one in England [Tottenham had a reliably documented interest in him], I didn't hesitate when he invited me back.'

Nor did Ferguson now hesitate when Queiroz suggested he take youngsters from Portugal. He paid Porto £18 million for Anderson, whom the fans hoped would be a more assertive Brazilian than Kléberson, and Sporting got £16 million for Nani, a winger who began like the next Ronaldo only to lose his way for a while. But Rooney and Ronaldo appeared to be acting like enough of a rejuvenation drug on Ferguson.

When Rooney was sent off during the 2006 World Cup in a match against Portugal and Ronaldo indulged in a sly wink at team-mates, the newspapers speculated that there would be pre-season trouble at Carrington. Ferguson scoffed. He knew his men. Rooney scored twice and Ronaldo once in the opening League match, a 5–1 victory over Fulham, and United led the table virtually all season.

Ferguson had rebuilt yet again. He had, in Edwin van der Sar, a £2.5 million signing from Fulham, his best goalkeeper since Schmeichel. Ferdinand, who had matured into one of the world's best defenders, enjoyed the worthy partnership of Nemanja Vidić. Ryan Giggs was well into an Indian summer so wonderfully prolonged that in 2009 he was to be voted BBC Sports Personality of the Year, and Paul Scholes was prompting more cleverly than ever. Michael Carrick, from Tottenham, was an elegant, soft-shoed and often deadly addition to the midfield, notably in the 7–1 triumph over Roma at Old Trafford that signalled United were on the march in Europe once more.

They had come through a group featuring Benfica and Lille but that quarter-final was a revelation. After a 2–1 defeat in the Olympic Stadium, United ran riot, Carrick and Ronaldo scoring twice each and Rooney and even the French full-back Patrice Evra chipping in along with Alan Smith, a £7 million signing from cash-strapped Leeds who had returned after horrifically breaking a leg at Liverpool.

Again it was Italian opposition in the semi-finals – shades of being drawn Juventus after Inter in 1999 – and, after Ronaldo had opened the scoring against Milan at Old Trafford only to have the brilliant Kaká reply twice, there was time for Rooney to equalise and then, in the ninetieth minute, hit the winner. United were badly prepared for the second leg and Milan won 3–0, Ferguson blaming it on tiredness even though the preceding programme had not been inordinately heavy and Milan had much the older side. Milan went on to beat Liverpool in Athens.

Ronaldo matched Rooney in scoring twenty-three goals that season. It was a remarkable return for a winger, even one who could pop up in the goalmouth and head them in like an old-fashioned English centre-forward, but we had seen nothing yet.

After Schmeichel, van der Sar

The 2007/8 League season began with a scoreless match against Reading. It was not until the last match of September, a 1-0 win at Birmingham City, that Ronaldo got his first League goal, but in twenty-nine appearances thereafter, three of them as a substitute, he scored a further thirty.

In the FA Cup, from which United were removed by Portsmouth with Ferguson and Queiroz delivering scathing verdicts on the referee, Martin Atkinson – they thought he had let Portsmouth players get away with too many fouls on the star man – Ronaldo scored three more.

And in the Champions League he got no fewer than eight. His forty-second and last of the season helped United to defeat Chelsea in Moscow. And that was just for his club. With three in European Championship qualifiers that season, he had taken his total for the Portugal campaign to eight in twelve matches and in the tournament itself he was to notch one in three before the 3–2 quarter-final defeat by Germany. Only then did he have a holiday.

The highlights of United's unbeaten progress through the Champions League group stage had been Ronaldo's winners on a sentimental journey back to the Alvalade and again when Sporting made the journey to Old Trafford; although United had already qualified for the next round, it was a truly memorable goal, an example of his ability to develop state-of-the-art techniques, a free-kick from nearly thirty yards struck so that it cleared the defensive wall, bending in and then outward so that the goalkeeper was helpless as it found a corner of the net.

Ferguson sent virtually a reserve side to Roma for the concluding group match and still drew 1–1. No one could live with any of the English clubs that season; three marched to the semi-finals and the exceptions, Arsenal, fell only to Liverpool, who in turn lost their semi-final to Chelsea.

United, after drawing in Lyon, beat the French champions with a Ronaldo goal and then reacquainted themselves with Roma in the quarter-finals, winning 2–0 away and then at home through a goal from Carlos Tévez, whom Ferguson was supposed to have signed from West Ham United but in fact was owned by a company in which his agent, Kia Joorabchian, had an involvement. West Ham, who lied to the Premier League about the so-called 'third-party ownership', were heavily fined, but Tévez was allowed to play on for Manchester United. He stayed until, at the end of the 2008/9 season, Ferguson decided he was not worth the £25 million or more that Joorabchian was demanding and the Argentine went to Manchester City.

In the semi-finals there followed a tactical triumph for Ferguson and the unquestionably influential Queiroz in Barcelona, where Scholes, now thirty-three, and Carrick were excellent in protecting a defence lacking Vidić from the threat of Samuel Eto'o and Lionel Messi. Park Ji-Sung, the industrious South Korean, also did a fine defensive job for the manager, helping to secure a scoreless outcome. Scholes won the second leg with a thrilling drive. Ferguson had publicly promised Scholes a place in the final if United got to Moscow. It was a bizarre thing for any manager to guarantee, but how Scholes had vindicated him. And so United proceeded to meet Chelsea on the Luzhniki Stadium's artificial surface, which was to have quite a bearing on the match.

In the shuffle that let Vidić back for the final, Park was left out; Ferguson preferred the destructive specialist Owen Hargreaves.

If Ferguson's first Champions League final had been a slow-burner, this one fizzed from the start. Both teams attacked and Ronaldo wasted little time in exposing Michael Essien's unfamiliarity with the right-back position. After twenty-six minutes, United's own right-back, Wes Brown, crossed and a towering Ronaldo headed United in front. Chelsea equalised just before half-time when Essien shot and the ball deflected off Vidić and Rio Ferdinand to Frank Lampard, who scored as Edwin van der Sar lost his footing on the liberally watered surface.

Chelsea then commanded the midfield and might have won in normal time: Didier Drogba struck a post, just as Mehmet Scholl had done in 1999. Lampard hit the crossbar, as Carsten Jancker had also done in 1999, during the extra thirty minutes.

Any sympathy the neutral may have felt for Chelsea disappeared as penalties loomed. Throughout the match they had been diving, feigning injury and harassing the Slovakian referee, Ľuboš Micheľ. On one occasion they even kicked the ball out of play for a case of cramp — and wanted it back! What next would impel them to hold up the match, we wondered — slight breathlessness? Now a posse led by John

Terry tried to bully Tévez and Vidić was slapped by Drogba. The red card cost Chelsea one of their prime penalty-takers.

The decider had gone to 2-2 when Ronaldo, of all people, had his kick saved by Petr Čech. The player of the European season appeared set to lose its biggest prize. Especially when Lampard scored. Hargreaves scored, as did Ashley Cole, and the United substitute Nani. Up stepped Terry to win the competition, but he slipped as he kicked and the ball flew behind the goal, forlornly glancing the post on its way. United were back in the contest. Anderson kept them there. After Salomon Kalou had scored, so did yet another substitute, Ryan Giggs. And finally there was Nicolas Anelka, who had been on the field less than a quarter of an hour. He had not wanted to take a penalty and his kick, struck to Van der Sar's right, was confidently stopped by the diving Dutchman.

It was to a tearful Terry that most media eyes swivelled and, as the England captain crumpled in anguish, a member of the United contingent – the only one of seven who had served their country alongside Terry – went to him. Gary Neville, who was recovering from injury, got his suit soaked as he ran across the pitch to offer consolation. Only after this did United's club captain and arch-supporter rejoin the celebrations. That was true sportsmanship from Neville, of the sort he and Ferguson had shown to Porto and Mourinho amid their own disappointment in Manchester four years earlier.

And it was conduct befitting the year; as Ferguson had often mentioned, it was the fiftieth anniversary of the Munich crash. Bobby Charlton enjoyed the moment with characteristic restraint. For all that the rub of post and bar had favoured them, Ferguson's United were worthy winners.

Talking a Blinder

The final ended long after midnight in Moscow – 1.34 on Thursday morning.

Late on Friday morning Ferguson appeared at Carrington and helped to dispense champagne to journalists. Immediately his future came up. He would have two more years. 'Three at the very, very, very most. I'll no' be managing at seventy. Definitely not. You have to think of time for yourself. And my wife's getting older. You have to think about that. She deserves a bit of my time. In fairness she never brings it up. But I think she'd like it.' We had heard all this before. 'Yes, but the older you get the more guilty you feel about it.'

He was later to appear to go back on this, as Mourinho mentioned, but maybe that was partly to prevent the players from switching off as he felt they had on a previous occasion. At Carrington that late spring day, it seemed, the champagne was talking a good game and on the question of Ronaldo's future it was more eloquent still, even implying that the Glazers would let the player 'sit in the stand' rather than let him follow the trail to Madrid.

'Believe me,' said Ferguson of the jewel he was to lose within a year, 'he'll no' be leaving in the next two years.' Almost spitting the name of Real, he compared the privacy of Carrington – he was proud that journalists called it Colditz – with Real's training ground. 'There's three thousand bloody supporters watching the training every day. The press are there. The TV stations are there. It's a jungle.' Once again Ferguson insisted we could take it from him: Ronaldo knew where he was better off. The following summer found Ronaldo all in white on a vast catwalk at the Bernabeú, waving at 80,000 of those bloody supporters, the new king of the jungle and looking very happy to be there.

But that day at Carrington was all about United and how they would strengthen – speculation correctly had Ferguson eyeing Dimitar Berbatov at Tottenham – and expand. Ferguson reiterated his hope that the stadium, now holding 76,000, would grow to accommodate more of those wishing to appreciate not only Ronaldo but the maturity of Wayne Rooney.

He spoke so fondly of Rooney and the selfless adaptability that had enabled the manager to include Hargreaves in Moscow: 'I just felt that, with Chelsea so strong in midfield, I had to give myself the option of Hargreaves [initially on the right] in case we needed to bring him into the central area at some point, which we did because of their dominance in the second half. They created a couple of chances. But bringing Hargreaves in stopped the rot.

'In order to do that, we put Rooney wide right and I know it's not his best position.'

Ferguson dwelt on Rooney's selflessness: 'He's not a selfish player, not a selfish boy. He's a committed winner and this leads him to make sacrifices to the detriment of his individual performance. As a team player, he is absolutely fantastic. He tells me things like "I can play centre-half – I played there for my school, you know." And I have to tell him, "Wayne, but we're playing Drogba today." The attitude he's got is a terrific asset to this club.' And, quite clearly, to the manager. Rooney had taken the exemplar role, following in the line of Cantona and Keane.

When someone mentioned Rooney's wife, Coleen, the response from Ferguson was interesting: 'Clever girl. Down-to-earth. Good.' For some reason an image of Victoria Beckham came to mind and you sensed that Alex Ferguson had seldom been happier in his work than now. As Ryan Giggs had said of his own elastic career: 'When you're young, you think it's never going to end. When you get older you get an appreciation of the finishing line. You want to enjoy every game . . . savour every moment.'

Not that Ferguson was relieved of life's little problems. Such as the necessity, once more, to find a new assistant. Early in the spring Queiroz had been courted by Benfica and Ferguson, reluctant to lose him again, mentioned the Old Trafford succession. Then the Portuguese national team, with whom Queiroz had a history – he had supervised the development of the so-called 'golden generation' of Luís Figo, Rui Costa and others – asked him to be their guide to the 2010 World Cup in South Africa, where he had also worked, as national team manager. He had to accept, and went with Ferguson's best wishes.

Queiroz, an affable man whose love of the game ran deep, told me that Ferguson, when first hiring him, had summarised the job by mentioning the renowned Jaguar marque of sports car and saying: 'Manchester United is one of those. Make sure it is ready to drive.' Queiroz had done more than this. He had come to do too much for the taste of an ageing Keane, who moaned about his tactical ideas, and other players thought him gifted but obsessive, but Ferguson, into whose ear he was never slow to whisper advice, had such a regard for Queiroz that he frequently recommended him as his own successor.

Ferguson had developed a habit of tipping people for this elusive job (McClaren, for example) who would be likely to show gratitude by keeping him on as a valued confidant. But three League titles and a Champions League in his five seasons marked Queiroz out as a particularly high-class assistant. In Europe especially, Ferguson's reputation had benefited from his acumen.

His role went to Ferguson's old utility player Michael Phelan, who, though not as convincing as the urbane Queiroz in post-match interviews in front of the *Match of the Day* cameras (Ferguson still would not do those), shared in a third consecutive title celebration.

An extraordinarily eventful season, even by Ferguson's standards, began with a scoreless Community Shield match against Portsmouth, who had won the FA Cup under his old friend Harry Redknapp. It involved a mid-season trip to Japan during which United became world champions, then a Carling Cup final in which he surrounded Ronaldo with reserves and yet still beat Redknapp's Tottenham on penalties, then an FA Cup semi-final in which the reserves lost on penalties to Everton. There was a Premier League title triumph despite the best challenge yet from Liverpool under Rafa Benítez, who launched an attack on Ferguson's dirty tricks, and finally a Champions League final defeat by Barcelona.

Ferguson also found time to blood an entire outfield team of youngsters, farm others out on loan and sell a couple, raising more than £6 million from Sunderland and Burnley for the striker Fraizer Campbell and defender Richard Eckersley, as if to prove that the income stream from United rejects still flowed.

Three of the youngsters – Rafael and Fabio da Silva and Rodrigo Possebon – came from Brazil. Kiko Macheda was from Italy (and you could still hear the howls of complaint from Lazio). Zoran Tošić was from Serbia, Ritchie de Laet from Belgium. Jonny Evans, a central defender from Northern Ireland, had been impressive on loan at Sunderland and was 'a Manchester United player', swore Ferguson. So was another Irishman, the midfielder Darron Gibson, a calm player with a ferocious shot.

A couple of them looked the part, it was true, but we remembered how Ferguson had sung the praises of, among others, a winger called Luke Chadwick who was supposed to offer a more direct and challenging alternative to Beckham but who ended up in the lower divisions. So, when he tipped the English striker Danny Welbeck to make Fabio Capello's squad for the 2010 World Cup, we reached for the salt cellar. In order to give them the best chance of making it, he had to keep their heads up. And, if it didn't work out and they had to be sold, it would be the price that stayed up.

Rafa's Rant

Ronaldo's final season at United began in his absence. The previous season had been a long one for him, with the European Championship, and he returned to the side as a substitute in the fourth League match, a bruising 1-1 draw at Chelsea. He then started scoring as if he had never been away: eight in as many League matches. He was sent off in a 1-0 win at Manchester City, and quite bizarrely, after he had seemed instinctively to handle a corner in the City penalty area. But United gathered pace in December. They were just behind Liverpool when the statement that came to be known as 'Rafa's Rant' was issued by the Anfield manager on 9 January.

Benítez was responding to a series of apparently crafty complaints Ferguson had made. About, for instance, fixtures being arranged in a way that put United at a supposed disadvantage. Benítez tried sarcasm: 'There is another option – that Mr Ferguson organises the fixtures in his office and sends it to us and everyone will know and cannot complain . . .'

On referees, he mentioned an FA campaign and asked: 'How can you talk of Respect and criticise the referees every week?' Not just criticise them: 'We know what happens every time we go to Old Trafford and the United staff. They are always going man-to-man with the referees, especially at half-time when they walk close to the referees and they are talking and talking.' In the manner David Elleray had noted when he was a leading referee.

As for the mind games, it had got to the stage where Ferguson's very existence was polluting the atmosphere. All he had to do was break wind and the press would portray it as an insult to a rival manager or club. At the start of the season, he had mentioned that Chelsea's average age was higher than United's and been accused of making mischief when all he had done was make a reasonable observation. That was hardly his fault. But his claim that the League fixtures were intended to hamper United by giving them difficult away matches in the first half of the season was nonsense and, as Benítez noted, any advantage in the second half of the season – which any manager would prefer – would go to United.

What Ferguson said might have been vaguely self-parodic – but it wasn't funny because it seemed casually to insult a game which most of us believed to have honest referees and, for that matter, fixture compilers. Moreover, it exposed for the umpteenth time the element of hypocrisy involved in railing against supposed trouble-making in the media while remaining such an arch-exponent of the black art himself.

The response from Benítez ran to several hundred words, including: 'I am surprised that United are starting the mind games so early. Maybe it is because we are top of the table.' Three weeks later, after draws with Stoke, Everton and Wigan, they were second.

United never relinquished the leadership, despite Liverpool's staggering 4-1 triumph at Old Trafford in March. Fernando

Torres utterly dominated Nemanja Vidić, who was sent off, as he had been in a 2–1 defeat at Anfield early in the season. At Fulham, where United lost 2-0, Wayne Rooney's frustrations with fellow players seemed to impel him to hurl the ball too near the referee, Phil Dowd, who showed him a second yellow card.

The match after won them the title, for they were losing at home to Aston Villa, one of the best away sides in the League, when Ronaldo equalised with his second majestic goal of the match and then the young substitute Macheda, having lost his marker with a deft flick, curled the ball round Brad Friedel's dive for a stunning winner two minutes into stoppage time. It was all so reminiscent of the Steve Bruce double against Sheffield Wednesday in the run-in to Ferguson's first title in 1993.

And that was it. Benítez's Liverpool, though the only points they dropped in their last eleven matches were in a 4-4 draw in which Andrei Arshavin scored all of Arsenal's goals from their only four attempts, could not catch Ferguson's United. Had the points dropped after Rafa's Rant made the real difference? Here the Machiavellians had a better case than in 1996, with Kevin Keegan. But who knows? Ferguson was just doing what came naturally.

Beaten by Barca

The 2008/9 title triumph was all the more praiseworthy because being European champions brought United extra commitments: the European Super Cup match in Monaco at the end of the summer, which they lost to Zenit St Petersburg without anyone taking much notice, and Fifa's Club World Championship. This was the tournament which the club had helped to launch in Brazil nine years earlier. It now took place in Japan. United, beating Gamba Osaka 5–3 and the Ecuadorian club Liga de Quito 1–0, won it, again evoking little reaction from the folks back home.

Defending the Champions League did matter and, after negotiating a group containing Celtic, Villarreal and Aalborg, Ferguson took on his friend Mourinho; Inter were no match for United, who were given more trouble by Porto, qualifying for the semi-finals through a stunning free-kick by Ronaldo at the Dragão. And so they met Arsenal, whose progress had been uncharacteristically dogged. United, however, swept Arsène Wenger's team aside. Although their goalkeeper, Manuel Almunia, restricted United to a John O'Shea goal at Old Trafford, the second leg proved electrifyingly one-sided.

Here was Ronaldo at his very best. Ferguson used him at centre-forward, flanked by Ji-Sung Park and Wayne Rooney with a tight trio of Darren Fletcher (by now one of Ferguson's big-match men), Michael Carrick and Anderson behind them. After seven minutes Ronaldo pulled the ball back and, after the young Arsenal full-back Kieran Gibbs had slipped on the turf, Park scored. Three minutes later a Ronaldo free-kick beat Almunia for pace at his near post. So it was all over long before United struck again on the hour with a devastating counter-attack. Ronaldo began it with a backheel and, after Park had found Rooney on the left, rounded it off from the Englishman's fine pass.

There was still time for a regret: as Cesc Fàbregas ran through on Edwin van der Sar, Fletcher snaked out a leg, but his tackle was deemed foul and a red card ruled him out of the final. Ferguson watched with a mixture of incredulity and contempt for the Italian referee, Roberto Rosetti, but it had been a reckless challenge given the state of the match. Robin van Persie's conversion of the penalty was incidental.

From Park's point of the view, the night was to end more happily. As usual, the post-match gathering of press featured a little group of South Koreans. Park had scored, they pointed out – but would he once again be disappointed when the team was picked for the final? 'I don't think he'll be disappointed this time,' said Ferguson, all but promising Park a place, just as he had done with Paul Scholes the year before.

And Park duly trotted out in Rome. The team shape was unchanged from the Emirates Stadium, with Ryan Giggs coming in for Fletcher. As for Barcelona, an unkind combination of injury and suspension had obliged Pep Guardiola, at the end of his first, extremely promising, season in charge, to recast the defence with Yaya Touré, normally a holding midfielder, next to Gerard Pique, once of United, in the middle. Both Andrés Iniesta, whose last-minute goal had won a roller-coaster semi-final against Chelsea, and Thierry Henry played with injuries that would have kept them out of a less important match.

In the first minute, Ronaldo struck a free-kick with such power that Víctor Valdés could only parry; Park tried to pounce but was thwarted by Pique. 'But for what Gerard did at that moment,' said Henry, 'it could have been a different match.' For another nine minutes, Barcelona were embarrassingly nervous. Unforced errors sent the ball out of play; Touré and Carles Puyol ran into each other.

'It was the narrow escape from the free-kick,' said Henry. 'We just couldn't settle. There was a corner kick straight after, and then a couple of crosses. You realise you're lucky not to be behind and you kind of forget who you are for a while. It's like when a great boxer gets knocked down. It doesn't mean he won't win the fight. But for the rest of the three minutes, until he hears the bell, he's going to struggle. In football, unfortunately, there's no bell.'

Yet it began to toll for United as early as the tenth minute. Guardiola had made a significant tactical change in starting with Samuel Eto'o rather than Lionel Messi to the right of the front trio so that Messi could link with Iniesta in the middle. Suddenly Iniesta broke from midfield and fed Eto'o, to whose teasing Nemanja Vidić responded by standing off, an extraordinary decision that the striker punished by squeezing a shot past Van der Sar.

'After that, we believed we would win,' said Henry. 'Once we are in front, we seldom lose the game. It suits the way we play. When the opponents come at us, we can get at them. And, as soon as guys like Andrés and Xavi got on the ball, we played our game. That was what the boss had told us to do. "No matter what happens today," he had said, "I want the world to know, and to appreciate, and to recognise, the way we play." Those were his words. Okay, he gave us all the tactical stuff as well, but those were his only words of motivation.'

From Xavi's cross, bent almost mischievously so that Rio Ferdinand, like Vidić earlier, was put in two minds, little Messi headed a second goal and it was left to Ferguson to congratulate the winners. Henry was talking to Patrice Evra on the pitch when he walked over. 'Well done,' he told Henry. 'You deserved it.'

He paid further tribute to Guardiola in the press conference, adding: 'It's a credit to them that they pursue their football philosophy.' Barcelona's passing game had indeed made them popular champions, though Henry stressed: 'The most important thing is the way everybody works. It's not just one or two pressing – it's everybody. If you want to win, you have to do it. Pressure, pressure, pressure. And it's tiring – I can tell you!'

Ferguson would have approved of that. But, as the inquest began, he wasted little time in letting it be known that something had gone wrong with United's preparation: something that could be put right if the sides met again. He did not define it. It was as Mourinho said. He was already playing the next game. In case fate was to bring United and Barcelona together again.

Ronaldo Goes, the Debt Grows

By the start of 2010, Manchester United's debts had grown to more than £700 million and it looked as if much of what would otherwise have been Ferguson's transfer budget was being diverted by the Glazers to pay their interest bill.

The Old Trafford crowd seemed to have turned into a vast protest meeting – 'Love United, Hate Glazers' was the slogan – and had even changed hue from the familiar red to green and gold, the club's colours in its original incarnation as Newton Heath, its name from inauguration in 1878 until 1902. Scarves in these colours became prevalent on the steep slopes. Meanwhile, a group of wealthy men known as the Red Knights and led by Jim O'Neill, head of global economic research at Goldman Sachs and a United fan of unquestionable credentials who had briefly served on the board in the mid-1990s, plotted a takeover from the Glazers.

The odd aspect was that Ferguson maintained a friendship with O'Neill. For he also maintained strong and boldly audible support for the Glazers. If he felt any sense of shame over the Glazers and the consequences of his having encouraged Magnier and McManus to buy into the club, he hid it under a mountain of praise for the stewardship of the Americans who had in turn bought out the Irish pair.

His most memorable paean was delivered, with perfect timing, in the wake of the Champions League triumph over Chelsea in Moscow in 2008. Back at Carrington less than thirty-six hours after the final penalty at the Luzhniki Stadium, he dispensed the club's champagne and lauded the Glazers for having 'balls', swearing that they would keep Cristiano Ronaldo out of Real Madrid's clutches for at least two years and maybe a lot longer, which proved hopelessly optimistic; within one year, a world record offer of £81 million had proved irresistible.

Now Ferguson's United, who used to break records as buyers, were sellers and Real, whom Ferguson had come to detest, appeared to be using them almost as a feeder club.

Ferguson had been able to claim that he wanted to sell Beckham. And that was certainly the view of the episode that Beckham conveyed to me four years on. Having been invited to the David Beckham Academy in the Docklands of east London the morning after England's removal from the European Championship by Croatia in 2007, I asked if he thought he could have continued at the top level with United. 'I believe I could still be playing for them now,' replied the thirty-two-year-old exile, now playing his club football with LA Galaxy, smiling as he added: 'But I'm not the manager.'

Nor was he going to leave the subject there. 'I've just read Bobby Charlton's autobiography,' Beckham said, 'and it was interesting to see what he wrote about me leaving United, because he talked about seeing the contract I was offered and the amount of money involved. Well, I didn't see any contract, let alone the "excellent, generous" offer he was talking about.

Whether it was kept back by certain people I don't know.' Would he have stayed if such riches had been tendered? Beckham's look verged on the withering. 'I'd have played for Manchester United,' he said, 'for free.'

So Beckham had left by Ferguson's choice. Ferguson had also, when he lost Ruud van Nistelrooy to Real, got away with a contention that the Dutchman had been too unpopular to keep; there were leaks of friction with Ronaldo. Nor did many of the supporters mind too much when Gabriel Heinze went to the Bernabéu, because Patrice Evra, the Frenchman signed from Monaco, seemed a livelier left-back. But Ronaldo was different. Ronaldo was Ferguson's top player. Even more so than Gordon Strachan had been at Aberdeen. And, just as Aberdeen had been unable to satisfy Strachan, the club that had developed Ronaldo lost out to the club of his heart.

Ferguson replaced him with Antonio Valencia, a quick and clever wide player from Ecuador who had been impressive at Wigan Athletic, and there was no complaint from the Glazers as they collected a £65 million profit.

They would have had to cough up nearly half of that if Carlos Tévez, the on-loan former West Ham player owned, in effect, by his agent, Kia Joorabchian, had been signed on a permanent basis – and the deal would have been done had the crowd's wishes been answered after the final home fixture of the season, the scoreless draw with Arsenal which clinched the title. But, as Tévez was withdrawn in the sixty-seventh minute, to thunderous cheers and the now-familiar chants of 'Fergie, Fergie, sign him up', the prolonged nature of his wave to all corners left little room for doubt that his future was elsewhere. Not far away, as it turned out; he went to

Manchester City. Ferguson claimed to have tried to make the Argentine an offer; Tévez denied having received the message.

But it did leave more money over for paying the Glazers' interest charges. As did Ferguson's idea of a replacement: Michael Owen on a free transfer. Owen eventually and inevitably succumbed to injury. Ferguson also signed the young French wide midfielder Gabriel Obertan for £3 million and, in mid-season, the Senegalese striker Mame Biram Diouf for £4 million. Meanwhile, it was revealed that, of a £72 million profit made by United the previous year, £69 million had been swallowed up by interest. Many United fans, though still happy with what they saw on the field, did what Americans would have called the 'math' with mounting outrage. But almost to the last fixture of the season, when the protests extended to a couple of smoke bombs in the Old Trafford forecourt before United beat Stoke City in vain, Ferguson exuded pro-Glazer sentiment.

He still appeared to believe what he had said at Carrington after the Champions League final: 'It's all nonsense. They are brilliant owners. All takeovers are done by debt. Do you think that, if I wanted to take over Marks & Spencer, I could just go and get £3 billion from under the floorboards? No – I'd go to the Bank of Scotland.'

Within a few months of his unfortunate analogy, the Royal Bank of Scotland was being rescued as a consequence of the collapse of the financial system. It was yet another hostage to fortune that Ferguson had offered with the Carrington champagne. But, because of his achievements, Ferguson was never going to be fully held to account for his unwitting role in the Glazers' takeover. To the supporters, his acquiescence with successive carpetbaggers – the Irish, then the Americans – was the truth that dare not speak its name.

All the supporters could do was watch developments: the switching of debt to a bond which let the Glazers continue to draw money from the club in the form of fees and raised the possibility of ultimate repayment of the loan through the sale and leaseback of Old Trafford and/or Carrington. And still it was insisted, not least by David Gill and the Glazers' spokespeople, that Ferguson could buy big if he wanted. And as Ferguson himself joined the chorus, the scorn of David Conn, as respected a writer on football and its finances as any since the subjects became inextricable, almost leapt from the pages of the *Guardian*.

'Imagine how United might look without the Glazer debt,' Conn wrote, outlining how the dividends paid by the club as a plc now appeared modest when compared with a 'mountain' of interest. 'Had the takeover never happened, how fearsomely United could now be swaggering. Three times Premier League champions and European champions in 2008, with a record income of £278 million [and] a £91 million operating profit, not plundered to meet the interest. On top of that, £81 million from selling Ronaldo. Would the manager, in these debt-free circumstances, really spend the autumn years of his brilliant career grumbling about the price of players? Can he be pictured allowing Ronaldo and Carlos Tévez to depart, leaving him to admit that United's thinner strike force is seriously reliant on one player, Wayne Rooney?'

Yet grumble about the price of players Ferguson did. As if he had never happily splashed United's cash to get the best he could. Even as it was calculated that, since the Glazer takeover, he had spent only £32.4 million net – less than £6.5 million a season – on reinforcements, he insisted: 'It's nothing to do with the Glazers or David Gill. It's because I am not going to pay £50 million for a striker who isn't worth it. I could easily have spent the Ronaldo money, but I didn't want to do it.' He preferred to wait for 'value in the market'. And, to be fair to him, the poor first season at Real Madrid of the French striker Karim Benzema, for whom he had refused to pay Olympique Lyonnais the required £35 million, did nothing to harm his case.

Towards the end of the 2009/10 season, Ferguson reiterated his scorn for the overpaid stars constantly being pushed his club's way: 'Agents get in touch with our chief scout and say this player will take a drop in wages from £10 million to £8 million a year. Oh, will he? That's very good of him. Jesus Christ! So that's only £42 million now in wages over a five-year deal instead of £50 million.' Not far off. 'So work it out. You bring in a player for forty-odd million and then you have to pay their salary on top. So with a five-year contract and wages you're suddenly talking of paying £82 million for a player over the term of his contract – it's ridiculous.'

He went on to declare that he would pay a £60 million fee for only one player – Ronaldo, whom he would take back any time – and to defend the acquisition of Owen. 'He was a popular signing among the players,' said Ferguson, 'and we felt if we could get fifteen goals out of him it was good business. Unfortunately he got injured in the League Cup final where the pitch was a killer.' No one asked Ferguson why, when the deficiencies of the Wembley surface were so well known, he had picked the notoriously injury-prone Owen in the first place.

And so he moved on to his concluding point: 'The clamour

to spend big will happen again but people are missing the point.' During the season he had signed Chris Smalling, a highly promising English defender, from Fulham in a deferred transfer for a basic £10 million; Javier Hernández, a young Mexican forward, for £7 million; and Diouf. 'That's twenty-odd million on young players who will develop in the long term. The proof of the pudding is in the eating, isn't it? The Glazers have given me £20 million for three players already and any time we've asked for money, like for Dimitar Berbatov, they've given it. There's no criticism for me because there's no criticism justified.'

Wisely, though, he avoided the ownership question in a final address to the fans after the Stoke match on 9 May, and was warmly cheered in consequence.

No More the Champions

The season had brought only one trophy – Aston Villa had been beaten in the League Cup final – but United had run Chelsea close in the Premier League, acknowledging that a record nineteenth title and unprecedented fourth in a row would not be theirs only on that last afternoon, in which they beat Stoke 4–0 while the visiting supporters gleefully celebrated each of the eight goals Chelsea put past Wigan Athletic without reply at Stamford Bridge; United had needed Chelsea to drop points. Ferguson's greatest frustration, however, had been visited in Europe.

It had been a season in which Ferguson had sometimes seemed to be caricaturing himself, blaming referees for several of United's defeats and, when they were beaten on away goals by Bayern Munich in the Champions League, calling their players 'typical Germans' for having encouraged the referee to send off United's young defender Rafael da Silva for incurring a second yellow card that, to most neutral observers, looked justified. No German member of the Bayern team had, in fact, been involved. But that was not the point.

High though emotions may have been running in the

aftermath of a bitter defeat – Ferguson was still furiously chewing gum as he spoke to the television interviewer afterwards – it was a needlessly hackneyed insult, one whose character reminded Ferguson-watchers of his supposedly jocular remarks about another nationality a few years earlier: 'When an Italian tells me it's pasta, I always look under the sauce, just in case.'

This defeat by Bayern, in the quarter-finals, cost Ferguson a date to which he had been looking forward. Earlier in the season, while United and the rest of Europe's more fancied clubs had been making their usual steady progress through the group stages, José Mourinho's mobile phone vibrated at the Inter training ground outside Milan. On it was a text message from Ferguson with a cheery PS that read: 'Let's meet in Madrid in May.' As it transpired, only Mourinho could turn up. Arjen Robben's controlled volley at Old Trafford put United out, but Inter marched on to the final at the Bernabéu, past Chelsea and then Barcelona to a meeting with not Ferguson but Louis van Gaal, whose Bayern Munich were comprehensively beaten.

Ferguson made no secret of his frustration. Right up to the week of the final, he seethed about United's absence.

From the start of the domestic campaign – though he had taken with good grace an extraordinary defeat at the raucously jubilant home of Alastair Campbell's beloved and newly promoted Burnley – there had been something of a scattergun approach to referees.

Alan Wiley, who had taken charge of a 2–2 draw at home to Steve Bruce's Sunderland in which United played poorly, had supposedly exemplified the deficient fitness of Premier League officials (a point ridiculed by statistics showing that

Wiley had covered more ground than all but four of Ferguson's players, and all but three of Bruce's).

Chris Foy had been berated for having allowed only six extra minutes at the end of the FA Cup tie in which Leeds United, then of League One, triumphed 1–0 at Old Trafford (the former referee Graham Poll explained in a newspaper article why Ferguson had got that one wrong too). And then, after a 1–1 draw at Birmingham, Ferguson went for the hat-trick.

'I've been watching Mark Clattenburg for a while,' he said, with the air of a Politburo member who had been reading too much *Pravda* or (to be more literal) a Manchester United manager who'd done too much MUTV, 'and I've not seen a softer sending-off in a long time.' This time video evidence revealed Darren Fletcher's two yellow cards as open and shut cases. Even by his own standards, Ferguson was overdoing it. The line between pique and mind games had become blurred.

His team's performances could be just as erratic. United were doing their manful best to cope with an unusually heavy list of casualties but sometimes the additional strain of a midweek Champions League encounter proved too much for the squad. They lost limply at Liverpool in October, were all too predictably beaten at Chelsea the next month and then encountered one of Ferguson's dodgy Decembers, going down at Aston Villa and Fulham. But things picked up when Manchester City, whose nouveau-riche crowing and brandishing of Tévez had been nicely put down by Ferguson's reference to 'noisy neighbours', were subdued over two legs of a League Cup semi-final and Patrice Evra spoke tellingly: 'Sir Alex . . . was jumping up and down like a child after that game. You could be forgiven for thinking he had never won a game before!'

That the fires burned as strongly as ever was emphasised by Wayne Rooney: 'There are days when I don't want to see the manager. Even after we have won a game maybe 2-0 or 3-0, we can go in the dressing room and everyone is smiling and happy and we think we have played well and done all right. Then he comes through the door and just lets loose. Everyone is looking around and thinking, "What's wrong?" But that's the way he is. He is a perfectionist.'

But even with Rooney in brilliant form, relentlessly striving to make up for the losses of Tévez and, especially, Ronaldo, scoring a career-best thirty-four goals in all competitions, the team remained short of perfect.

Chelsea demonstrated as much in April as, well rested thanks to their Champions League knockout by Mourinho's Inter (United had spent the midweek in Munich), they came to Old Trafford and were much the better side, even if it took a Didier Drogba goal that should have been disallowed for offside to give them all three points. They went on to be worthy champions in Carlo Ancelotti's first season, as Ferguson generously admitted.

The Footballer of the Year, though, was rightly Rooney. Ferguson accompanied him to the Football Writers' Association dinner and, after paying tribute to his star player, sat back on the top table to watch Rooney be briefly interviewed by Sky's Jeff Stelling and tell a story involving the manager. At the beginning of the season, Rooney said, Ferguson had asked him to score more goals with his head. 'I said to him last season it was me crossing the ball – I asked him if he wanted me to get on the end of my own crosses.' As the audience laughed, the hitherto beaming Ferguson retained his smile, but with apparent difficulty.

He had hardly been more amused when David Beckham returned to Old Trafford with Milan in March, shortly before the former England captain sustained the Achilles-tendon injury that ruled him out of the World Cup.

Beckham had spoken affectionately about Ferguson in the build-up to the match, calling him a 'father figure', but, when the first question put to Ferguson at his briefing was about Beckham, the manager reacted with sarcasm. 'That was three seconds – bloody hell!' he said. 'Can't you build it up a bit?' Beckham played only as a substitute and, Milan having lost 4–0, left the arena wearing a green and gold scarf provided by one of the legion of dissident supporters. He later felt obliged to explain that it was not a significant gesture.

All in all, the occasion turned out pretty much as Ferguson would have wished. The past was gone. United would live to fight another day and, despite what Ferguson was to call the 'absolute travesty' of Munich, another season.

THE LEGACY

'Not Today but Tomorrow'

For most managers United's achievements in the 2009/10 season would have constituted success. Yet so accustomed had we become to Ferguson lifting prizes more glittering than the League Cup that he went on holiday without garlands. Nothing he or his team had done earned more praise than an eloquent tribute to Sir Bobby Robson which Ferguson delivered at Durham Cathedral during the much-loved former England manager's memorial service on 21 September 2009.

Without notes, as ever, he captured the essence of Robson as seen by his peers: 'Bobby never lost that enthusiasm. That enthusiasm, you just can't explain it – special people have got it.' According to Ferguson, Robson had even influenced one of his decisions to stay on at Old Trafford by inquiring 'You're not going to retire, are you?' in a tone that left room for only one answer. 'He always influenced me,' said Ferguson. From way back in 1981, after Aberdeen had beaten Ipswich Town. 'In true Robson fashion, he finished by saying, "Go and win it – anyone who can beat my Ipswich team must be able to win the Cup."'

Ferguson had mounted the pulpit steps a day after a dramatic

4-3 victory over Manchester City at Old Trafford. A few weeks later, though, came dismal defeat at Liverpool and, when United went to visit the leaders, Chelsea, it was hard, for those of us trying to preview the match in our newspapers, to recall one with a fellow member of the established top four in which they had gone as such underdogs.

And yet the song I could not get out of my head was 'My Back Pages'. When Bob Dylan wrote it in 1964, Ferguson was forsaking the toolmaker's trade for a full-time contract with Dunfermline and, given his mainstream musical tastes he would more likely have been listening to Sinatra or the 'awful Glaswegian' mentioned by Gordon Strachan than the poet Dylan. But a couple of lines seemed apposite to what Ferguson had so gloriously made of his life in football, so I used them to introduce a piece in *The Times*:

> Ah, but I was so much older then,
> I'm younger than that now.

He had certainly looked older on that May evening in 2005 when Chelsea came to Old Trafford, their first title under Mourinho secured, and won 3-1 as if for the fun of it, causing the stadium to half-empty long before Ferguson joined his players on the pitch for the customary lap of honour after the final home match of the season. Ferguson was eighteen months short of senior-citizen status at that time – and beginning, with his limp, to look the part.

He was younger than that now, four and a half years on. You could see it in the training-ground banter he shared with Rooney. Between the night of the limping lap and the morning of the Chelsea match in 2009 he had won three championships in England (to Chelsea's one) and one in Europe. But the most important substance with which he seemed to have endowed the club was not silverware but deoxyribonucleic acid. Ferguson had referred to it by its more common name, DNA, after United had fought back from 3–1 down against CSKA Moscow five days earlier to secure a place in the Champions League's last sixteen. It struck me that, although Ferguson was not entirely responsible for that, he had revived and even enhanced the spirit of Sir Matt Busby.

Busby had survived the Munich crash and rebuilt. United's great fortune was to have identified, largely through the acumen of Sir Bobby Charlton, the most venerable Busby Babe, one of the few men who could have invested the Busby legacy and made a profit. No wonder everyone connected with United was dreading the day when Ferguson went to the board and said it was time to go. No one had ever practised rejuvenation like him.

My mind was cast back to 1992. He had not won his first United championship at that stage and yet, as we talked at The Cliff, on one of those early mornings when he would offer a journalist ten minutes – the deal was that you had to arrive well before the staff and players started to come in – and keep nattering for an hour, until people were banging on his door and pleading for the day's first decisions, I turned the talk to legacy and, amazingly, he had a full and detailed response.

'Only one club in the history of the game,' he said, 'has been able to do it.' He meant Liverpool. 'To maintain success over two generations. Now that will be out of my remit because my lifespan as manager here will probably stretch no more than another six or seven years – if I'm successful. I'm trying to be realistic. But, whatever I do, I have to lay down a really good foundation that will continue the success. All the work that goes on in this club is not about today but about tomorrow.'

Tomorrow, as it turned out, was to be Ferguson's. And the day after tomorrow. But his vision of the day he would go was clear: 'The takeover should be sweet.' By which he meant that the staff and players would be in place for continued success. 'That's my key job now.' At that moment, he was working on the assumption that United would beat Leeds to the 1992 title, but it took them another season and from then a smooth transition, with none of the trauma involved in the departure of Jock Stein from Celtic, remained high on his list of priorities.

Heroes

Stein was one of the great formative influences on Ferguson's management style. The other was Scot Symon. 'I was only four months with him,' said Ferguson, 'but in that time I learned what it is to be a strong manager. He wasn't the easiest with the press. A bit like Sir Alf Ramsey – he couldn't be bothered with them. But Scot Symon knew the game. He'd been manager of East Fife when they won the League Cup and reached the Scottish Cup final in 1949/50 and even devised a 4–2-4 system [the Hungarians were not to unveil this until a few years later]. He called the players together and said, "We're going to play 4–2–4. But don't tell anybody – you know what the press are like." They were a good team, East Fife, and Scot Symon was a brilliant thinker about the game. When he came into the dressing room, every player stopped talking. There was a sort of reverence.'

Stein taught Ferguson a different way of exerting power. 'I wish I'd had longer with Jock,' he said. 'Jock had it all summed up. He knew everything about everyone. He knew every weakness in a person. Even the journalists. "Here they come," he'd say, as the room filled up for a press conference.

"There's so-and-so – he's had a few bets on the horses today."
He was in control. Because he knew everything. Because
everybody told him a bit. He's be sitting there like a big Buddha.
"What's happened today, son?" He used to phone me sometimes on a Saturday night. "Oh, I see you were at the game
today – were you watching so-and-so?" And you felt forced
to tell him. Because if you told him a lie he'd know.'

Then there was the gambling connection. 'Alex has always
liked a bet,' said Bobby Seith, his old Rangers coach, 'and so
did Jock. These men are prepared to take the kind of chances
the rest of us might not.' Or, as Ferguson put it after the young
substitute Macheda had secured a breathless 3-2 win over
Aston Villa in 2009: 'Risk – that's what this club is built on.'

Seith also mentioned Stein's fondness for the mind game.
'Jock played them all the time,' he said. 'A good example was
on the day before the European Cup final in 1967. Both sides
had gone to look at the stadium in Lisbon. Inter's manager
was Helenio Herrera and, while both sides were on the field,
Jock quite deliberately engaged Herrera in an argument in the
full view and earshot of his players. Because Herrera was a
god in football and the message Jock wanted to convey to his
players was "I'm as good as him – and you're as good as Inter."
He was always doing that sort of thing.'

It was Shankly who, as Celtic were celebrating their victory,
strode into the dressing room at the National Stadium and
told Stein: 'John, you're immortal.' To Ferguson he certainly
was. About eighteen months after Ferguson had won his first
Champions League in 1999, he travelled to Lisbon with a film-
maker and went to the National Stadium, now hardly used,
to have himself recorded 'savouring what Jock had experienced'. The film was for personal use.

Power and Control

Power and control. Those were the words Ferguson flourished in front of an audience of philosophy students at Trinity College, Dublin, in January 2010. 'Through my development,' he said, 'I've come across two issues – power and control.' Not necessarily in that order. 'Control is important, very, very important. My control is the most important thing. If I lose control of these multimillionaires in the Manchester United dressing room, then I'm dead. So I never lose control. If anyone steps out of my control, that's them dead.'

It might have been a florid way of outlining the background to the departures from Old Trafford of, among others, Paul Ince, Ruud van Nistelrooy, David Beckham and Roy Keane – but the message got across.

The handling of success was another subject he discussed. He had learned to do that, he told the students. 'I'm more worried about how the players handle it. I'm very conscious of that and always will be. That's my job.' How perfectionism with humility was incorporated into the club ethos – the DNA – was described in an interview given to a French newspaper by Patrice Evra. 'Manchester United,' said Evra, 'is a factory workers' club. You have to respect that culture. It's a club where we work hard.

'They will not congratulate you after each win. Sir Alex frequently says, "Well done, my son" and that says it all. For them it is normal when you play well. It is normal to win the championship. It is Manchester United. We don't have the right to make mistakes.'

Any manager can be demanding. Ferguson is equally ruthless with himself. He was quoted in *Mandelson*, a biography of Lord Mandelson by Donald Macintyre, as having warned Alastair Campbell at the start of the 1997 election campaign that it was all too easy to be distracted by thinking of life after victory, rather than what had to be done to achieve victory: 'You're in the position of a manager a month out from the end of the championship when you're seven points ahead. What you have to develop is tunnel vision. If you see anything that doesn't need to be there, get rid of it.'

In the spring of 2009, a special edition of the *New Statesman* was guest-edited by Campbell, who interviewed Ferguson. Asked to name the three most important qualities required for leadership, he replied: 'Control. Managing change. And observation.'

The first was no surprise.

The second had been evident throughout his time at United, in how football's evolution from a team to a squad game had been recognised at Old Trafford before anywhere else, in how the value of freshness was acknowledged by an ever-changing team; even Sir Bobby Charlton confessed in 2009 that he could seldom predict more than eight starters in a match. In how the spiralling fortunes of the players had somehow failed to blunt their hunger. And in how Ferguson had been obliged to accept things he could not control. As he told the Dublin students: 'When somebody scored, everyone used to celebrate together. Today, they run across [to the crowd]. I don't know whether it's self-adulation or what. Tattoos, earrings – it's not my world. I'm sorry. But I've had to adjust to it.'

Campbell asked what he meant by observation. 'Spotting everything around you,' he said, 'analysing what is important. Seeing dangers and opportunities that others can't see. That comes from experience and knowledge.'

And what was the key to a winning mentality? 'There's two for me. A will to win. And attention to detail.' When they combined, it struck me, perhaps the defining images of the Ferguson era at Manchester United were composed: the late, late winners, notably Steve Bruce's in 1993, Ole Gunnar Solskjær's in 1999 and Kiko Macheda's, after a substitution as inspired as any, in 2009.

The infinite capacity for taking pains was always there. The early starts, the first-light arrivals at The Cliff or Carrington for a bit of exercise before work; Ferguson believes in the link between physical health and mental alertness and, in 2004, after having a pacemaker fitted in order to regulate his heartbeat, was proudly back at his desk within twenty-four hours. And in the latter half of his sixties a distaste for the very notion of retirement became prevalent, prompting the thought that his place in the managerial pantheon might not be decided until the obituaries.

But here goes . . .

Where Stands He?

Ferguson is not a genius, as Brian Clough (with Peter Taylor) was in the early years of Ferguson's career in management and José Mourinho has been towards the end. But he outlasted Clough and has since set standards of one-club achievement that cause Mourinho to throw up his arms in admiring despair.

He stands above both Bill Shankly and Bob Paisley because, in not only rebuilding Manchester United on a scale above anything that English football had known before but maintaining success with an aesthetic dimension, he has emulated each of the Liverpool legends.

Without being any cleverer than Jock Stein, he has repeatedly refused to allow success to form a rod for his back as Celtic's nine consecutive Scottish titles had done for his friend and hero; the classic example of indomitability, surely, was Ferguson's defiance in the face of Chelsea's Mourinho-era dominance.

To compare him with Busby is inevitable but hazardous because we shall never know what the Munich victims would have achieved, especially in Europe, where many observers felt they were the natural successors to the great Real Madrid by whom Ferguson was to be enthralled in 1960 at Hampden Park. If anything like that had happened, an impossible standard would have been set for Busby's successors, Ferguson included.

Moreover, Busby built his United from a post-war shell; the club then was anything but the relatively prosperous institution at which Ferguson arrived. It ought also to be said that Shankly found Liverpool in an under-developed second-division state, as were both Derby County and Nottingham Forest when Clough took charge.

Herbert Chapman built triple-championship-winning teams at both Huddersfield Town and Arsenal. Death cut short his career. Bill Nicholson, of Tottenham Hotspur, and Don Revie, of Leeds United, created great football, but even the latter could not sustain it as Ferguson has done.

Arsène Wenger was responsible for the most handsome football played since the top-level English game was rebranded as the Premier League in 1992 but chose to redefine success as winning while balancing the books. In this he was ahead of Uefa's thinking on 'financial fair play'. But Arsenal went several years without a trophy. Wenger is probably the most closely comparable to Ferguson – dedicated to improving youngsters, passionate, football-mad – and on at least the same level of talent, if not solid-metal achievement.

In Europe, Ferguson bears scrutiny along with such veterans as Marcello Lippi, Giovanni Trappatoni and Ottmar Hitzfeld but cannot be said to have exceeded any because so much of what he has done has taken so long. There was a twenty-year span between his first European trophy and his fourth. José Mourinho won three in seven years. But Ferguson is up with the very best of the rest.

Loyal to the Last

Ferguson has also been involved in more controversy than any famous manager since Brian Clough, at least until Mourinho came along.

From the start, his belligerent nature was visited on Scottish referees sheltering from the thunder outside their dressing-room door. It seemed that the Scottish FA tried at first to control Ferguson with escalating punishments before gradually giving up, and he appeared to have learned from that in his dealings with the FA in London, pushing them as far as he could and, in the end, controlling their disciplinary bodies with a mixture of intimidation and the flattery of a personal appearance in which he not only ventured but sought opinions. 'We agree with a lot of what you say, Alex,' he was told as late as 2009, 'but we'll have to fine you.' He said he quite understood and took a light slap on the wallet with equanimity. No wonder Liverpool's erstwhile manager Rafa Benítez became so wound up by Ferguson's manipulative tactics.

The truth was that the FA's so-called 'Respect' campaign, to which Benítez alluded, was having a coach and horses repeatedly driven through it by a leading light of the League Managers' Association, which had pledged full support to this worthy attempt to improve behaviour towards referees and linesmen at every level of the game.

Was Ferguson always setting a good example to the young and impressionable? Amid all the scorn he expressed for aspects of the young society around him – tattoos, earrings, self-adulation – there was seldom a glimmer of self-recognition or acceptance of any personal contribution to change or decay. While maintaining admirable discipline at Manchester United, did his behaviour towards authority undermine that very quality in the world outside the stockade that was always fundamental to his professional *modus operandi*? And, finally, did the more extreme elements of his workplace behaviour ever infinge the principles supplied to him in that Govan youth? The answer to each question would have to be a guarded 'Yes'.

It was Mark McGhee, Ferguson's first signing for Aberdeen and as perspicacious a man as any to whom I have spoken in connection with this book, who confirmed the impression that Ferguson's life has been, in essence, a quest to please his father. 'I think he would feel he is proving himself to his father more than anything else,' said McGhee. 'I think he would want to prove to his father that he could maintain his standards. Everyone who gets close to him feels that, if you are performing badly, you are letting *him* down and I think he doesn't want to let his family down. It's a very working-class ethic.'

If a thing's worth doing, said Alexander Ferguson Senior, it's worth doing well. Sir Alex Ferguson has done football management so extraordinarily well for so long that his life in the game is not only unprecedented but, in near-certainty, unrepeatable.

Discipline and good manners were also in the family tradition. Along with something else. And, before we come to that, let it be said with utter confidence that, if Alexander Ferguson Senior were here to be asked what he felt of his elder son's life, he would – after manifesting a reluctance to be boastful or effusive – express nothing but pride.

But, then, the Fergusons always did believe in loyalty.

Bibliography

Auclair, Philippe, *Cantona: The Rebel Who Would Be King* (Macmillan, 2009)

Bose, Mihir, *Manchester DisUnited: And the Business of Soccer* (Aurum Press, 2007)

Campbell, Alastair, *The Blair Years: Extracts from the Alastair Campbell Diaries* (Hutchinson, 2007)

Charlton, Sir Bobby, *My Manchester United Years* (Headline, 2007)

Cole, Ashley, *My Defence: Winning, Losing, Scandals and the Drama of Germany* 2006 (Headline, 2006)

Crick, Michael, *The Boss: The Many Sides of Alex Ferguson* (Simon & Schuster, 2002)

Crick, Michael, and David Smith, *Manchester United: The Betrayal of a Legend* (Pelham Books, 1989)

Ferguson, Alex, *A Light in the North: Seven Years with Aberdeen* (Mainstream Publishing, 1985)

Ferguson, Alex, *Alex Ferguson: Managing My Life* (Hodder & Stoughton, 1999)

Holt, Oliver, *If You're Second You Are Nothing: Ferguson and Shankly* (Macmillan, 2006)

Kelly, Ned, *Manchester United: The Untold Story* (Michael O'Mara Books, 2003)

Macintyre, Donald, *Mandelson: The Biography* (HarperCollins, 2000)

Marr, Andrew, *A History of Modern Britain* (Macmillan, 2007)

McIlvanney, Hugh, *McIlvanney on Football* (Mainstream Publishing, 1996)

Mitten, Andy, *Glory! Glory!* (Vision Sports Publishing, 2009)

Strachan, Gordon, *Strachan: My life in Football* (Little, Brown, 2006)

Strachan, Gordon, with Jack Webster, *Gordon Strachan: An Autobiography* (Stanley Paul, 1984)

Taylor, Daniel, *This Is the One. Sir Alex Ferguson: The Uncut Story of a Football Genius* (Aurum Press, 2007)

Index